D1201511

Introduction to
Physical System Modelling

Introduction to

Physical System Modelling

P. E. Wellstead

Control Systems Centre,
University of Manchester
Institute of Science and
Technology

1979

ACADEMIC PRESS
London · New York · Toronto · Sydney · San Francisco
A Subsidiary of Harcourt Brace Jovanovich, Publishers

ACADEMIC PRESS INC. (LONDON) LTD
24/28 Oval Road,
London NW1

United States Edition published by
ACADEMIC PRESS INC.
111 Fifth Avenue,
New York, New York 10003

British Library Cataloguing in Publication Data
Wellstead, P E
    Introduction to physical system modelling.
    1. System analysis
    2. Mathematical models
    I. Title
    511'.8   QA402

    ISBN 0–12–744380–0   LCCN 79–50528

Typeset in Great Britain by C. F. Hodgson and Son Ltd, London
Printed in Great Britain by Whitstable Litho Ltd, Whitstable, Kent

Preface

This book has arisen from efforts to formulate a simple unified approach to system modelling. In particular, the aim was to develop modelling in such a way that it would compliment dynamical systems analysis and control systems studies. Experience has shown that the modern heavily theoretical approach to control systems analysis and design has caused a decline in the intuitive understanding of engineering systems and the way in which they behave. One way of establishing this understanding is through an appreciation of system modelling methods. Of corresponding importance is a knowledge of the fundamental properties which are shared by all physical systems.

The unifying theme used in this book is the interpretation of systems as energy manipulators. The idea being that the perceived dynamical behaviour of a physical system is the outward manifestation of the energy transactions within the system. In this way a wide range of systems can be handled in a common framework, with energy as the central concept.

The notion of energy as a unifying agent is not new. It flows directly from the theories of Hamilton and Lagrange and occurs in the work of Firestone and his contemporaries. In recent years it has come into prominence by way of the bond graphic methods of H. M. Paynter. However, this is the first point at which all the established methods of system modelling have been drawn together in one text. In fact a key feature of the book is the way in which network modelling, variational modelling and bond graph methods are presented with energy handling as a common theme..

The potential range of a book on modelling is enormous, and to make the task manageable I have been selective. To this end the book is restricted to lumped parameter systems. In the same spirit, the highly specialized areas such as chemical process and reaction modelling have been excluded. The space gained in this way has been used to introduce a series of case studies. These are brief discussions of real modelling problems in which the dynamical equations are obtained in a number of ways each of which is linked to the subsequent use of the model. The aim here is to underline the fact that the modelling process is often intimately associated with subsequent simulation, design or control studies.

In preparing the lectures upon which this book is based I have drawn extensively upon the existing literature. In particular, the work of Paynter on bond graphs has had a substantial influence. In addition, the book by Shearer, Murphy and Richardson[1] was useful in the discussion of system components, while the excellent book by Crandell, Karnopp, Kurtz and Pridmore-Brown[2] was extremely helpful on variational methods.

One of the most rewarding and pleasant aspects of writing this book has been the opportunity which it afforded of constructing laboratory scale models which demonstrate particular forms of dynamical behaviour. In this respect I am particularly indebted to the Control Systems Centre technicians and students who assisted in the design and construction of scaled versions of the systems which are used as illustrative examples in the text. It is also gratifying that these laboratory scale models are now to be produced commercially[3] in a form which complements and extends the formal teaching material presented here. The commercial exploitation is being undertaken by TecQuipment Limited, Bonsall Street, Long Eaton, Nottingham, NG10 2AN, England.

In the same spirit, it is a pleasure to acknowledge the stimulation provided by collegues and students at the Control Systems Centre. Professor H. H. Rosenbrock in particular played a crucial role in providing the opportunity and encouragement needed to write this book. Likewise, Professor A. G. J. MacFarlane gave valuable guidance through his published work and by personal communication.

[1] Shearer, J. L., Murphy, A. T. and Richardson, H. M. (1967). "Introduction to System Dynamics", Addison-Wesley, Reading, Mass.
[2] Crandell, S. H., Karnopp, D. C., Kurtz, E. F. and Pridmore-Brown, D. C. (1968). "Dynamics of Mechanical and Electromechanical Systems". McGraw-Hill, New York.
[3] Wellstead, P. E. (1979). Laboratory Models for Control System Analysis and Design. TecQuipment Limited, Nottingham, England.

Contents

PART 2: SYSTEMATIC MODELLING METHODS

PART 3: CASE STUDIES

Introduction

1

This introductory discussion will attempt to put system modelling into the context of control system analysis and design. The kind of system models which are appropriate to control are outlined, with particular attention to their subsequent use. An outline of the book's structure is then presented in conjunction with a justification of the approach to system modelling presented here.

1. WHAT KIND OF MODEL?

First of all one should state that system modelling is as much an art as a scientific pursuit. This means on the one hand that only certain aspects of the subject can be taught. More significant is the implication that the term modelling will have a great many shades of meaning. For example, a control systems analyst will interpret a system model as a mathematical abstraction in terms of a set of differential equations. At the other extreme a prototype engineer interprets model in the classical sense of a scaled replica of the system.

The variations in interpretation can be clarified by a classification of models along the lines shown in Fig. 1.1. At the most heuristic level is the intuitive model; this often exists only in the engineer's mind as his personal conception of the system. Such models need have neither physical existence or mathematical substance. At a more tangible level a distinction (Fig. 1.1) can be made between models intended for analysis and design of controllers and those used for detailed investigation of fundamental properties of the system.

Dynamic model is the generic name given to mathematical system models which exist as a set of coupled differential or transform equations. They are used in the theoretical analysis of system behaviour and in the subsequent reconfiguration of the system and controller design. This class contains in principle two forms of model.

1

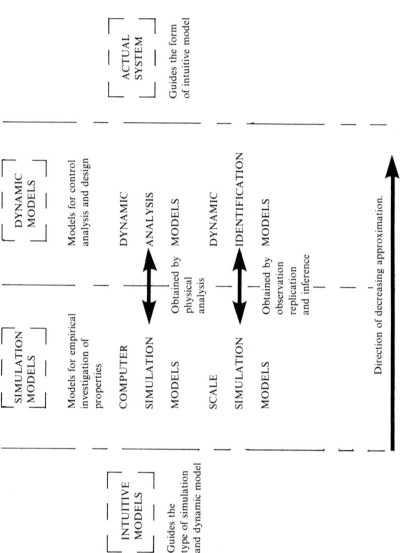

Figure 1.1 The relationships between various types of model

(i)   Dynamic analysis models: being those obtained by analysis of the physical system at a fundamental level, yet involving approximations sufficient to simplify the model to a differential equation form.

(ii) Dynamic identification models: being those obtained by (statistical) inference from the observed behaviour of the physical system. This form of modelling leads to an identical type of description as does dynamic analysis. The difference lies in the mode of obtaining the equations of motion.

Simulation model is the term used to include all forms of model which are explicitly aimed at investigating basic phenomenological features of a system or process. This class of model includes two forms.

(i)   Computer simulation models, whereby an exact and detailed analysis of the system leads to a mathematical formulation of its behaviour which can be implemented on analogue or digital computer. Such simulations tend to be extremely complex in nature involving many intricacies which would be omitted from a dynamic model.

(ii) Scale simulation models. Some phenomena are so complex that they defy useful analysis. In order to simulate such processes it is common practice to construct a physical replica of the process under study with appropriate dimensional scaling. Such scale simulations allow a variety of design and operational conditions to be studied in a controlled environment often at a more realistic level than other model forms would permit.

It must be emphasized that the segregation given above and illustrated in Fig. 1.1 is, to a degree, arbitrary. Indeed there is strong cross-linking between simulation models and dynamical models on at least two levels. First the distinction between models for computer simulation and dynamic analysis only exists in the degree of approximation involved. Both models are obtained by analysis of the physical laws underlying the system, but where a simulation model would take account of all the system's properties, the dynamic analysis model would seek to capture only the key dynamic features in a simplified form. Secondly, and in the same spirit, scale models and identification models are related, since they are both derived from a process of observation and replication of the original system's appearance and behaviour respectively.

To summarize, simulation and dynamic models are related and merge at a certain point. The factor which separates the two is the degree of approximation involved. Simulation models in general involve fewest approximations, whereas dynamic models may contain gross simplifications but nevertheless include certain germane features. In this vein, an ordering of the techniques can be made as indicated in Fig. 1.1 by the direction of decreasing approximation ranging from intuition through to the actual system itself.

2. MODELLING IN PERSPECTIVE

The scope of this book extends only to dynamic models obtained by direct analysis, the intention being to lay a foundation whereby the behaviour of a wide class of physical systems can be understood. As such the main use will be in the analysis of control systems for which a (relatively) simple differential/ transform description is required. In this spirit it will be useful to outline the relationship of modelling to other aspects of the control engineering task. The basic steps in control systems (Fig. 1.2) are: modelling, controller design and controller validation. These phases proceed in an interactive fashion, although in the diagram a circular procession has been indicated in order to indicate that this is the normal chronological sequence. The modelling process may be achieved by any combination of the approaches outlined previously. However, the result which is passed to the controller design phase will usually be a dynamic model in terms of a set of ordinary differential or Laplace transform equations. By these remarks it is intended to emphasize that the state of the art is such that, no matter what degree of complexity or fidelity can be achieved in the modelling phase, controller design algorithms require a fairly simple (albeit approximate) dynamic representation of the system. It is this aspect of approximation which leads to the closure of the circle from controller validation to modelling. If a control law does not perform adequately it usually points to some weakness in the model. When the model deficiency is rectified, the design process is re-applied and circular iteration continues.

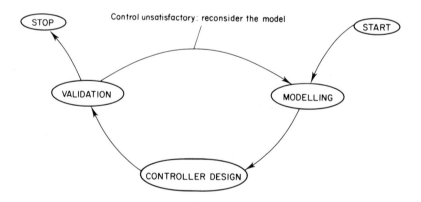

Fig. 1.2. The iterative nature of the modelling process.

3. GENERALIZED MODELLING AND LAYOUT OF THE BOOK

It is because of the direct relevance to the control design process that the ambit of this book is limited to the modelling of physical systems, with the goal of producing descriptions in terms of ordinary differential/transform equations. Partial differential equation models of distributed parameter systems are not considered. The aim is to develop methods for specifying system motion in the form of

coupled first-order differential equations,

coupled second-order differential equations,

and for linear, time-invariant systems, Laplace transform descriptions.

Even with such severe restrictions upon the range of models the potential scope and diversity of systems is rather large. With this thought in mind, an attempt is made to unify basic modelling procedures as they occur in electrical, mechanical, hydraulic, pneumatic and some thermal systems. The approach used is to consider systems as devices for the handling of energy. Dynamical behaviour is then interpreted as our perception of internal energetic trans- actions. Such an interpretation is not new, and has been employed by a number of authors. In particular, bond graphs (considered in this book) were conceived in terms of energetic bonding between the elementary parts of the system.

The book is divided into three parts:

Part 1. The idea of energy handling systems is abstracted in terms of generalized system variables and elements. This is linked to specific engineer- ing disciplines and used to formulate the fundamental rules of system interconnection in an energetic framework.

Part 2. Here the established methods of formulating mathematical models are developed in detail. These are:

(i) Network methods, where the energetic interactions of the component parts of a system are codified into a linear system graph.

(ii) Variational methods, in which energy transactions in a system are associated with a function of the total system energy which balances to zero when the system dynamical behaviour is correct.

(iii) Bond graph methods, whereby a graphical representation of the energetic interactions is used to obtain the system model.

Part 3. We examine a series of case studies in which the various modelling procedures are applied to a range of physical systems drawn from engineering applications.

4. CONCLUSION

The foregoing discussion is only a partial rationalization of modelling as a subject. In this connection the ideas expressed here reflect a personal viewpoint which has been influenced by the approaches adopted in certain text-books.

In particular the approach suggested by H. M. Paynter in "Analysis and Design of Engineering Systems" (MIT Press, 1961) is fundamental. Likewise the variational approach used here is based upon that adopted in "Dynamics of Mechanical and Electromechanical Systems" (McGraw-Hill, New York, 1968) by S. H. Crandall and his co-workers. In addition, the first part of the book was heavily influenced by the form of presentation adopted in "Introduction to System Dynamics" (Addison-Wesley, Reading, Mass. 1967) by J. L. Shearer, A. T. Murphy and H. H. Richardson.

Lastly, it was the book "Dynamical Analogies" by H. F. Olsen (Van Nostrand, Princeton, 1958) which first introduced me to the notion of a generalized approach to the modelling of dynamical systems.

5. NOTES AND REFERENCES

[1]   The use of laboratory scale models has declined dramatically with the introduction of electrical circuit analogues and more recently analogue and digital computation. However, certain phenomena are either too difficult or complex to model in the analytical sense. In such cases scale models are of direct use, as is demonstrated in:

Schuring, D. J. (1977). "Scale model engineering, fundamentals and applications". Pergamon Press, Oxford.

[2]   Dynamic identification models are obtained by combination of statistical inference and estimation in a way which can be interpreted as a macroscopic approach to the measurement of constitutive relationships. For a comprehensive treatment of these methods see:

Eykhoff, P. (1974). "System identification". Wiley, New York.

[3]   The view of modelling expressed here is from an engineer's viewpoint. Other disciplines would place different constructions on the subject. See for example:

Deutsch, R. (1969). "System analysis techniques". Prentice-Hall, New York.

Part 1: Basics

The idea of systems as energy handling devices is introduced. Sets of generalized energy variables and system elements are developed.

The ideas are then made more specific with reference to electrical, mechanical, hydraulic, pneumatic, magnetic and thermal systems. The energetic restrictions introduced by interconnecting system elements are used to specify certain basic interconnective constraints and hence obtain mathematical models.

Generalized Variables and System Elements

2

INTRODUCTION

The aim of the system modeller is to obtain in mathematical form a description of the dynamical behaviour of a system in terms of some physically significant variables. As the nature of the system changes, the system variables change. For example, the variables commonly used in electrical systems are voltage and current, in mechanical systems force and velocity, and in fluid systems pressure and volumetric flow rate. Despite the differences in the physical variables used to characterize systems in various disciplines, certain fundamental similarities exist, and it is in the analyst's interest to seek out and exploit these similarities in such a manner that the task of modelling is eased and our overall insight into the dynamic performance of physical systems is increased.

A suitable unifying concept which can be used for this purpose is energy. A physical system can be thought of as operating upon a pair of variables whose product is power (or proportional to power). The physical components which

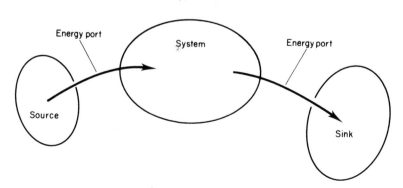

Fig. 2.1.

9

make up the system may thus be thought of as energy manipulators which, depending upon the way they are interconnected, process the energy injected into the system in a characteristic fashion which is observed as the system dynamic response. In the same spirit, the input–output behaviour of a system follows if energy can be considered as being injected into a system via an energy port (Fig. 2.1), with a similar port applied to read out the system response.

In this chapter a class of systems is identified which has a pair of variables associated with energy transfer. The generalized forms of these system variables are the abstract quantities effort and flow. Basic system elements are then postulated for the fundamental phenomena of energy storage, energy generation and energy dissipation.

1. SYSTEM VARIABLES

The idea of systems as energy manipulators which interact with inputs and outputs via energy ports is a conceptual model which encompasses a wide range of physical systems. In order to develop this notion however it is necessary to examine the mechanism of energetic interactions in terms of so-called "system variables" which determine just how and in what sense energy is transmitted. A simple example of energy transmission is an electrical source (which might be a battery or laboratory power supply) connected to a single resistive load, as shown in Fig. 2.2. In terms of Fig. 2.1 the power supply is an energy source, the resistor is the system and the energy port connecting them is the pair of conducting wires. The transmission of power to the resistor is given as the product of the system variables voltage v and current i:

$$\text{Power delivered to resistor} = vi \qquad (1)$$

with the energy delivered between time $t = 0$ and t_1 being the time integral of the power:

$$\text{Energy delivered to resistor} = \int_0^{t_1} vi \, dt$$

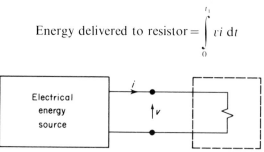

Electrical
energy
source

Fig. 2.2.

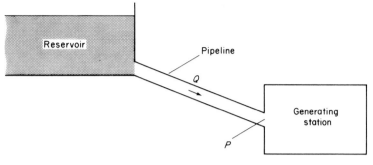

Fig. 2.3.

In a fluid system the energy transmission phenomena can be illustrated by a hydro-electric generating scheme. Figure 2.3 shows a reservoir connected by a pipe to a hydro-power generating station. The reservoir is a source of hydro-energy connected by an energy port (the pipeline) to a system (the hydro-energy generating station). The system variables which give the power supplied to the generating station are the fluid volumetric flow rate Q and the pressure P measured at the intake with respect to some pressure datum:

$$\text{Power delivered to station} = PQ \qquad (3)$$

Again the energy delivered between time $t = 0$ and t_1 is just the time integral of the power:

$$\text{Energy delivered to station} = \int_0^{t_1} PQ \ dt. \qquad (4)$$

A simple mechanical system which may be used to illustrate the idea of system variables is shown in Fig. 2.4. It depicts a mechanical dashpot anchored at one end, with the other end moving with velocity V under the action of a force F. The system variables which determine the energetic interchange in the

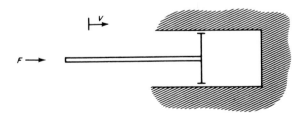

Fig. 2.4.

system are the force F in the shaft of the dashpot and the velocity V measured with respect to a velocity datum. The energy port is the shaft connecting the force input and the dashpot, and the energy delivered via this port is

$$\text{Energy delivered to dashpot} = \int_0^{t_1} FV \ dt. \tag{5}$$

1.1. Effort and flow: generalized system variables

Further examples can readily be drawn from everyday experience to show that the energy coupling of many systems can be represented by a pair of system variables whose product is the instantaneous power being transmitted through an energy port. In addition, the act of delivering energy is associated with one intensive variable (e.g. current, fluid flow) giving the flux of energy flow, and an extensive variable (e.g. voltage, pressure) giving the pitch of energy flow. In a generalized sense the two energy variables can be thought of as an *effort* variable and a *flow* variable. Thus an abstract energy port can be diagrammatically represented by a pair of terminals with a pair of generalized variables, effort (e) and flow (f) which together represent the energy transfer mechanism. Such an abstract description is given in Fig. 2.5.

An appealing way in which to further rationalize the generalized variables of effort and flow has been provided by the mobility analogy. This involves the classification of system variables according to the measurement scheme required to meter them. Two measuring devices are required, an across meter and a through meter. The former requires a datum to which measurements may be referred, in this sense it is a two-terminal meter, connected *across* two points in space and thus measures a *spatially extensive* variable (Fig. 2.6(a)). Examples of across meters are voltmeters, pressure gauges, thermometers and velocity transducers. A through meter, on the other hand, requires no separate

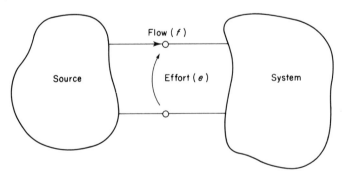

Fig. 2.5.

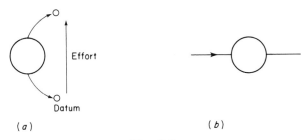

(a) *(b)*

Fig. 2.6.

datum point, it is inserted *into* a system and measures the rate of flow through itself of a *physically intensive* variable (Fig. 2.6(*b*)). Examples of through meters are flow meters, ammeters and force transducers.

In terms of the generalized variables, effort is normally visualized as an across variable and flow as a through variable. In specific disciplines however the assignment of effort and flow is (in a formal sense) arbitrary since it makes little difference to the final mathematical model if voltage is considered as an effort variable and current a flow or vice versa. Nevertheless, the across/through variable concept gives a uniform way of assigning system variables which in most cases is consistent with physical intuition.

The distinction between spatially extensive and physically intensive variables is sometimes made by using Latin prefixes. In this convention across variables are referred to as transvariables and through variables are denoted as pervariables.

1.2. Power and energy

In the generalized scheme of energy handling systems the product of the flow variable (f) and the effort variable (e) is the instantaneous power associated with the energy port or terminal pair which the pair (e, f) characterizes (Fig. 2.7). The energy which is transferred over the terminal pair *ab* in the interval of time 0 to t_1 is given by

$$E_{ab}(t_1) = \int_0^{t_1} ef \; dt. \tag{6}$$

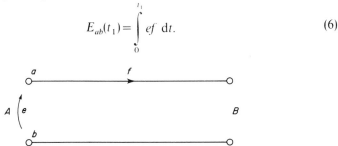

Fig. 2.7. Power associated with terminal pair *ab* = *ef*.

Notice that power and energy are both directed variables, whose sign depends upon the arbitrary sign conventions used for the effort and flow variables. If in Fig. 2.7, e and f are both in the assumed positive direction at time t, then the instantaneous power is positive and is from a to b. The energy $E_{ab}(t_1)$ thus indicates the magnitude and sense of the net energy transfer in the interval 0 to t_1, but must be considered with respect to the conventions for positive effort and flow.

1.3. Stored energy and state

A system which has no memory has no capacity to store information concerning its past history. It will respond in a way determined only by its instantaneous inputs. From practical observation it is clear that such systems only exist in idealized situations, for the unlikely implication is that a zero-memory system will respond instantaneously to changes at its inputs. In most cases therefore we will encounter systems which store information concerning their past behaviour such that their response to stimuli is a function of both past and present input values.

In the energetic interpretation of system behaviour, the storage of information is synonymous with storage of energy, and the simplest form of storage which can be conceived is by pure time integration. Thus

$$\text{Stored energy} \equiv \int_0^t ef \, dt. \qquad (7)$$

Two fundamental mechanisms exist for the storage of energy. The first is in terms of stored effort and the second in terms of stored flow. Two new variables can be defined to account for energy stored in this manner. For effort the stored effort can be defined as the effort accumulation e_a associated with a component and given by

$$e_a = \int_0^t e \, dt \quad \text{or} \quad e = \frac{de_a}{dt}. \qquad (8)$$

By substituting equation (10) in equation (7), the stored energy associated with flow accumulation f_a is

$$\text{Stored energy} = \int_0^{e_a} f \, de_a. \qquad (9)$$

The stored flow can be defined as the flow accumulation f_a associated with a system component and given by

$$f_a = \int_0^t f \, dt \qquad \text{or} \qquad f = \frac{df_a}{dt}. \tag{10}$$

By substituting equation (10) in equation (7), the stored energy associated with flow accumulation f_a is

$$\text{Stored energy} = \int_0^{f_a} e \, df_a. \tag{11}$$

The elementary stored energy variables e_a, f_a, together with the applied efforts and flows specify the time history of energy flow within a system. It is in this manner that effort and flow accumulation are related to the *state* of a dynamical system. To be more specific, the time behaviour of a lumped parameter system can be expressed in terms of a set of first-order differential equations of the form:

$$\dot{x}_i = f_i(x_1, x_2, \ldots, x_n, u_1, u_2, \ldots, u_r),$$
$$i = 1, 2, \ldots, n,$$

where the x_i are termed state variables, and the u_j are system inputs.

The details of the state variable representation will be discussed later, the point of mentioning it now is to indicate that the stored energy variables (effort accumulation and flow accumulation) form a natural set of system state variables with which to describe a dynamical system. An example may serve to clarify some of the points made concerning system variables and stored energy. The electrical system shown in Fig. 2.2 can be idealized as shown in Fig. 2.8(a) as a source of current i supplying a resistor R. In this form the system is memory-less, since the remaining system variable v (the voltage across the resistor R) responds instantaneously to the supplied current according to Ohm's Law. A crude way of protecting against failure' or fluctuations in an electrical source is by building memory into the system in the form of a capacitor connected across the source, as shown in Fig. 2.8(b). The system

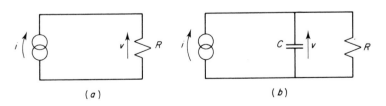

(a)   (b)

Fig. 2.8.

variable v no longer responds immediately to changes in i, since it is now a function of the input and the stored energy in the capacitor. The accumulated variable in the capacitor is the charge (time integral of current) and the charge on C forms a natural state variable for the system.

2. BASIC SYSTEM ELEMENTS

The physical variables at work in a system are the media by which energy is manipulated, and by suitable interpretation of physical variables, many systems can be reduced to a common, energy handling, basis. However, to extend the idea of energy handling systems further it is necessary to examine the components which make up physical systems, and most important of all, classify them according to how they process energy. In this manner, it should be possible to build up a catalogue of system elements with distinct energy handling properties. A detailed study of the types of system elements in the physical sciences is given the next chapter, it is however useful to consider a simple physical system and hence speculate on the possible energy handling roles of typical elements. The mechanical system in Fig. 2.9(a) depicts a pair of trucks each of mass m being pulled by a force F against rolling friction. The coupling between the two trucks acts like a spring: as the first truck is pulled away, the coupling extends. The question which is now posed is: How many different energy handling elements exist in this system? Clearly, there is a source of energy in the force input F, and a dissipator of energy in the rolling friction. In addition, two means of energy storage can be discerned; the energy stored in the moving trucks and the energy stored in the extended spring.

Another simple system is shown in Fig. 2.9(b); this depicts a simplified suspension unit in which m is the effective mass of a vehicle and the velocity

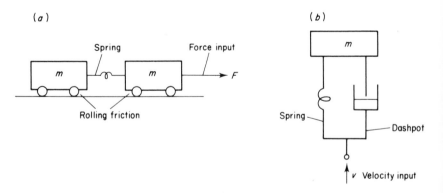

Fig. 2.9.

input v represents the stimulus the suspension gets when a vehicle moves over an incline. In this system as in the previous example, two energy storage elements are present, and one dissipator of energy. The energy source however, is different, in that it is a source of velocity. It is thus possible to distinguish two types of source, one which supplies energy via the across (extensive) system variable and another which imparts energy via and through (intensive) system variable. A little thought will reveal that energy storage also takes two complementary forms. In masses energy is stored in terms of momentum, while springs store energy in terms of the displacement from the unextended position. In one case the energy is stored as the time integral of an across variable and in the other it is stored as the time integral of a through variable.

The study of various lumped parameter systems will support these specific findings, and suggest that the basic energy handling elements can be classified as follows:

(1)   **Energy sources.** Two types of generalized energy sources exist: (a) sources of across variables, which are denoted *effort sources*: (b) sources of through variables, which are denoted *flow sources*.

(2)   **Energy stores.** Two types of generalized energy stores exist: (a) stores of across variables, which are denoted *effort stores*: (b) stores of through variables, which are denoted *flow stores*.

(3)   **Energy dissipators.** Apparently just one form of dissipator exists: this is termed a generalized energy dissipator.

These five types of generalized system elements, along with a few others to be introduced later, form a basic set of energy handling elements from which most physical systems can be modelled. Although the type of elements can be standardized, the performance of individual components of similar types may differ markedly. For example, an electrical diode and a carbon resistor are both energy dissipators, but they behave in completely different ways because of fundamental differences in their physical nature. The performance of the two devices can be quantified by experimentally determining their voltage–current characteristic, and this curve together with the knowledge that the device is an energy dissipator is sufficient to completely describe the diode and carbon resistor. Any experimental curve or law which specifies the physical characteristic of a system element is called a *constitutive relation* or a *material relation*, and in order to fully specify the five generalized system elements mentioned above, it is helpful to examine the type of constitutive relations which might be anticipated in each case.

2.1. Constitutive properties of energy sources

An energy source can be associated with each member of the system variable pair, that is to say one can have sources of flow and sources of effort. The ideal

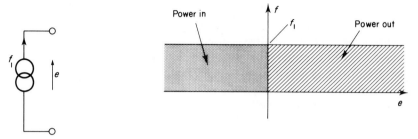

Fig. 2.10. Flow source.

flow source delivers a specified flow determined by its constitutive relation. The symbolic representation of an ideal flow source is (in common with most symbols used here) drawn from the electrical engineers' symbol for a current source and is shown in Fig. 2.10 along with the constitutive relation for a constant flow source. In practice the constitutive relation may well be a function of time (e.g. an electrical sine-wave generator), but should be independent of the effort at the terminals.

The ideal effort source delivers an effort determined by a specific material relation which may be an arbitrary function of time, but independent of the source flow. The symbol and constitutive relation for a constant source of effort are shown in Fig. 2.11. The power delivered by a source is simply the product of directed effort and flow variables, thus the hatched regions of the constitutive relations in Fig. 2.10 and 2.11 represent areas where power is delivered by the sources. The dotted regions indicate areas where the source is receiving energy.

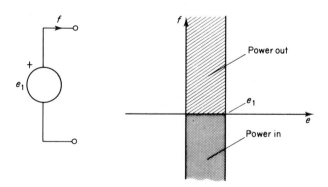

Fig. 2.11. Effort source.

2.2. Constitutive properties of energy stores

An energy storage device can be associated with each of the system variable pair, effort and flow. A device which stores energy by a time integral accumulation of flow is termed a flow store. If the flow accumulation is defined as f_a by equation (10), then the physical properties of a specific flow store are determined by a constitutive relation which expresses the flow accumulation in a device as a static function of the effort at the device output:

$$f_a = \varphi(e). \tag{12}$$

An example of such a constitutive relation is the simple law which relates the heat (flow accumulation) H in an object to the temperature difference $T_2 - T_1$ (effort) between the object and its surroundings as a linear function of the object's mass M and a constant of proportionality termed the specific heat C_P,

$$H = C_P M T_{21}. \tag{13}$$

In general, flow store constitutive relations are not linear, and a general constitutive relation together with the symbol for a flow store are shown in Fig. 2.12.

The energy stored in a flow store can be computed directly from the constitutive relation. If the stored flow energy is U, defined by

$$U = \int_0^t ef \, dt, \tag{14}$$

where $U(t=0)=0$, then recalling the definition of flow accumulation (equations (10) and (11)), the stored energy can be rewritten as

$$U = \int_0^{f_a} e \, df_a. \tag{15}$$

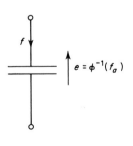 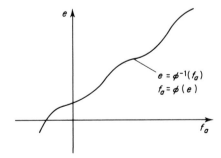

Fig. 2.12. Flow store.

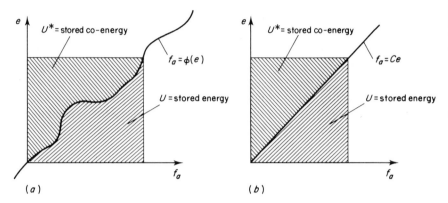

Fig. 2.13. Stored energy in flow stores.

This energy is illustrated in Fig. 2.13 as the area under the single-valued constitutive relation for both a linear and a non-linear flow store. For the non-linear device the stored energy is evaluated as

$$U = \int_0^{f_a} \varphi^{-1}(f_a) \, df_a. \tag{16}$$

For a linear store with constitutive relation

$$f_a = Ce, \tag{17}$$

the stored energy is simply

$$U = \tfrac{1}{2}Ce^2. \tag{18}$$

The right-hatched region of the constitutive relation represents a complementary energy function termed the stored co-energy U^*, and is defined (cf. equation (15)) as

$$U^* = \int_0^e f_a \, de. \tag{19}$$

In the case of a linear constitutive relation the energy U and co-energy U^* are equal. In the general, non-linear, case they are related by the Legendre transformation:

$$U = ef_a - U^*. \tag{20}$$

If the flow energy is a known function of the flow accumulation then equation (15) can be used to determine the corresponding effort. Similarly, the flow accumulation can be determined if the flow co-energy U^* is a known function

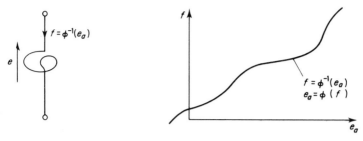

Fig. 2.14. Effort store.

of effort. The relevant equations (obtained from equation (15) and (19)) are

$$e = \partial U / \partial f_a, \qquad f_a = \partial U^* / \partial e \qquad (21)$$

The co-energy variable may seem superfluous to the current discussion. However, complementary energy functions take on a vital role in the development of variational techniques considered later.

A device which stores energy in terms of accumulated effort and whose flow is a function of effort accumulation is termed an effort store. The symbol for an effort store, together with a typical constitutive relation is shown in Fig. 2.14. A general non-linear effort store has a constitutive relation which expresses effort accumulation as a function of the device flow:

$$e_a = \varphi(f). \qquad (22)$$

For example, a mechanical spring has a displacement x (effort accumulation) from its equilibrium point which is specified by the force F (flow) on the spring, and the spring's physical characteristic. For a linear spring the stiffness parameter k fixes constitutive properties and one can write, analogously to equation (22),

$$x = (1/k)F. \qquad (23)$$

In terms of the generalized effort store the constitutive relation is

$$e_a = LF. \qquad (24)$$

The stored energy in the effort store T can be evaluated from the constitutive relation since the following holds:

$$T = \int_0^t ef \; dt = \int_0^{e_a} f \; de_a = \int_0^{e_a} \varphi^{-1}(e_a) \; de_a. \qquad (25)$$

Thus the stored effort energy T is simply the area under the constitutive relation, as indicated in Fig. 2.15. In the case of a linear effort store the stored energy is

$$T = \tfrac{1}{2} L f^2. \qquad (26)$$

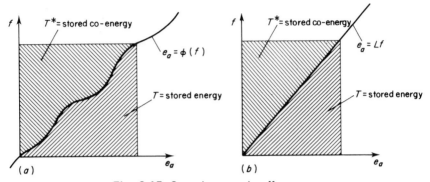

Fig. 2.15. Stored energy in effort stores.

The complementary energy function, the effort co-energy T^* is indicated in Fig. 2.15, from which the following definition is derived:

$$T^* = \int_0^f e_a \, df. \tag{27}$$

In the case of a linear effort store, the energy and co-energy are equal. In general however they are related by the following Legendre transformation:

$$T = e_a f - T^*. \tag{28}$$

Furthermore, if the co-energy associated with an effort store is a known function of flow, then the effort accumulation is, from equation (27), given by

$$e_a = \partial T^* / \partial f. \tag{29}$$

Similarly, if the energy associated with an effort store is a known function of effort accumulation, the corresponding flow variable is

$$f = \partial T / \partial e_a. \tag{30}$$

Like the co-flow energy U^*, the co-effort energy T^* plays an important role in the variational analysis of systems.

2.3. Constitutive properties of energy dissipators

Unlike the stores and sources mentioned above there is only one basic device for dissipating energy. In fact it would be strictly correct to say that a true dissipating element does not exist, since the devices which are modelled in this way are actually energy converters which transform energy into a form (usually thermal) which is not recoverable by the system. The simple dissipator considered here is a device whose constitutive relation statically relates the

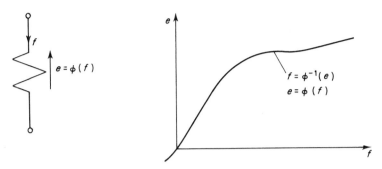

Fig. 2.16. Energy dissipator.

device flow and effort variables. A typical constitutive relation, together with the symbolic representation is shown in Fig. 2.16.

The general single-valued constitutive relation takes the form

$$e = \varphi(f). \tag{31}$$

In the linear form this becomes

$$e = Rf. \tag{32}$$

An example of a nominally linear energy dissipator is the carbon resistor referred to earlier. A highly non-linear energy dissipator is the electrical diode.

By definition a dissipator stores no energy. However the instantaneous power absorbed by a dissipator is given by

$$ef = \int_0^f e \; df + \int_0^e f \; de \tag{33}$$

$$= G + J,$$

where the quantities dissipator content G and the dissipator co-content J are defined graphically in Fig. 2.17. From equation (33) it is clear that content and

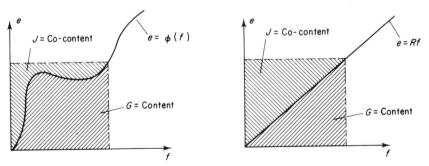

Fig. 2.17. Absorbed power in dissipators.

co-content are linked by a Legendre transformation, and that properties can be ascribed to them which are similar to those of the energy functions. In particular, if the dissipator content is a known function of flow then the corresponding effort is given by

$$e = \partial G / \partial f. \tag{34}$$

A similar relation gives the flow from the dissipator co-content:

$$f = \partial J / \partial e. \tag{35}$$

For a linear dissipator the content G and co-content J are equal, and have a value given as one-half the power being absorbed by the dissipator. In the general non-linear case, the sum of content and co-content gives the power being absorbed by the dissipator. The notions of dissipator content and co-content will be of direct use later when we discuss variational methods of system modelling.

3. ADDITIONAL SYSTEM ELEMENTS

The set of generalized system elements considered in the previous section are sufficient to describe a wide class of systems. They are however limited, in that they do not model basic energy manipulation functions like energy transformation, or coupling of sub-systems. For example, it would not be possible to model the behaviour of a gear train, or an electrical transformer with the basic elements treated so far. Neither could coupling elements like transducers or control actuators be modelled in a satisfactory manner.

The inadequacies of the basic five system elements arise because they are *one-port* or *two-terminal* devices, and to represent energy transforming and coupling devices *two or more energy ports* are needed. To be more specific, an effort store can be drawn, as in Fig. 2.18(a) as an element which can communicate with its surroundings through one energy port or one pair of terminals. Whereas, the mechanical gearbox of Fig. 2.18(b) has two energy ports, one associated with torque τ_1, velocity ω_1 and the other with torque τ_2,

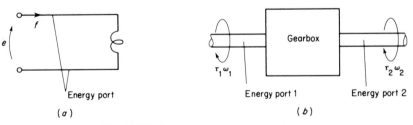

Energy port

(a)

Energy port 1   Energy port 2

(b)

Fig. 2.18. One- and two-port devices.

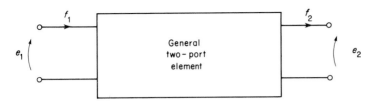

Fig. 2.19. General two-port element.

velocity ω_2. Furthermore, the energy ports are, in the ideal case statically coupled by a constitutive relation of the form:

$$\omega_2 = n\omega_1, \qquad \tau_1 = n\tau_2, \qquad (36)$$

where n is the gearing ratio of the gearbox.

A feature of the ideal gearbox is that there is no power stored or dissipated in it, since the power at port 1, is at all times equal to the power at port 2. It is therefore improbable that an interconnected set of stores and dissipators could model the ideal gearbox, and special *multi-port* system elements are needed to model such devices.

The generalized two-port, (or four-terminal) element which caters for this need is the power conserving two-port depicted in Fig. 2.19 and with general constitutive relation:

$$e_2 = \varphi_1(e_1, f_1), \qquad f_2 = \varphi_2(e_1, f_1). \qquad (37)$$

In addition, the following power conserving constraint is placed upon the system variables:

$$e_1 f_1 = e_2 f_2. \qquad (38)$$

The ideal power conserving two-port therefore transforms energy according to the non-linear constitutive equations (37), without intermediate dissipation, generation or storage of energy. The general linear power conserving two-port has constitutive relation given by

$$\begin{bmatrix} e_2 \\ f_2 \end{bmatrix} = \begin{bmatrix} a_{11} & a_{12} \\ a_{21} & a_{22} \end{bmatrix} \begin{bmatrix} e_1 \\ f_1 \end{bmatrix}, \qquad (39)$$

where again the power conserving constraint, equation (38) applies.

Two specific forms of the linear power conserving two-port are of especial importance: the ideal transformer and the ideal gyrator. The ideal transformer has a constitutive relation of the form:

$$\begin{bmatrix} e_1 \\ f_1 \end{bmatrix} = \begin{bmatrix} n & 0 \\ 0 & n^{-1} \end{bmatrix} \begin{bmatrix} e_2 \\ f_2 \end{bmatrix}, \qquad (40)$$

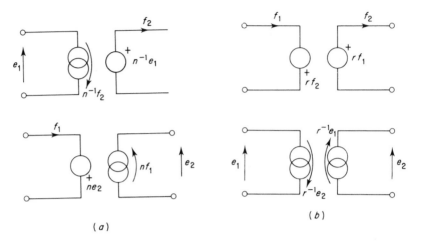

Fig. 2.20. Standard representations for transformers and gyrators: (*a*) transformer equivalents; (*b*) gyrator equivalents.

where n is the transformer modulus. The ideal gyrator has a constitutive relation of the form:

$$\begin{bmatrix} e_1 \\ f_1 \end{bmatrix} = \begin{bmatrix} 0 & r \\ r^{-1} & 0 \end{bmatrix} \begin{bmatrix} e_2 \\ f_2 \end{bmatrix}, \tag{41}$$

where r is the gyrator modulus.

These two power conserving two-ports are widely used in system modelling to represent power transformation and transduction phenomena. For power transformation within a specific energy medium, the gyrator occurs infrequently, the gyroscope is the only example which is commonly encountered. On the other hand, gyrators and transformers occur with equal probability in the modelling of devices which transduce energy from one domain to another. For example an electric motor transduces electrical energy to mechanical energy, and depending upon how the system variables are assigned in the electrical and mechanical domains, either a transforming or gyrating two-port will be required to model it.

In certain cases, notably the network method of system modelling, it is necessary to split all system components into equivalent sets of one-port elements. For this reason it is often convenient to represent ideal transformers and gyrators as pairs of coupled energy sources as shown in Fig. 2.20.

4. CONCLUSION

The generalized system variables and elements discussed in this chapter provide a uniform basis upon which to analyse a wide class of physical systems. The system elements required to model most energy handling functions reduce to a set of five one-port (or two-terminal) devices, together with a simple power conserving two-port (or four-terminal) device to represent energetic transformation and transduction. Although these elements suffice in most applications, it is sometimes necessary to utilize special multi-ports for specific large system components which defy detailed analysis. When such cases arise they are best treated on an individual basis.

In the next chapter the generalized one-port elements are considered again, this time in terms of the specific components which they represent in various energy handling media.

5. NOTES AND REFERENCES

[1]   The idea of generalized variables stems from the notions of dynamical analogies between electrical and mechanical systems. In particular, the mobility analogy which is associated with across and through measurements is ascribed to Firestone. See for example:

Firestone, F. A. (1957). American Institute of Physics Handbook, "The Mobility and Classical Impedance Analogies." McGraw-Hill, New York.

Firestone, F. A. (1938). *Journal of Applied Physics*, **9**(5), 373.

Firestone, F. A. (1933). *Journal of the Acoustic Society of America*, **4**(3), 249.

Firestone, F. A. (1957). *Journal of the Acoustic Society of America*, **28**(6), 1117.

[2]   The selection of effort and flow as our arbitrary generalized variables brings the terminology into line with that used in bond graph methods which are considered in this text.

Basic System Elements in Mechanical, Electrical, Fluid, Magnetic and Thermal Systems 3

INTRODUCTION

In this chapter the ideas concerning system variables and generalized system elements are used to put a wide range of physical system components into a uniform framework.

Five types of energy handling media are considered: mechanical, electrical, fluid, magnetic and thermal. Each medium is discussed separately, and system variables, together with the five basic energy handling elements, are treated. For simplicity, mechanical system elements are discussed in two classes — simple translatory motion and rotary motion about a fixed axis. In addition, the discussion of thermal systems is restricted to the simplest forms of heat transfer.

Only one-port system elements are treated, the class of multi-port elements are discussed in a subsequent chapter.

1. MECHANICAL SYSTEMS

The dynamical behaviour of mechanical systems is specified by a set of vector velocities, displacements, forces and moments. An appropriate set of these variables is sufficient to specify the general motion of a mechanical assembly moving in three-dimensional space. In general, the movement will combine translation and rotation of the system with respect to some reference framework. In practice, however, a wide variety of situations exists where the motion is either translatory or rotary. Alternatively, the translation and rotation of a system may be considered as separate but interacting energetic mechanisms. In any event, it is convenient to distinguish between two types of mechanical one-port elements:

(i)   mechanical one-ports for translation along a fixed direction co-ordinate;
(ii)   mechanical one-ports for rotation about a fixed co-ordinate axis.

1.1. Mechanical elements (translational)

The translational motion of a mechanical system is characterized by a set of energetically interacting components, where the nature of the interaction is determined by a set of applied and reaction forces and a corresponding set of component velocities. For instance, one thinks of a force applied to an ideal mass resulting in an acceleration of the mass such that an equal and opposite reaction force is generated. Moreover, the scalar product of the force and the resultant velocity is the power being delivered to the mass. Hence, in our generalized scheme of things, the variables, force and velocity, form a valid effort–flow pair. According to the across variable and through variable notion, velocity is an across variable, since two points are required to specify the velocity of an object, an inertial reference and a point on the object. Similarly, force can be readily visualized as a through variable since it may be measured by reference to one point alone.

With this reasoning in mind the following assignment of variables results:

$$\left.\begin{array}{l}\text{Velocity is analogous to effort}\\\text{Force is analogous to flow.}\end{array}\right\}\ \begin{array}{l}\textbf{A.1}\\\text{(Mobility Analogy)}\end{array}$$

Despite the rationale provided by the across and through variable idea, this assignment is completely arbitrary. The dual assignment is equally valid as a way of conceiving and modelling mechanical systems. In fact, historically the analogy of force to effort precedes the mobility analogy. For this reason, the two analogies, A.1 and A.2 (defined below) are used interchangeably in the text, although the development in this chapter is predominantly in terms of A.1.

$$\left.\begin{array}{l}\text{Velocity is analogous to flow.}\\\text{Force is analogous to effort.}\end{array}\right\}\ \begin{array}{l}\textbf{A.2}\\\text{(Classical Analogy)}\end{array}$$

1.2. Translational mass

A pure translational mass is a rigid mechanical object which is moving through a non-dissipative environment. Then, according to Newton's second law, the momentum p of the mass is linearly related to the object's velocity v:

$$p = mv, \tag{1}$$

where m is the Newtonian mass of the object. The quantity p, the momentum, is defined by

$$p = \int_{t_0}^{t} F \, \mathrm{d}t + p(t_0) \qquad \text{or} \qquad F = \frac{\mathrm{d}p}{\mathrm{d}t}, \tag{2}$$

where *upper case* F is used to signify force.

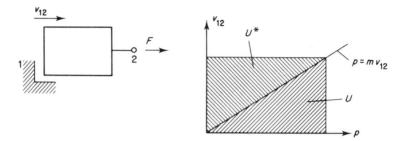

Fig. 3.1. Translational mass: symbol and constitutive relation.

The analogy A.1 indicates that the quantity momentum is formally analogous to flow accumulation and thus a pure translational mass can be classified as a flow store with the constitutive relation and symbol shown in Fig. 3.1. Notice that, in Fig. 3.1, v_{12} is considered positive if there is a net movement of terminal 2 in the direction indicated.

The Newtonian mass has an intrinsically linear constitutive relation and consequently the stored energy U (kinetic energy) and the co-energy U^* (kinetic co-energy) are equal:

$$U = U^* = \tfrac{1}{2}mv_{12}^2. \tag{3}$$

The ideal translational mass moving without resistance is completely described by the dynamical relation (equation (2)) and the constitutive (or material) relation (equation (1) and Fig. 2.1). The remarkable thing about the material behaviour of mass as specified by Newton's second law is its linearity. From the special theory of relativity it is now established that this is only an approximation which is valid for velocities much less than the velocity of light. When this condition does not prevail the constitutive relation takes the form

$$p = \frac{mv_{12}}{(1 - v_{12}^2/c^2)^{1/2}}, \tag{4}$$

where c is the velocity of light.

1.3. Translational spring

A mechanical object which when subject to a force either compresses or elongates without significant acceleration of its component parts, or loss of energy due to friction or unrecoverable deformation is a pure translational spring. The energy storage mechanism of a pure spring is the net displacement of the spring from its quiescent state. The variable displacement is defined as

$$x = = \int_{t_0}^{t} v \, dt + x(t_0) \qquad \text{or} \qquad v = \frac{dx}{dt}. \tag{5}$$

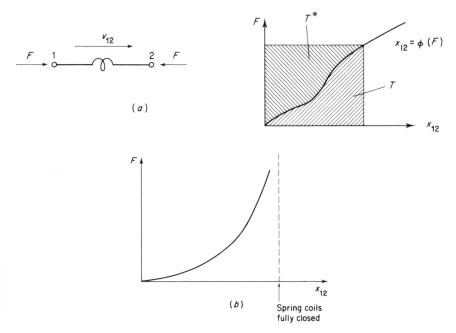

(a)

(b)   Spring coils
       fully closed

Fig. 3.2. Translational spring: (a) symbol and constitutive relation; (b) typical coil spring constitutive relation.

The material properties of a spring are specified by the constitutive relation which relates the applied force and the resultant spring deformation

$$x_{12} = \varphi(F). \tag{6}$$

The symbolic spring representation and a typical constitutive relation are shown in Fig. 3.2(a). Fig. 3.2(b) shows a typical characteristic for a coil spring under compression. A linear ideal spring obeys Hooke's law and has constitutive relation

$$x_{12} = (1/k)F, \tag{7}$$

where k is known as the spring stiffness, while the inverse k^{-1} is commonly known as the compliance.

From the above argument it will be clear that an ideal spring is (according to analogy A.1) an effort store, since the displacement x represents an accumulation of the effort variable (velocity). The stored energy in a spring is T (potential energy), and both the potential energy T and the potential co-energy T^* can be evaluated from the constitutive relation. In the linear case the stored energy and co-energy are given by

$$T = T^* = (1/2k)F^2. \tag{8}$$

Physical examples of objects which can be modelled as ideal springs are:
(a)   the familiar coil spring used in clock and meter movements;
(b)   the leaf spring used in motor car suspension systems;
(c)   the pipe U joint common in heating systems to absorb expansions and contractions in the pipework.
Actually any mechanical object where compliance effects dominate massive and power absorbing characteristics can be modelled as a spring.

1.4. Translational dissipation

A mechanical object which requires a steady force to maintain a certain velocity displays dissipative effects. Usually, the dissipation of power occurs because energy is being transformed from kinetic energy to thermal energy by viscous friction. Viscous forces have to be overcome whenever neighbouring bodies have a relative velocity. Thus, any arrangement which involves the relative motion of adjacent objects will incur power dissipation. A pure dissipator is one in which the kinetic and potential energy storage phenomena are absent. Thus a light, rigid object moving through a viscous fluid or sliding along a rough surface will have a constitutive relation which statically relates the applied force and relative velocity of the object:

$$F = \varphi(v_{12}). \qquad (9)$$

In the linear case the constitutive relation becomes

$$F = bv_{12}. \qquad (10)$$

The pure dissipator is symbolically represented by the dashpot of Fig. 3.3(a). This schematically evokes the dashpot devices used to damp the motions of motor car suspension systems and electrical meter movements.

The power absorbed by a dissipator is the product of the effort and flow variables, and is obtained from the constitutive relation as the sum of the dissipator content and co-content. For a linear dissipator with the constitutive relation of equation (10), the content and co-content are given by

$$J = G = \tfrac{1}{2}bv_{12}^2. \qquad (11)$$

The net power absorbed is

$$\text{Power} = bv_{12}^2 = F^2/b. \qquad (12)$$

In practice frictional losses are almost always non-linear in nature. In particular the characteristics of sliding friction have the form shown in Fig. 3.3(b).

1.5. Translational energy sources

It follows from the pattern of analogy A.1 that an ideal source of force is a pure flow source. Similarly, an ideal source of velocity is a pure source of effort. It is difficult to visualize idealized translational source elements, since actual translational sources exhibit losses and storage effects which are intimately

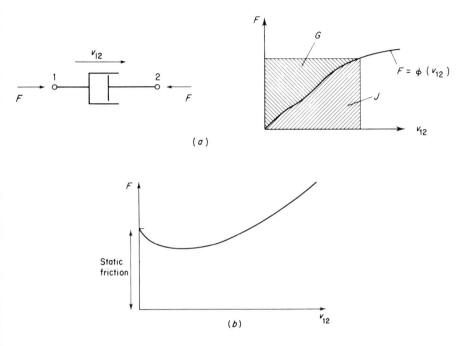

Fig. 3.3. Translational dissipator: (*a*) symbol and constitutive relation; (*b*) typical frictional characteristic.

associated with the actual energy generating phenomenon. As a consequence, actual energy sources are modelled as ideal sources associated with dissipator and store elements to represent the imperfections. Despite this practical point, it is still possible to find energy source phenomena which are, to a good approximation, ideal. A specific example is the gravitational attraction of the earth, this is conventionally modelled as an ideal source of force $-mg$, where g is the gravitational constant and m is the mass of the object under the influence of gravity.

1.6. Mechanical elements (rotational)

Rotational motion about a fixed axis is governed by a set of torques and angular velocities. Torque is the moment of a force about a point and is consequently a through variable in the same way as force is. In a similar fashion angular velocity about a fixed axis is readily seen to be an across variable, thus for rotational motion the complementary statement to analogy A.1 is

Angular velocity is analogous to effort. $\left.\right\}$ **A.1**
Axial torque is analogous to flow.

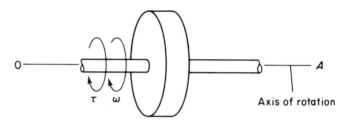

Fig. 3.4. Rotational motion.

1.7. Rotational mass

A pure rotational mass store is a rigid mechanical object rotating without resistance about a fixed axis OA (Fig. 3.4). Then according to Newton's second law the angular momentum h is related to the angular velocity ω_{12} of the mass with respect to the inertial framework and is given by

$$h = I\omega_{12}, \tag{13}$$

where I is defined as the moment of inertia of the object about axis OA. The axial torque τ applied to the object is defined by the dynamical relationship:

$$\tau = dh/dt. \tag{14}$$

A rotational mass store is represented symbolically in Fig. 3.5. The figure also depicts the constitutive relation for a rotating mass; because of our choice of analogy A.1, the constitutive properties are represented as those of a flow store. Note that the flow accumulation (angular momentum h) is linearly related through the constitutive relation to the effort variable (angular velocity ω_{12}). As a result the stored kinetic energy U and the kinetic co-energy U^* are equal and given by

$$U = U^* = \tfrac{1}{2}I\omega_{12}^2 \tag{15}$$

As with the translational mass, the linear constitutive relation (equation (13)) is a direct consequence of neglecting relativistic effects.

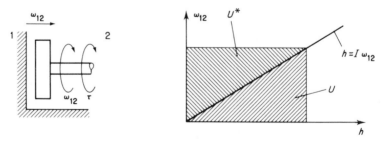

Fig. 3.5. Rotational mass: symbol and constitutive relation.

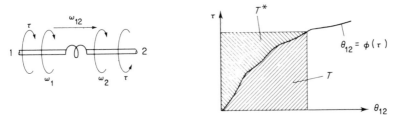

Fig. 3.6. Rotational spring: symbol and constitutive relation.

1.8. Rotational spring

Any object which when subject to a torsional moment has a resultant angular displacement measured across the object and along the axis displays the essential features of a rotational spring. If the object is nominally massless and moves without dissipation, then it is a pure torsional spring. The constitutive relation of a pure torsional spring is

$$\theta_{12} = \varphi(\tau). \tag{16}$$

With reference to Fig. 3.6, equation (16) states that the angular displacement θ_{12} measured across the spring is statically determined by the torque applied at the ends 1 and 2. The displacement variable is defined in terms of the angular velocity by the dynamic relationship:

$$\omega_{12} = d\theta_{12}/dt. \tag{17}$$

In the convention of Fig. 3.6, the relative velocity ω_{12} is defined as positive if the terminal velocities ω_1 and ω_2 (themselves measured with respect to an inertial framework) are such that ω_1 is larger in an anticlockwise sense than ω_2.

If the constitutive relation of the spring is linear, then

$$\tau = k\theta_{12}, \tag{18}$$

where k is the torsional stiffness and k^{-1} is the torsional compliance.

According to analogy A.1 the rotational spring is an effort store with stored potential energy T and co-energy T^* given by the shaded regions of the constitutive relation (Fig. 3.6). If the store is linear then the potential energy and co-energy are given by

$$T = T^* = \tfrac{1}{2}k\theta_{12}^2. \tag{19}$$

1.9. Rotational dissipation

A rotational dissipator of energy displays material behaviour which determines the device angular velocity as a function of the device torque. The

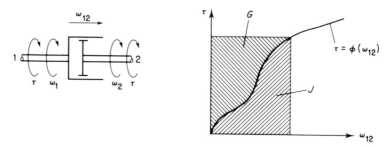

Fig. 3.7. Rotational dissipator: symbol and constitutive relation.

dissipator actually converts mechanical energy to thermal energy by the phenomenon of viscosity or friction. Symbolically a rotational dissipator is represented by a rotational dashpot (Fig. 3.7) with a constitutive relation:

$$\tau = \varphi(\omega_{12}), \qquad (20)$$

where the angular velocity ω_{12} is measured across the dissipator terminals. In its linear form the constitutive relation of a rotational dissipator is

$$\tau = b\omega_{12}. \qquad (21)$$

The power dissipated by a rotational dissipator is the sum of the dissipator content G and co-content J:

$$\text{Power dissipated} = G + J.$$

In the linear case G and J are equal and are given by

$$G = J = \tfrac{1}{2}b\omega_{12}^2. \qquad (22)$$

1.10. Rotational energy sources

Pure sources of torque and angular velocity are respectively the rotational sources of flow and effort (analogy A.1). They rarely appear in forms which resemble ideal sources and are modelled as pure source elements with appropriate stores and dissipators to emulate the imperfections of the energy source.

2. ELECTRICAL SYSTEMS

2.1. Voltage and current

The generalized concept of effort and flow variables as an energy transporting mechanism finds a ready parallel in the variables voltage and current of electrical systems. The conceptual similarity of the variable sets leads naturally to the assignment:

> Voltage is analogous to effort.
>
> Current is analogous to flow.

This assignment is compatible with the notions of across and through variables, and is used universally.

2.2. Inductance: Electrical effort storage

In the seventeenth century Joseph Henry in America, and Michael Faraday in England, discovered that current flowing in a circuit displayed properties analogous to mechanical momentum. The electricity flowing in a long circuit displays what Maxwell termed "an electrokinetic momentum", which is proportional to the current flowing and a constant dependent upon the physical arrangement of the circuit. The quantity electrokinetic momentum is now known as "flux linkages" λ and is the total magnetic flux linked by the electrical circuit. Similarly, the physical constant which together with the current i determines the flux linkage is the circuit inductance L:

$$\lambda = Li. \tag{23}$$

The flux linked by the circuit determines the voltage v developed across the inductor via Faraday's Law:

$$v = d\lambda/dt. \tag{24}$$

Equation (23) is the linear form of the inductive constitutive relation; in general the relation is non-linear and may be multi-valued:

$$\lambda = \varphi(i). \tag{25}$$

For an inductor composed of a coil of N turns wound on a homogeneous core of permeability μ of uniform cross-sectional area, the inductance is given by

$$L = N^2 \mu a/l, \tag{26}$$

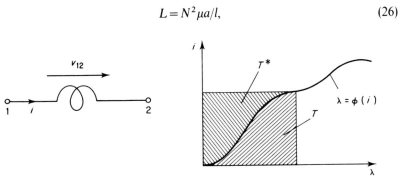

Fig. 3.8. Inductor: symbol and constitutive relation.

where a is the cross-sectional area of the magnetic circuit and l is the length of the magnetic circuit. For non-magnetic core materials the magnetic permeability is constant. However for ferrous cored inductors the permeability is a function of the current, such that the inductive constitutive relation is non-linear.

The symbol for a pure inductor and a typical single-valued constitutive relation are shown in Fig. 3.8. The energy stored in an inductive field is given from the graph in Fig. 3.8 as

$$T = \int_0^\lambda i \, d\lambda. \tag{27}$$

The inductive co-energy is given by the complementary integral:

$$T^* = \int_0^i \lambda \, di. \tag{28}$$

If the inductor is linear then the energy and co-energy are equal and given by

$$T = T^* = (1/2L)\lambda^2 = \tfrac{1}{2}Li^2. \tag{29}$$

2.3. Capacitance: Electrical flow storage

The inductor stores energy in a magnetic field. The complementary storage element, the capacitor, stores energy in an electric field. Whenever two electrical conductors are at different potentials there is storage of charge upon them. The amount of charge q which is accumulated in this way is determined by the voltage difference v across the conductors and the physical properties of the conductors and the medium which separates them. The constitutive relationship of a capacitor therefore has the general form:

$$q = \varphi(v). \tag{30}$$

In the linear case this becomes

$$q = Cv, \tag{31}$$

where C is termed the capacitance of the capacitor. For a pair of parallel plates separated by a distance a and with a homogenous filling of permittivity ε, the capacitance is given by

$$C = \varepsilon a/d, \tag{32}$$

where d is the effective cross-sectional area of the plates. For almost all dielectric materials used in capacitors the permittivity is a constant such that the capacitive constitutive relation is a constant. The electrical charge q is related to the current i flowing in the capacitor circuit by the dynamic relationship:

$$i = dq/dt \tag{33}$$

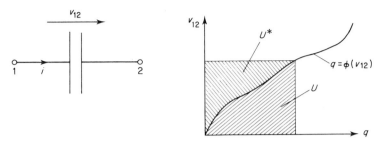

Fig. 3.9. Capacitor: symbol and constitutive relation.

Fig. 3.9 shows the symbol for an electrical capacitor, together with a typical constitutive relation. The electrical energy stored in a capacitor is given by

$$U = \int_0^q v \, dq. \tag{34}$$

The co-energy is defined in a complementary fashion:

$$U^* = \int_0^v q \, dv. \tag{35}$$

If the capacitor is linear the capacitative energy and co-energy are equal and given by

$$U = U^* = \tfrac{1}{2}Cv^2 = (1/2C)q^2. \tag{36}$$

2.4. Resistance: Electrical dissipation

An electrical device in which the terminal voltage v is statically related to the current flowing through the device is a dissipator of electrical energy. If the device is free from storage and source effects, it is said to be a pure electrical resistance. The general constitutive relation for a resistance is

$$v = \varphi(i). \tag{37}$$

The linear form of equation (37) was first discovered by Georg Ohm, and bears his name. Ohm's law states

$$v = Ri, \tag{38}$$

where R is termed the resistance of the electrical dissipator. For a homogeneous electric circuit of length l and uniform cross-sectional area a, the resistance is given by

$$R = \rho l / a \tag{39}$$

where ρ is the resistivity of the circuit material.

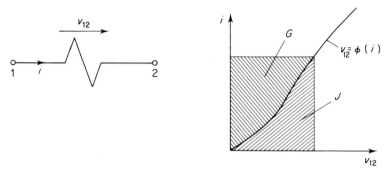

Fig. 3.10. Resistor: symbol and constitutive relation.

The symbol for an electrical dissipator together with a typical constitutive relation are shown in Fig. 3.10. The total power dissipated by a resistor is the product of current and terminal voltage; this is just the sum of the electrical content G and co-content J of the resistor. For a linear device the content and co-content are equal and given by

$$G = J = \tfrac{1}{2} R i^2. \tag{40}$$

The total power dissipated is

$$\text{Power} = i^2 R = v^2 / R. \tag{41}$$

3. FLUID SYSTEMS

In a similar way to mechanical systems fluid motion can be modelled in terms of elementary source, storage and dissipative mechanisms. However, fluids are generally less dense and more compliant than solids so that the distinction between massive and compliant parts of fluid systems cannot generally be made. Nevertheless, a wide variety of engineering systems which use fluids as a working medium are susceptible to the lumped parameter treatment given here. The type of fluid systems dealt with here are the most simple to analyse, consisting of one-dimensional flow in pipe-work, with the energy handling phenomena isolated at specific points.

3.1. Pressure and fluid flow rate

In contemplating the energy transport mechanism in fluid systems, one is led to conclude that fluid pressure (P) and fluid flow rate (Q) form a valid pair of variables with which to associate the generalized energy variable pair:

> Fluid pressure is analogous to effort.
> Fluid flow rate is analogous to flow.

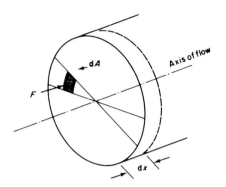

Fig. 3.11. Fluid flow in pipes.

Consider a closed pipe (Fig. 3.11) in which the fluid pressure is P at a certain cross-section. Pressure is defined as the fluid force per unit area; thus if the cross-sectional area of the pipe is A, the total fluid pressure F is

$$F = \int_A P \, dA. \qquad (42)$$

If the pressure is constant over the area, the total force is the product of fluid pressure and the cross-sectional area. The energy associated with fluid flow can now be determined by using the relation (cf. potential energy T of a translational or rotational spring):

$$\text{Work done} = T = \int_0^{x_1} F \, dx = \int_0^{x_1} PA \, dx, \qquad (43)$$

where x is displacement of fluid along the axis of flow past the reference cross-section.

By recalling that the incremental fluid flow rate δQ past the reference cross-section is

$$\delta Q = \frac{d(A\delta x)}{dt}, \qquad (44)$$

hence the work done T can be written

$$T = \int_0^t PQ \, dt. \qquad (45)$$

This expression means that, in addition to being intuitively valid, the fluid pressure and fluid flow rate are true energy variables with a product which equals the fluid power and time integral which is the fluid energy.

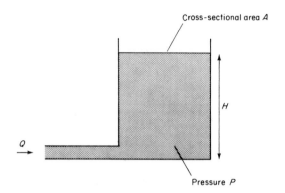

Fig. 3.12. Fluid flow store: open reservoir.

3.2. Fluid flow store

There are several fluid elements which store flow energy, the two most important are the fluid reservoir and the pressurized tank.

3.2.1. Fluid reservoir

An open tank or reservoir which is fed from the bottom with working fluid is a store of fluid flow energy. As fluid flows into the reservoir the potential energy of the fluid mass is increased by raising the fluid level in the tank. The increase in energy manifests itself in an increase in the relative fluid pressure P measured at an arbitrary fixed point in the tank (Fig. 3.12). The principle of conservation of material can be applied to get

$$\rho Q = \frac{\mathrm{d}(\rho A H)}{\mathrm{d}t},\tag{46}$$

where ρ = the mass density of the fluid; A = the cross-sectional area of the reservoir; H = the fluid height in the reservoir. This expression can be rearranged in the form:

$$V = \frac{A}{\rho g}P,\tag{47}$$

which is the constitutive relation for the reservoir, and relates fluid pressure P to the fluid volume V in the reservoir. The fluid volume is related to the fluid flow rate by the dynamical equation:

$$Q = \mathrm{d}V/\mathrm{d}t.\tag{48}$$

Note that the constitutive relation (equation (47)) is linear, this is because incompressible flow and vertical tank sides have been assumed. The coefficient

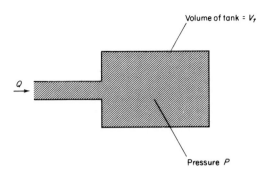

Fig. 3.13. Fluid flow store: sealed tank.

of a flow store is termed the fluid capacitance C_f; for the open reservoir this is given by

$$C_f = A/\rho g. \tag{49}$$

3.2.2. Pressurized tank

A second fluid flow store is the pressurized tank; these devices store fluid flow energy by compressing the fluid in a sealed chamber as indicated in Fig. 3.13. Suppose the tank is filled with fluid of uniform density ρ, with pressure P and absolute temperature T. The principle of conservation of material may be applied to get

$$\rho Q = \frac{d\rho}{dt} V_t, \tag{50}$$

where Q is the fluid flow rate into the tank and V_t is the volume of the tank which is assumed constant (rigid tank).

The constitutive relation of the pressurized tank now depends upon the nature of the working fluid. More specifically it depends upon how the mass density of the fluid ρ is related to the absolute fluid pressure. For liquids a good approximation to this dependence is given by

$$d\rho = \frac{\rho}{\beta} dP, \tag{51}$$

where β is the fluid bulk modulus of elasticity and is a measure of the "stiffness" of the fluid (cf. equation (7)).

For gases (pneumatic systems) the situation is more complex since the bulk modulus at a given temperature and pressure is dependent upon the precise specification of the heat transfer which accompanies the strain upon the gas. Only two specifications are normally considered — isothermal heat transfer and adiabatic heat transfer. These determine two distinct thermodynamic constraints, respectively constant temperature processes and zero-heat-exchange processes. Under these conditions two distinct bulk moduli arise — the isothermal elasticity k_i and adiabatic elasticity k_a. For an ideal gas these are:

> Bulk modulus (constant temperature) $\equiv$ isothermal elasticity $k_i = P$.
> Bulk modulus (constant heat) $\equiv$ adiabatic elasticity $k_a = \gamma P$.　　(52)

where $\gamma = C_P / C_V$ the ratio of principal specific heats and P is the gaseous pressure.

By manipulating equations (50) and (51) the constitutive relation of a pressurized tank flow store is

$$V = \frac{V_t}{\beta} P,$$　　(53)

where $\beta = $ a constant for most fluids; $\beta = k_i = P$ for isothermal gaseous processes; $\beta = k_a = \gamma P$ for adiabatic gaseous processes.

The total fluid volume V in the pressurized tank is determined from the fluid flow rate Q by the dynamical relation:

$$Q = dV/dt.$$　　(54)

The pressurized tank fluid flow store is characterized by the capacitance C_f given by

$$C_f = V_t/\beta.$$　　(55)

The constitutive relation of a general fluid flow store is shown in Fig. 3.14. The stored flow energy U is given by

$$U = \int_0^V P \, dV = \int_0^V \varphi^{-1}(V) \, dV.$$　　(56)

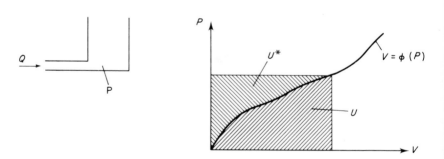

Fig. 3.14. Symbol and constitutive relation for a fluid flow store.

Similarly, the flow co-energy U^* is given by

$$U^* = \int_0^P \varphi(P)\, dP. \tag{57}$$

In the linear case the two energy functions are equal and given by

$$U = U^* = \tfrac{1}{2} C_f P^2. \tag{58}$$

3.3. Fluid effort store

The fluid mechanism for storing effort energy is the kinetic energy associated with a moving body of fluid. Consider an incompressible fluid flowing without dissipation in a tube; suppose that a plug of fluid of length l can be considered as a rigid mass with a uniform velocity v (Fig. 3.15). From Newton's second law the effective force on the plug is related to the acceleration of the fluid plug by

$$F = A(P_2 - P_1) = \rho A l \frac{dv}{dt}, \tag{59}$$

where $P_2 - P_1$ is the pressure difference across the fluid plug, ρ is the fluid density and A is the cross-sectional area of the tube.

The constitutive relation of the fluid effort store can be obtained by manipulation of equation (59):

$$\Gamma_{21} = \frac{\rho l}{A} Q \tag{60}$$

where Γ_{21} is defined as the fluid momentum and is related to the pressure difference P_{21} across the plug by

$$P_{21} = P_2 - P_1 = d\Gamma_{21}/dt. \tag{61}$$

The material properties of a fluid effort store are defined by its inertance L_f, defined from equation (60) as

$$L_f = \rho l / A. \tag{62}$$

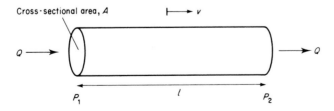

Fig. 3.15. Fluid flow in a pipe.

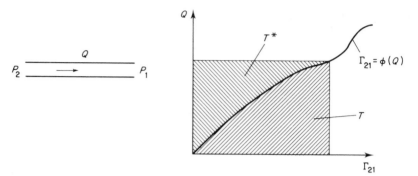

Fig. 3.16. Symbol and constitutive relation for a fluid effort store.

Fig. 3.16 shows the symbol for a fluid effort store, together with a typical constitutive relation. The kinetic energy stored in a fluid effort store is given by

$$T = \int_0^{\Gamma_{21}} Q \, d\Gamma_{21} = \int_0^{\Gamma_{21}} \varphi^{-1}(\Gamma_{21}) \, d\Gamma_{21}. \tag{63}$$

The stored kinetic co-energy is defined by the complementary integral:

$$T^* = \int_0^Q \Gamma_{21} dQ = \int_0^Q \varphi(Q) \, dQ. \tag{64}$$

In the linear case these energy functions are equal and given by

$$T = T^* = \tfrac{1}{2} L_f Q^2 \tag{65}$$

3.4. Fluid dissipation

Since fluid flow always involves the relative motion of close objects there are many fluid devices in which viscous effects can cause conversion of fluid kinetic energy to thermal energy and hence dissipate power. There are, however, two basic mechanisms which fliud dissipators employ:
(i)   viscous forces between the fluid and the retaining pipework;
(ii) viscous forces between fluid particles.
Fluid dissipators which occur because of the former effect are:
(a)   Flow through a porous medium: D'Arcy's law for incompressible flow through a porous medium inserted in a fluid line is linear. It relates relative pressure across the plug P_{21} to the effective fluid flow rate through it as

$$P_{21} = R_f Q \tag{66}$$

where $R_f = $ fluid resistance.

(b)   Laminar flow through a capillary pipe: For small values of Reynolds number the Hagen–Poisenille law predicts that power dissipation follows a linear constitutive relation with fluid resistance given by

$$R_f = \frac{128\,\mu l}{\pi d^4} \qquad (67)$$

where μ = fluid viscosity; l = capillary pipe length; d = capillary pipe diameter.

Fluid dissipators which rely upon viscous forces between fluid particles are:

(a)   Turbulent flow through a long pipe: For incompressible flow at Reynolds numbers in excess of about two thousand, the flow is normally turbulent. In this situation fluid power is dissipated and the dissipator constitutive relation is approximately

$$P_{21} = aQ|Q|^{3/4} \qquad (68)$$

where a is a constant dependent upon the fluid properties and pipe geometry.

(b)   Incompressible flow through an orifice: A sudden restriction or change in cross-sectional area over a short length of a pipe constitutes an orifice. Fluid is rapidly accelerated through the orifice with resultant turbulent flow downstream of the restriction. An approximate expression for the constitutive relation of an orifice dissipator is

$$P_{21} = \frac{\rho}{2C_d^2 A_o^2} Q|Q| \qquad (69)$$

where ρ = the fluid density; C_d = the orifice coefficient of discharge; A_o = the cross-sectional area of the orifice; P_{21} = the pressure difference measured upstream and downstream of the dissipator.

A general fluid dissipator is represented by the symbol and constitutive relation of Fig. 3.17. Formally the constitutive relation is given by

$$P_{21} = \varphi(Q). \qquad (70)$$

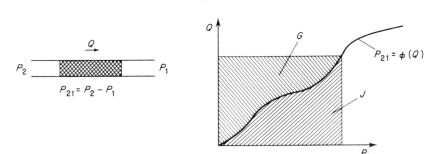

Fig. 3.17. Symbol and constitutive relation for a fluid dissipator.

The power dissipated by a fluid resistance is

$$P_{21}Q = G + J, \tag{71}$$

where the dissipator content G and co-content J are defined in the normal way:

$$G = \int_0^Q P_{21} \, dQ, \qquad J = \int_0^P Q \, dP_{21}. \tag{72}$$

For linear dissipators the power dissipated is given by

$$P_{21}Q = Q^2 R_f. \tag{73}$$

3.5. Fluid energy sources

The most frequently encountered source of fluid energy is the mechanical fluid pump. In general these devices are neither pure flow or pressure sources and are modelled by a pure source with auxiliary components to represent imperfections. For a variety of applications positive displacement pump types can be modelled as pure flow sources. If a constant pressure hydraulic source is required a fluid flow store is frequently employed to smooth the pressure variations from a constant displacement pump.

4. MAGNETIC SYSTEMS

4.1. Magnetomotive force and flux

In almost all cases the properties of magnetic circuits can modelled indirectly via their reflected electrical circuit properties. Situations arise however when the magnetic circuit must be considered in its own right. The extensive variable in a magnetic circuit is magnetomotive force (M). The intensive variable is associated with the total magnetic flux (Φ). Hence according to the across and through variable analogy:

Magnetomotive force is analogous to effort.
Magnetomotive flux is analogous to flow.

The storage of energy in magnetic circuits is usually modelled by the reflected electrical characteristic of inductance. In magnetic terms, the property of inductance is a flow storage phenomenon in that it is associated with an accumulation of magnetic flux. The complementary form of magnetic energy storage is not normally discernible.

4.2. Magnetic reluctance

The magnetizing force at any point in a magnetic system is the magnetomotive force per unit length required at that point to maintain the magnetic flux. Lines

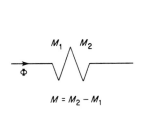

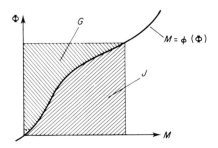

Fig. 3.18. Symbol and constitutive relation for a magnetic dissipator.

of magnetic flux form closed loops and if H represents the magnetizing force then the total magnetomotive force is the integral of H along the centre flux line, i.e.

$$M = \oint H \, dl. \tag{74}$$

Now consider a closed iron circuit having a cross-sectional area of a square metres and a mean length l. The total flux is Φ and is the product of flux density B and cross-sectional area. Hence

$$\frac{\Phi}{M} = \frac{Ba}{Hl}. \tag{75}$$

However, the ratio B/H defines the magnetic permeability μ of the medium supporting the flux, giving

$$M = S\Phi, \tag{76}$$

where $S = l/\mu a$ is the reluctance of the magnetic circuit and is the magnetic form of energy dissipation.

Equation (76) is the constitutive relation of a magnetic dissipator. Recalling that permeability is a function of the magnetic flux level, magnetic dissipators are usually non-linear in nature with constitutive relation:

$$M = \varphi(\Phi). \tag{77}$$

Fig. 3.18 shows a typical constitutive relationship for a magnetic dissipator together with the symbol adopted.

4.3. Magnetic energy sources

The most basic form of magnetic energy source is the permanent magnet which is a source of magnetomotive force. Most magnetic systems display some element of permanent magnetism either as an explicit source or as residual magnetism in the ferrous medium which supports the magnetic flux. Another form of magnetic energy source is an electric coil of N turns carrying a current I coupled to the magnetic circuit such that the magnetomotive force of the equivalent magnetic source is

$$M = NI. \tag{78}$$

5. THERMAL SYSTEMS

5.1. Heat and temperature

The concept of heat arises from intuitive judgements of how objects "feel" when touched. The experience of our tactile sensations is that objects can be ordered in a sequence of "hotter" or "colder". Furthermore, this conceptual property "heat" exhibits flow properties. Two bodies, one hotter than the other, tend to retain this difference if isolated one from the other, but if they are brought into close contact they tend to lose any temperature difference. These notions are systematized by the introduction of "temperature" as a measure of the degree of hotness and a quantity "heat" which tends to flow from hotter to cooler bodies. A quantitive measure of temperature is obtained by fixing a scale of measurement against some controlled events which are characterized by specific degrees of hotness. Temperature scales in common use, Celsius and Fahrenheit, are now fixed with respect to the characteristic temperature of water. The amount of heat can be similarly quantified by an interaction experiment between two bodies of initially different temperatures T_1 and T_2. Then postulating that the amount of heat associated with a body is proportional to the product of mass and temperature, the conservation principle for energy can be envoked to determine the constant of proportionality which characterizes the substance. In this way the phenomenon of heat can be rationalized as follows: If a mass m_1 of substance is heated from temperature T_1 to T_2 the amount of heat H which it acquires is given by

$$H = m_1 C_P (T_2 - T_1), \tag{79}$$

where C_P is the specific heat of the substance.

Thus the quantities heat flow rate (q) and temperature (T) apparently qualify as an effort/flow pair. Heat is readily thought of as a flow variable, and temperature is an across variable since a temperature datum is required for thermometer calibration. This notion is valid, but should be used with care since heat (H) itself is an energy variable, so that generalizations concerning energy will not carry over.

5.2. Thermal flow store

The ability of a specific material to store heat is a measure of its thermal capacity. The constitutive relation (equation (79)) of a thermal flow store

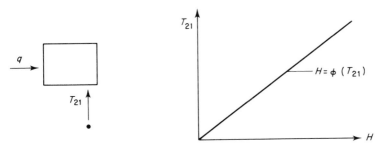

Fig. 3.19. Symbol and constitutive relation for a thermal flow store.

relates in a linear fashion the total heat transferred and the temperature change. The total heat is related to the heat flow rate q by the dynamic relation:

$$q = dH/dt. \tag{80}$$

The constitutive relation for a thermal flow store, together with its symbolic representation, is shown in Fig. 3.19. The total energy stored in the flow store is the time integral of the heat flow variable.

5.3. Thermal effort store

There is apparently no thermal element which displays an energy storage mechanism which is complementary to the flow store.

5.4. Thermal dissipation

The flow of heat through a substance is accompanied by thermal resistance and a consequent temperature gradient. The material relation which governs the flow of heat by conduction is Fourier's law:

$$q = \frac{\sigma_c A}{l}(T_2 - T_1), \tag{81}$$

where σ_c is the thermal conductivity of the material; A is the cross-sectional area of the object; l is the length of the object; and $T_2 - T_1$ is the temperature difference across the ends of the object.

If the transport of heat is by convection, the resistance to heat flow is difficult to analyse. In this instance the notion of an overall heat transfer coefficient for a specific physical object is employed. The resultant constitutive relation is

$$q = C_h A(T_2 - T_1), \tag{82}$$

where the heat coefficient C_h is defined in terms of the constitutive relation of a particular object.

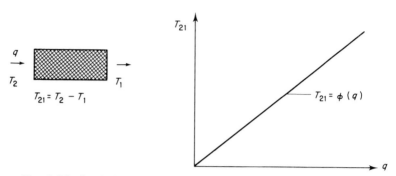

Fig. 3.20. Symbol and constitutive relation for a thermal dissipator.

The third mechanism for heat transfer is radiation, this is described analytically by the Stefan–Boltzmann law:

$$q = C_r(T_2^4 - T_1^4), \tag{83}$$

where C_r is a constant determined by the geometry of the surfaces radiating and receiving heat.

The symbol for a thermal dissipator is depicted in Fig. 3.20, as is a typical constitutive relation. Like other types of dissipator elements, thermal dissipators do not lose energy. The heat flow is associated with a net increase in the entropy of the transporting medium and a net decrease in "useful" heat energy.

6. NOTES AND REFERENCES

[1]. The discussion of basic system elements given here can be found in similar forms in a number of text books. A particularly clear exposition is given in:

Shearer, J. L., Murphy, A. T. and Richardson, H. H. (1967). "Introduction to systems dynamics". Addison Wesley, Reading, Mass.

[2]. We have also found useful the perspective set in:

Feather, N. (1959). "Mass, length and time". Pelican Books, London.

[3]. The representation of thermal energy in terms of a pair of variables is questionable on a number of levels. First, temperature and heat flow are not a true energy pair (entropy flow rate and temperature are more appropriate). Second, the class of thermal systems which can be modelled by a pair of variables is limited. Fortunately, the dynamics of heat conduction dominate most other aspects of thermal systems and in a practical sense justify the restrictions invoked here.

[4]. A good discussion of spring and dissipator constitutive relations encountered in practice is given in:

Shigley, J. E. (1977). "Mechanical Engineering Design", 3rd edn. Series in mechanical engineering design. McGraw–Hill, New York.
See especially chapters, 3, 8, 10.

7. PROBLEMS

7.1. Determine the constitutive relation for a spherical fluid reservoir of radius r. Obtain the stored energy as a function of the volume of stored liquid, and the stored co-energy as a function of the pressure at the tank bottom.

7.2. The open top container shown in Fig. 3.21 is used as a reservoir for an incompressible fluid. Sketch the constitutive relation of the reservoir, and obtain equations for the stored co-energy and energy.

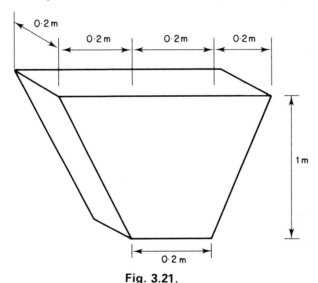

0·2 m

0·2 m   0·2 m   0·2 m

1 m

0·2 m

Fig. 3.21.

7.3. An electrical inductor has inductance which is a function of current:

$$L = 0.01(i)^{-1/2}$$

Sketch the constitutive relation of the device and evaluate the stored energy and co-energy when a current of 0·2 amperes passes through the inductor.

7.4 A mechanical dissipator consists of a paddle rotating in a viscous fluid. A torque of 0·1 newton metre is required before the paddle will rotate, the torque then increases linearly with angular velocity given by 0·2 newton metres per rad/second. Find the content and co-content of the device at a velocity of 0·5 rad/second.

7.5   Mechanical systems are sometimes analysed by constructing analogous electrical circuits. Write down a list of analogous one-port elements, starting with inductance analogous to a translational spring. Compare this list with the analogy which results from the notions of across and through variables.

7.6.   The mechanical system shown in Fig. 3.22 consists of a mass m_1 sliding without friction in a guide-way. A force $F(t)$ is applied to the mass m_1, and a light, flexible, shaft connects m_1 to another mass m_2, which is sliding in a viscous fluid.

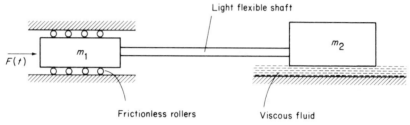

Fig. 3.22.

Decompose the system into a set of one-port elements, identify the energy handling properties of each element, and sketch typical constitutive relations for each type of element.

7.7.   A problem with non-linear constitutive relations is that they are often unsuitable for analysis. One approach to this problem is to linearize the constitutive relation about specific operating points. Apply this procedure to the non-linear electrical dissipator whose constitutive relation is shown in Fig. 7.23. Obtain equivalent linear circuits for the device operating at points A, B, C.

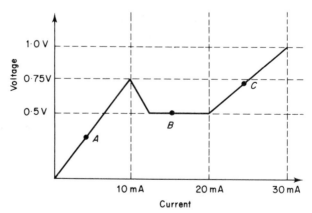

Fig. 3.23.

Special Multi-port System Elements

4

INTRODUCTION

The catalogue of basic one-port elements presented in the previous chapter allows fundamental energy handling processes to be modelled in a uniform way. The discussion now naturally turns to the additional multi-port elements needed to model realistic systems. Most important among these devices are two-ports which allow coupling of different energy handling media, and converters which change the ratio by which effort and flow jointly transport energy. Couplers provide a means of bridging an energy interface and are at the heart of models for transducers, actuators, motors and generators. Convertors on the other hand are necessary in order to model the basic transforming or gyrating functions of devices like levers, pulleys, and electrical transformers. A distinctive feature of these devices is that they are energy conserving, this immediately excludes the possibility of thermal transformers since one of the effort/flow pair in thermal systems is itself a power variable. In addition most of the energy converting two-ports are power conserving, implying that all energy dissipation and storage effects can be modelled separately or ignored. An additional class of devices which deserve special discussion are modulated multi-ports. There are basically two types which attract our interest: The modulated one-port and the modulated two-port. The former class permits straightforward modelling of controlled sources and dissipators, while the latter form a valuable class of power conserving two-ports.

1. ENERGY CONVERTERS

1.1. Electrical transformers

If two electric circuits affect one another by a mutual magnetic field, then a transforming action occurs whereby each circuit induces a voltage in the other.

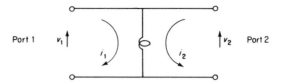

Fig. 4.1. A simple circuit displaying mutual inductance.

When this occurs the circuits are said to exhibit mutual inductance. The simplest case occurs when two circuits share a common branch (Fig. 4.1). The more interesting instance is a pair of circuits linked via a common (mutual) magnetic field (Fig. 4.2). The flux linkages in one coil depend now upon the current flowing in both circuits, as a result the constitutive relations take the form

$$\lambda_1 = \varphi_1(i_1, i_2), \qquad \lambda_2 = \varphi_2(i_1, i_2), \tag{1}$$

where λ_1 is the flux linking circuit 1, and λ_2 is the flux linking circuit 2.

When the material properties of the two-port are linear, the constitutive relation becomes

$$\lambda_1 = L_{11}i_1 + M_{12}i_2, \qquad \lambda_2 = M_{21}i_1 + L_{22}i_2, \tag{2}$$

where the positive signs in equation (2) imply a choice of current orientations such that positive current flow enters the coils of Fig. 4.2 at the dotted ends. (The dot notation indicates the *sense* of the coil windings, dots at corresponding ends (cf. Fig. 4.2) indicate that the coils are wound in a common sense, opposing dots indicate coils wound in the opposite sense.)

The port voltages are given by Faraday's Law:

$$v_1 = d\lambda_1/dt, \qquad v_2 = d\lambda_2/dt. \tag{3}$$

In equation (2), the parameters L_{11}, L_{22} are the inductances of the coils 1 and 2 respectively; M_{12}, M_{21} are the mutual inductances of port 2 into port 1 and port 1 into port 2. If the two-port is conservative, the mutual inductances M_{12} and M_{21} are necessarily equal. This is readily demonstrated by comparing the energies supplied from port 1 and port 2 when the work increment is integrated round a closed path.

The energy supplied from port 1 is

$$T_1 = \int_S i_1 d\lambda_1. \tag{4}$$

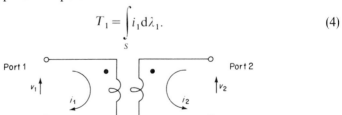

Fig. 4.2. Coupled inductive circuits.

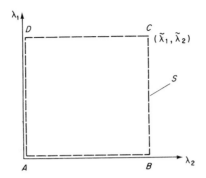

Fig. 4.3. Integration path for energy evaluation in an inductively coupled circuit.

Similarly for port 2:

$$T_2 = \int_S i_2 d\lambda_2. \tag{5}$$

If the contour S is that indicated in Fig. 4.3, and the inverse constitutive relation is

$$i_1 = \Gamma_{11}\lambda_1 + \Gamma_{12}\lambda_2, \qquad i_2 = \Gamma_{21}\lambda_1 + \Gamma_{22}\lambda_2, \tag{6}$$

then the net energy transfer at port 1 and port 2 is given by

$$T_1 + T_2 = (\Gamma_{12} - \Gamma_{21})\tilde{\lambda}_1 \tilde{\lambda}_2. \tag{7}$$

For conservation of energy this expression must vanish, implying that Γ_{12} and Γ_{21} are equal. Elementary matrix algebra then indicates that M_{12} and M_{21} are equal. The constitutive relation (equation (2)) can now be rewritten with the mutual inductances replaced by a common symbol M:

$$\begin{bmatrix} \lambda_2 \\ i_2 \end{bmatrix} \begin{bmatrix} L_{22}/M & \dfrac{M - L_{11}L_{22}}{M} \\ 1/M & -L_{11}/M \end{bmatrix} \begin{bmatrix} \lambda_1 \\ i_1 \end{bmatrix} \tag{8}$$

The magnitude of the mutual inductance depends upon the degree of coupling of magnetic flux. A non-parametric measure of this quantity is the "coefficient of coupling" defined by

$$k = \frac{M}{(L_{11}L_{22})^{1/2}}. \tag{9}$$

When k is zero, the circuits are de-coupled and have no common flux. At the other extreme, when all the flux in coil 1 links coil 2 and vice versa, the coils are

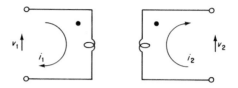

Fig. 4.4. Mutual inductance with positive current convention.

perfectly coupled and k is unity. In this ideal situation the constitutive relation takes the form:

$$\begin{bmatrix} \lambda_2 \\ i_2 \end{bmatrix} = \begin{bmatrix} (L_{22}/L_{11})^{1/2} & 0 \\ (L_{11}L_{22})^{-1/2} & -(L_{11}/L_{22})^{1/2} \end{bmatrix} \begin{bmatrix} \lambda_1 \\ i_1 \end{bmatrix} \quad (10)$$

If the medium supporting the magnetic field has a high permeability, the off-diagonal term in equation (10) will be negligible. The coupled electric circuit now approximates an ideal transformer since, using equations (3) and (10), one obtains

$$v_1 = nv_2, \qquad ni_1 = -i_2, \quad (11)$$

where the transformer modulus is defined by

$$n = (L_{11}/L_{22})^{1/2}. \quad (12)$$

Notice the minus sign in equation (11) is the result of the reference orientation chosen for the currents in Fig. 4.2. This discrepancy is removed by reversing the sign convention on one of the currents i_1, i_2, (e.g. Fig. 4.4).

1.2. Mechanical transformer (translational)

A transformer of translational motion is the well known lever mechanism depicted in Fig. 4.5. The force/velocity variables F_1, v_{01} on port 1 are related to

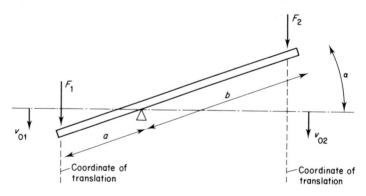

Fig. 4.5. Mechanical lever (translational converter).

the force/velocity variables F_2, v_{02} by a constitutive relation which depends upon the geometrical and physical properties of the lever. The relationship between the port velocities is found by differentiation of the geometrical constraint imposed between point 1 and 2. By assuming that the lever is rigid (i.e. no effort storage):

$$x_{01} = a \sin \alpha, \qquad x_{02} = -b \sin \alpha. \tag{13}$$

Hence:

$$v_{01} = -(a/b)v_{02}, \tag{14}$$

where the minus sign occurs because of the reference direction taken for positive velocities.

The corresponding relationship for the forces F_1 and F_2 is found under the assumption that the lever is massless (i.e. no flow storage) and the pivot is free of friction (i.e. no dissipation). By the principle of virtual work:

$$F_1 \delta x_{01} = F_2 \delta x_{02}, \tag{15}$$

and hence

$$F_2 = (a/b)F_1. \tag{16}$$

Together, equations (14) and (16) define the constitutive relations for an ideal mechanical translational transformer with transformer modulus:

$$n = a/b \tag{17}$$

1.3. Mechanical transformer (rotational)

An ideal rotational transformer relates the angular velocity at port 1 linearly to the angular velocity on port 2, with a similar relation between the port torques. Simple examples of rotational transformers are the belt drive system (Fig. 4.6) and any gear wheel mechanism. Consider the belt drive in Fig. 4.6, if the belt is stiff (no effort storage) then the angular displacements θ_{01} and θ_{02} (measured with respect to a common reference 0) are related by a common linear displacement x at the periphery of the pullies, such that

$$x = a\theta_{01}, \qquad x = b\theta_{02}, \tag{18}$$

where a and b are the radii of the respective pulleys.

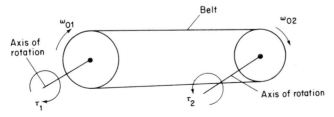

Fig. 4.6. Belt and pulley system (rotational converter).

Thus

$$\omega_{01} = (b/a)\omega_{02}. \tag{19}$$

Under the corresponding assumptions that the belt system is light and frictionless the port torques are related by equating the forces at the belt periphery:

$$\tau_1/a = \tau_2/b. \tag{20}$$

Hence the torque relation:

$$\tau_2 = (b/a)\tau_1. \tag{21}$$

The equation pair (19) and (21) together define an ideal rotational transformer with transformer modulus:

$$n = b/a. \tag{22}$$

1.4. Fluid transformer

Consider a fluid element which consists of two pipes of different cross-sectional areas A_1 and A_2 connected by a piston arrangement as shown in Fig. 4.7. The pressures P_{01} and P_{02} are measured relative to some datum which, in this instance, is conveniently taken to be atmospheric pressure. If the connecting pistons are assumed to be rigid and the fluid incompressible then the fluid volume changes (V_1 on port 1 and V_2 on port 2) are related by the linear displacement of the pistons, x:

$$x = V_1/A_1, \qquad x = V_2/A_2. \tag{23}$$

Hence:

$$Q_2 = \frac{A_2}{A_1} Q_1, \tag{24}$$

where Q_1 and Q_2 are the fluid flow rates at ports 1 and 2 respectively.

By similar reasoning, if the inertia of fluid and pistons is negligible and dissipation forces are small, the port pressures P_{01} and P_{02} are linearly related by the common force transmitted through the connecting rod:

$$P_{01}/A_1 = P_{02}/A_2. \tag{25}$$

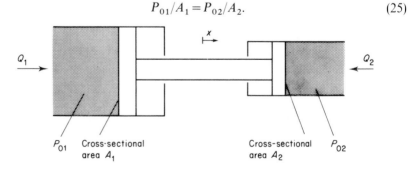

Fig. 4.7. Fluid converter.

Hence the pressure relation:

$$P_{01} = (A_1/A_2)P_{02}. \tag{26}$$

The equations (24) and (26) define the constitutive relations of an ideal fluid transformer with modulus:

$$n = A_1/A_2. \tag{27}$$

2. ENERGY COUPLERS

This class of devices includes any object which couples one kind of energy to another. A broad definition such as this encompasses a vast number of physical elements, including primary energy sources and energy sinks. However, these devices are not treated since, by hypothesis, the input and output ports of sources and sinks respectively are *excluded* from the collection of objects which are referred to as "the system". Of the couplers wholly contained within the system boundary, our treatment will cover only energy conserving couplers. Within this class of elements two important sub-classes can be discerned: power conserving couplers and energy storing couplers. It is important to note that this distinction could have been made earlier in connection with general two-ports, but it only attains significance when the storage mechanism plays an indispensible role in the energy conversion process. Energy storage couplers accumulate energy in some intermediate form, this can then be removed subsequently from either port.

2.1. Power conserving couplers

2.1.1. Rotational/translational transformers

A mechanism which converts rotational motion about a fixed axis to translation along a fixed coordinate displays energetic coupling. If the conversion is achieved without energy storage or dissipation the device is a pure power conserving rotational/translational coupler. Physical objects which display this phenomenon are: rack and pinion devices, crank mechanisms and belt/pulley mechanisms. For convenience only the last form is considered here, although crank mechanisms are discussed subsequently under modulated two-ports. Figure 4.8 shows a belt/pulley coupler in which the rotational and translational port variables are related by the slip-free motion of the belt and pulley. If storage and dissipation can be neglected then the port velocities are related by

$$\omega_{01} = (1/a)V_{02}. \tag{28}$$

The torque and force are related by

$$F_2 = (1/a)\tau_1. \tag{29}$$

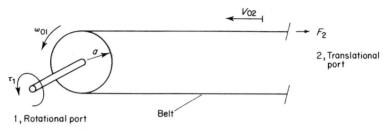

Fig. 4.8. Translational/rotational coupler.

Equations (28) and (29) together define the constitutive relation of an ideal rotational/translational coupler; because of the assignment of effort/flow variables (analogy A.1) the coupler is an energy transforming device, with transformer modulus:

$$n = 1/a. \tag{30}$$

It is now evident that the rotational energy *converter* of Fig. 4.6 can be viewed as two rotational/translational *couplers* connected back-to-back. There is no particular merit in this viewpoint except when the energy storage and dissipation are considerable, then a detailed treatment involving two couplers is essential.

2.1.2. Electromechanical transformers

The constitutive properties of most electromechanical couplers depend upon magnetic fields to provide the basic energy transforming (or gyrating) action. The fundamental relationships which govern induced voltages and forces in moving objects within a magnetic field are therefore at the heart of all such devices. A basic result which is a direct consequence of Faraday's Law gives the increment of electromotive force de induced in an element of conductor dl as a function of the magnetic field flux density B and the velocity of the object V (see Fig. 4.9):

$$de = V \times B.dl. \tag{31}$$

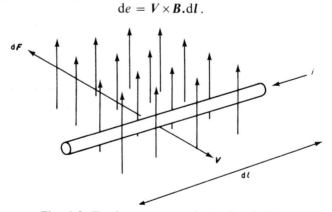

Fig. 4.9. The force on a conductor in a field.

where the dot and cross refer to the normal products of vector algebra. The second fundamental relation is a consequence of the Lorentz force law which relates the force of the field $d\boldsymbol{F}$ on the element $d\boldsymbol{l}$ to the current flowing i and the flux density $\boldsymbol{B}$:

$$d\boldsymbol{F} = i d\boldsymbol{l} \times \boldsymbol{B}. \tag{32}$$

If the conducting element is a straight uniform conductor of length l carrying current i and moving through a field of uniform flux density B with velocity V then the electromotive force across the conductor is

$$e = VBl, \tag{33}$$

and the force F, directed opposite to the direction of motion, is

$$F = iBl \tag{34}$$

Clearly, equations (33) and (34) define an energy coupler, and according to analogy A.1, the conductor is an energy transformer with constitutive relation:

$$V = (Bl)^{-1}e, \qquad F = Bli. \tag{35}$$

Note that the mechanical port has been taken as the second port and the electrical port is considered as the first port.

A more familiar form of electromechanical coupler is the direct current electric motor/generator. This consists of a set of conductors wound on an armature and arranged to rotate in a magnetic field. It follows from equation (33) that if the conductors are correctly commutated and the magnetic field is uniform, the armature voltage v is a function of the total flux Φ and the angular velocity ω of the armature (Fig. 4.10):

$$v = k_1 \Phi \omega. \tag{36}$$

Furthermore, the torque at the armature shaft will be determined (neglecting energy loss and storage) by the net armature current i and the flux Φ:

$$\tau = k_2 \Phi i, \tag{37}$$

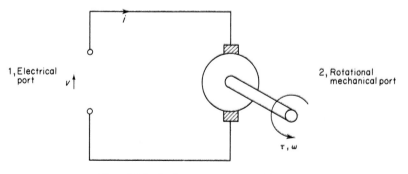

Fig. 4.10. A direct current machine.

where the constants k_1 and k_2 are equal, either by appeal to the principle of power conservation or direct application of expressions (33) and (34).

The constitutive relations of the ideal electromechanical motor/generator are

$$v = n\omega, \qquad \tau = ni, \tag{38}$$

where from the above $n = k_1\Phi$ is the transformer modulus.

2.1.3. Fluid–mechanical transformer

The most straightforward fluid–mechanical coupler is the piston arrangement depicted in Fig. 4.11. This simple device transforms fluid energy to translational mechanical energy and if storage and dissipation affects can be ignored the constitutive relations are

$$V_{01} = (1/A)Q, \qquad P = (1/A)F. \tag{39}$$

The simple piston arrangement of Fig. 4.11 forms the basis of many hydraulic pumps of the positive displacement variety. In essence these devices are sets of pistons arranged to move to and fro at a rate proportional to the speed of rotation of a shaft. If this arrangement is equipped with appropriate porting (analogous to the commutator of a d.c. electromechanical machine), the net fluid flow through the motor will be proportional to the shaft angular velocity:

$$Q = k_1\omega. \tag{40}$$

Furthermore, the net torque applied at the shaft is proportional to the increase in pressure in the pump:

$$\tau = k_2(P_2 - P_1). \tag{41}$$

If the pump is lossless and energy storage phenomena are negligible then power is conserved at the mechanical and fluid ports; this implies that the constants k_1 and k_2 are equal. Because of the effort/flow assignment (analogy A.1) this particular converter has gyrational constitutive relations:

$$\omega = rQ, \qquad P_2 - P_1 = r\tau, \tag{42}$$

where r is the gyrator modulus.

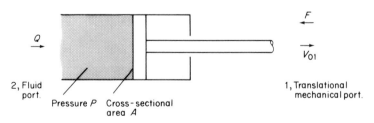

Fig. 4.11. Hydro–mechanical coupler.

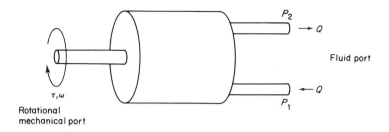

Fig. 4.12. A positive displacement fluid/mechanical machine.

A positive displacement pump is shown in schematic form in Fig. 4.12. Practical fluid pumps which employ this principle are hydraulic axial piston pumps and radial piston pumps. Pneumatic pumps include both positive displacement and compressor types, the latter are not amenable to the simplistic treatment used here. In practice compressors are modelled using measured constitutive relations. An idea of the complexity of these constitutive relations is conveyed by the sketched curves of Fig. 4.14. The legend of the figure refers to the schematic axial flow compressor depicted in Fig. 4.13.

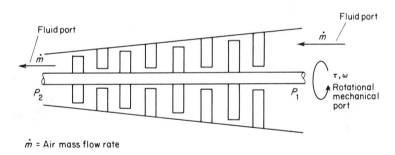

$\dot{m}$ = Air mass flow rate

Fig. 4.13. An axial flow compressor.

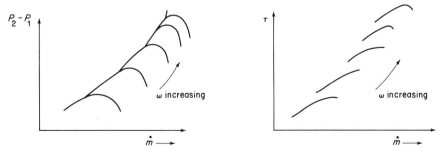

Fig. 4.14. Compressor constitutive relations.

2.2. Energy conserving couplers

2.2.1. Electromechanical (electric field)

An example of a two-port coupler where energy storage in an electric field is central to the behaviour of the device is the movable-plate capacitor depicted in Fig. 4.15. The capacitor plates hold a charge q, the attractive force of which is countered by a force F applied to the movable plate. The potential across the plates is denoted e (to avoid confusion with velocity v) and the plates are parallel and separated by a distance x.

If the ideal situation is assumed, whereby all dissipation and storage of energy is neglected (except that stored in the electric field) the constitutive relations for the device take the general form:

$$e = \varphi_1(x, q), \qquad F = \varphi_2(x, q). \tag{43}$$

If it is assumed that the arrangement is electrically linear, the first relation of equations (43) will have the form:

$$e = q/C(x), \tag{44}$$

where $C(x)$ is the capacitance, a non-linear function of displacement x. The stored energy in the electric field is given by

$$U(x, q) = \int_S e\,dq + \int_S F\,dx. \tag{45}$$

In equation (45), S is an arbitrary path of integration from a datum point to (x, q). With a known energy function the constitutive relations can be recovered using relations which follow from equation (45). Specifically:

$$F = \frac{\partial U}{\partial x}(x, q), \qquad e = \frac{\partial U}{\partial q}(x, q). \tag{46}$$

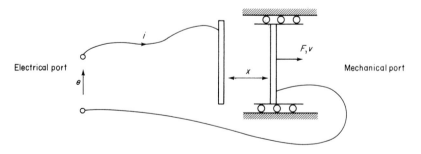

Fig. 4.15. A moving-plate capacitor.

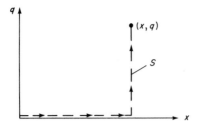

Fig. 4.16. Integration path S for the capacitor.

Alternatively the co-energy $U^*(e, x)$ defined by the Legendre transformation (equation (47)) could be used to recover the constitutive relations (equations (48)):

$$U^*(e, x) = eq - U(x, q), \tag{47}$$

$$F = -\frac{\partial U^*}{\partial x}(e, x), \qquad q = \frac{\partial U^*}{\partial e}(e, x). \tag{48}$$

The stored energy $U(x, q)$ can be found by integrating along any path S. Because the force F is zero for all x when the stored charge is zero, a convenient path is that indicated in Fig. 4.16. The electrical energy stored with an initial state $(x, q) = (0, 0)$ is therefore

$$U(x, q) = \int_0^q \frac{q}{C(x)}\, \mathrm{d}q = \frac{q^2}{2C(x)} \tag{49}$$

The remaining constitutive relation (equation (43)) is then found by equation (46):

$$F = \frac{\partial U}{\partial x} = \frac{q^2}{2}\left(\frac{\mathrm{d}C(x)}{\mathrm{d}x}\right)^{-1} \tag{50}$$

Use of the co-energy function leads to identical results.

2.2.2. Electromechanical (magnetic field)

The magnetic counterpart of the moving plate capacitor is the solenoid depicted in Fig. 4.17. A coil supporting flux linkages λ and current i creates a magnetic field. An iron core at position x has a mechanical force F applied to it in order to counter the magnetic attraction. The constitutive relations for the device take the form:

$$i = \varphi_1(x, \lambda), \qquad F = \varphi_2(x, \lambda). \tag{51}$$

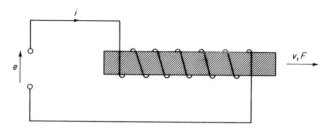

Fig. 4.17. An electromechanical solenoid.

If the device can be assumed electrically linear the first of the constitutive relations takes the form:

$$i = \frac{\lambda}{L(x)}, \tag{52}$$

where $L(x)$, the inductance is a non-linear function of displacement x.
The stored magnetic energy in the solenoid is given by

$$T(x, \lambda) = \int_{S} i \, d\lambda + \int_{S} F \, dx, \tag{53}$$

where S is an arbitrary path between the datum and the point (x, λ). Once the energy function is established the constitutive relations follow by differentiation:

$$F = \frac{\partial T(x, \lambda)}{\partial x}, \qquad i = \frac{\partial T(x, \lambda)}{\partial \lambda}. \tag{54}$$

The complementary energy function $T^*(x, i)$ is defined by the Legendre transformation

$$T^*(x, i) = i\lambda - T(x, \lambda). \tag{55}$$

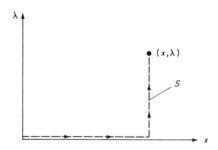

Fig. 4.18. Integration path S for the solenoid.

The constitutive relations are recovered from the co-energy according to

$$F = -\frac{\partial T^*(x, i)}{\partial x}, \qquad \lambda = \frac{\partial T^*(x, i)}{\partial i}. \tag{56}$$

The stored energy $T(x, \lambda)$ can be found by integrating along any path S. If the datum point is $(x, \lambda) = (0, 0)$ then a convenient path is that indicated in Fig. 4.18. In this case the stored energy is simply

$$T = \int_0^{\lambda} \frac{\lambda}{L(x)} \, d\lambda = \frac{\lambda^2}{2L(x)} \tag{57}$$

The remaining constitutive relation is then obtained from equation (54):

$$F = \frac{\partial T}{\partial x} = \frac{\lambda^2}{2} \left(\frac{dL(x)}{dx}\right)^{-1} \tag{58}$$

3. MODULATED MULTI-PORTS

A recurring feature in system modelling is the modulation of constitutive relations by an auxiliary variable. This phenomenon occurs frequently in power conserving two-ports and in one-port devices. In this section some specific examples are indicated, together with the general form of the modulated constitutive relation.

3.1. Modulated two-ports

A general modulated two-port has constitutive relations which express the state variable (effort or flow accumulation) as a function of the port variables effort, flow *and* some auxillary variable ρ. If the two-port is an ideal transforming element, the constitutive relations for the modulated transformer are

$$e_1 = n(\rho)e_2, \qquad f_2 = n(\rho)f_1. \tag{59}$$

Likewise the constitutive relations for a modulated gyrator are

$$e_1 = r(\rho)f_2, \qquad e_2 = r(\rho)f_1. \tag{60}$$

3.1.1. Rotational–translational transformer

Modulated couplers occur frequently in the transformation of rotational to translational energy. The simple crank mechanism shown in Fig. 4.19 is a specific example. The force F_1 applied along the coordinate of translation is balanced by a torque τ_2 about the axis of rotation. In the absence of dissipation or inertial effects the torque and force are related by

$$\tau_2 = (a \cos \theta)F_1. \tag{61}$$

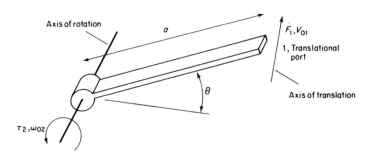

Fig. 4.19. A crank mechanism as a modulated two-port.

Similarly the angular velocity ω_{02} about the axis of rotation is related to the translational velocity V_{01} by the equation

$$V_{01} = (a \cos \theta)\omega_{02} \qquad (62)$$

The constitutive relations of the crank are defined by equations (61) and (62). The device is therefore a modulated transformer with modulus

$$n(\theta) = a \cos \theta. \qquad (63)$$

Notice that the crank provides a non-linear coupling of rotational and translational motion since the transformer modulus is a function of the angular displacement on port 2. This indicates an important practical distinction between dynamical systems which are non-linear because of the component material properties and others whose non-linearity arises from the nature of the component interconnections. Mechanical systems which combine translation and rotation fall into the latter category.

3.1.2. Variable field motor/generator

The d.c. motor/generator can, under ideal circumstances, be viewed as a pure transforming coupler with constitutive relations (cf. equation (38)):

$$v = k_1 \Phi \omega, \qquad \tau = k_1 \Phi i, \qquad (64)$$

where Φ, the total flux, was previously assumed constant. In practice, the field is often controlled by varying the current i_f through electric coils (field windings). The flux is then a function of the field current and is defined by the constitutive relation of the field coils (see Fig. 4.20):

$$k_1 \Phi = n(i_f). \qquad (65)$$

If this relation is substituted into the constitutive relations, the d.c. motor/generator with controlled field is seen to be a modulated transforming coupler with material relation:

$$v = n(i_f)\omega, \qquad \tau = n(i_f)i. \qquad (66)$$

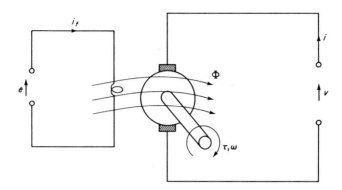

Fig. 4.20. A DC machine as a modulated two-port.

In general the transformer modulus is a non-linear function of field current, however over appropriate operating regions the relationship can be assumed linear.

Other examples of modulated two-ports are the variable stroke axial piston pump, variable eccentricity radial piston pump and alternating current motors/generators.

3.2. Modulated one-ports

Source and dissipator elements at the interface of a system and its environment are frequently modulated in order to provide some means of controlling the dynamical behaviour inside the system. Control is done in this way for two reasons. Firstly there is nominally no direct access to the system variables and secondly, the power levels required to modulate a source or sink are usually very much lower than the average power level within a system.

Realistic examples of modulated one-port elements are electrical amplifiers, most engines, and dynamometers. Of course, the modulated couplers mentioned above can be (and are) used to control systems and may be legitimately viewed as modulated one-ports.

4. NOTES AND REFERENCES

[1] Many of the multi-port systems considered here are concerned with the transduction of mechanical motion into electrical signals and vice versa. The moving plate capacitor and the electromagnetic solenoid are specific examples. The properties of such devices are of great significance in control system studies in which almost always the actuation and transduction process are critical factors.

For a detailed study of electromechanical/electroacoustic two ports, including moving plate capacitors and solenoids see:

Olsen, H. F. (1958). "Dynamical Analogies", chs VIII and IX. Van Nostrand, New Jersey.

[2] Detailed consideration of rotating electromechanical two-ports is given in a number of books on rotating machines. A good treatment which uses network analysis methods is given in:

Koenig, H. E. and Blackwell, W. A. (1961). "Electromechanical system theory". McGraw-Hill, New York.

[3] Similar considerations apply to hydraulic and pneumatic multi-port systems. In this connection we have found useful the following:

Blackburn, J. F. (ed.) (1960). "Fluid power control". Wiley–MIT Press, New York.

Merritt, H. E. (1967). "Hydraulic control systems". Wiley, New York.

[4] The book:

Shigley, J. E. (1977). "Mechanical Engineering Design", 3rd edn. Series in mechanical engineering design. McGraw-Hill, New York

gives details on mechanical multi-port devices, especially belt couplings, clutches, gears, etc. See particularly chapters 12, 14 and 15.

5. PROBLEMS

5.1 Determine the constitutive relation of the equivalent one-port device as seen through the terminal pair 11′ for the electrical circuits shown in Figure 4.21. Comment on the circuit involving two gyrators.

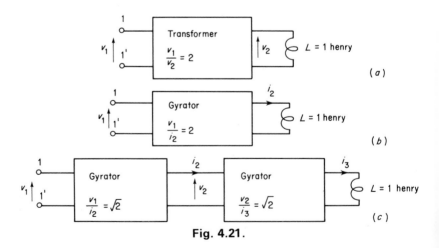

Fig. 4.21.

5.2 The belt and pulley system shown in figure 4.22. may be used to transform mechanical energy.

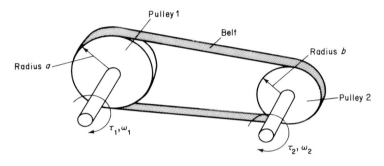

Fig. 4.22.

If the second shaft drives a dissipative load with a constitutive relation

$$\tau_2 = b\omega_2,$$

determine the equivalent constitutive relation seen at the first shaft.

5.3 Develop a model of the belt and pulley system described in the previous problem, which accounts for inertia in the pulleys and compliance in the belt.

Interconnection of System Elements

5

INTRODUCTION

The discussion so far has centred upon the individual properties of system elements and the physical variables associated with them. In the energetic interpretation, system elements can be specified according to how they process energy. Similarly the physical variables are related by simple dynamical relations which define the stored energy variables. In the sequel we consider what happens when the basic system elements are joined together to model an entire system. Evidently the act of interconnecting elements will introduce a new set of constraints which determine the interaction of the system components. Furthermore, the interconnective relationships will evidently constrain the system variables in a manner which is independent of the material and dynamic properties discussed so far.

Consider the generalized energy handling one-ports with power variables effort and flow. There are just two ways in which one-port elements can be interconnected: in series, as depicted in Fig. 5.1(a) or in parallel, as depicted in Fig. 5.1(b). In each case two sets of constraints can be written as a result of the interconnection. For the series connected elements, the constraints are

(a)
$$e = e_1 + e_2$$

(b)
$$f = f_1 = f_2$$

For the parallel connected elements the constraints take the dual form:

(c)
$$e = e_3 = e_4$$

(d)
$$f = f_3 + f_4$$

74

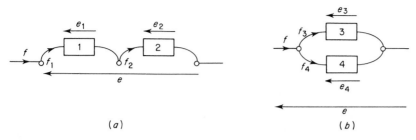

Fig. 5.1.

These basic equations relate or constrain the effort and flow variables in two fundamental ways. Relation (*a*) on the effort variables means that the effort across series connected elements is the sum of the efforts across each element, condition (*c*) then follows as a direct consequence. The constraints on the flow variables are translated as, "if two elements are connected in parallel then the total flow into the elements is the sum of the individual flows" (condition (*d*)). The complementary constraint (*b*) follows as a direct consequence of this condition.

These relationships can be stated in general terms as *compatibility* and *continuity* constraints upon the effort and flow variables. The compatibility constraint is placed upon the effort variables and demands that if a set of energy ports are connected so as to form a closed loop, then the sum of all the efforts around the loop must be zero (for compatibility of effort). The complementary constraint is upon the flow variables and requires that if a set of energy ports have one common terminal, then the sum of all the flows at the common terminal must be zero (for continuity of flow). These simple, but fundamentally important relations are depicted in Figs. 5.2 and 5.3

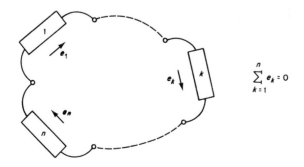

$$\sum_{k=1}^{n} e_k = 0$$

Fig. 5.2. Compatibility constraint on effort variables.

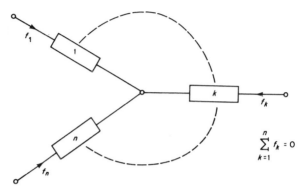

Fig. 5.3. Continuity constraint on flow variables.

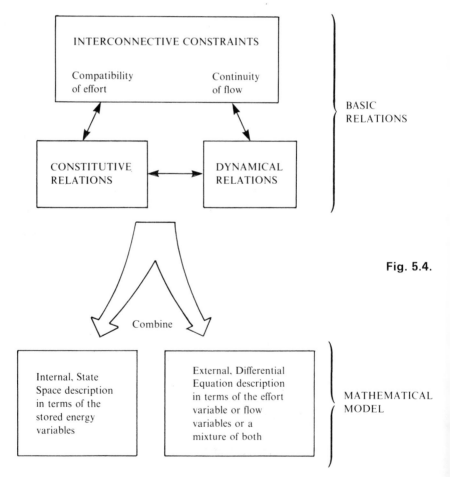

Fig. 5.4.

respectively. The consequences of these interconnective constraints are pursued against a generalized framework in subsequent chapters. For the moment however, the roots of the interconnection rules are traced in specific disciplines together with illustrations of how mathematical modelling consists of combining the interconnective constraints with the constitutive and dynamic relations of the system elements (cf. Fig. 5.4).

1. MECHANICAL SYSTEMS

The interconnective constraints in mechanical systems can be most simply studied with reference to the forces and velocities associated with an object in plane motion, the concepts which arise are immediately applicable to the general case. In addition, the constraint laws are interpreted as applying to the variables assigned in the mobility analogy. Thus the phrases "continuity of force" and "compatibility of velocities" are used.

1.1. Interconnective relations for force and velocity

Newton's second law states that in a specified inertial reference frame the time rate of change of the linear momentum p of a particle of mass m is proportional to the vector sum of the forces acting on the particle. With reference to Fig. 5.5, and recalling the constitutive properties of Newtonian mass, the second law implies

$$\sum_{i=1}^{n} F_i + F_m = 0, \tag{1}$$

where

$$F_m = \mathrm{d}p/\mathrm{d}t \tag{2}$$

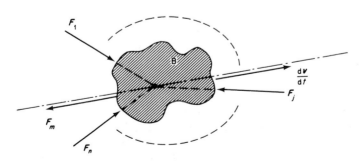

Fig. 5.5. Dynamic continuity constraint on forces acting on mass B.

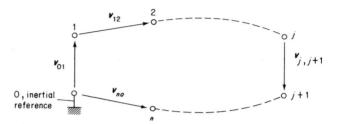

Fig. 5.6. Compatibility constraint on velocities.

and

$$p = mv \tag{3}$$

with v the velocity of the particle. Equation (1) is the continuity constraint on the forces in a mechanical system.

The complementary interconnective constraint for mechanical systems concerns the velocity vectors measured at various points throughout a system. Consider the collection of points $\{j\}$ ($j = 0, 1, ..., n$) shown in Fig. 5.6; it is a basic expression of the continuity of space that the velocities $v_{j,j+1}$ ($j = 0, 1 ... n-1$) are such that their vector sum is equal to velocity v_{0n}. Analytically this is stated

$$\sum_{j=0}^{n-1} v_{j,j+1} = v_{0n}. \tag{4}$$

Equation (4) is the compatibility constraint on the velocities in a mechanical system.

1.2. Application of the interconnective rules

The generalized compatibility and continuity relations as they occur in mechanical systems are statements about the balance of forces on an object and the geometric constraints arising from the continuity of space. The following example shows how these basic rules are used, along with the constitutive and dynamic relations, to specify the dynamical behaviour of a mechanical system.

Consider the object C of mass m shown in Fig. 5.7. The mass is constrained to move horizontally on frictionless rollers and is attached to a linear spring (stiffness, k) and a linear damper (coefficient, b). The problem is to obtain a mathematical model which describes the time variation of the displacement of the object C when subject to the force $F(t)$. First disconnect the spring and

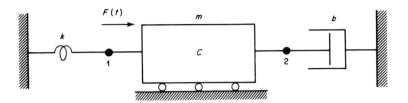

Fig. 5.7. A simple mechanical system.

damper and replace them by their action forces upon the object. This results in the free-body diagram of Fig. 5.8. The continuity law for forces (equation (1)) gives the first interconnective relation as

$$F(t) + F_k - F_b - F_m = 0. \tag{5a}$$

From Fig. 5.9, the complementary interconnective relations concerning the compatibility of velocities may be written

$$v_{10} = -v_{0c}, \qquad v_{20} = v_{0c}. \tag{5b}$$

The constitutive relations for the system elements, with reference to Fig. 5.9, are given by

$$F_k = kx_{10}, \qquad p = mv_{0c}, \qquad F_b = bv_{20}. \tag{6}$$

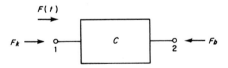

Fig. 5.8. Continuity of force on C (free body diagram).

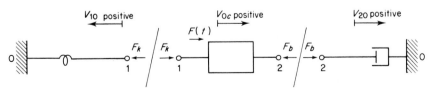

Fig. 5.9. Force and velocity conventions.

The dynamic relations for the system variables are

$$F_m = dp/dt, \qquad v_{10} = dx_{10}/dt. \tag{7}$$

If the momentum p and displacement x_{10} are taken as the natural state variables of the system, then by combining equations (5), (6) and (7) a state description of the system behaviour results:

$$dp/dt = -kx_{10} - (b/m)p - F(t),$$

$$dx_{10}/dt = -(1/m)p, \tag{8}$$

where the momentum p and displacement x_{10} are the system states.

The state space description of equation (8) forms a so-called internal model of the system, in that the system response is specified via the system variables which indicate the energies stored within the system stores. An alternative way of expressing the system dynamic behaviour is to reduce the set of first-order state equations to a single ordinary differential equation in terms of the variable of interest. Such a description of the mechanical system of Fig. 5.7 is readily obtained as

$$m\ddot{x}_{10} + b\dot{x}_{10} + kx_{10} = -F(t), \tag{9}$$

where the dot notation indicates differentiation with respect to time.

Given the time history of $F(t)$ and the initial state of the system, the dynamical behaviour of $x_{10}(t)$ follows from either the internal (state) description or the external (differential equation) description of the system. The reason for the distinction between internal and external system descriptions should now be evident. The former entirely specifies the dynamic performance of a system, whereas the latter is an incomplete description. This means in practical terms that given equation (9) alone we cannot make a statement concerning the variations in (say) momentum occurring in the system; supplementary information is required in order to do this. An additional important feature of external descriptions is that it is always possible to find two complementary equation sets, one in terms of the displacement variables and another in terms of the momentum variables. Equation (9) is in terms of the system displacements, the complementary form is

$$-F(t) = \dot{p} + (b/m)p + (k/m) \int p \, dt. \tag{10}$$

Both displacement and momentum representations yield a legitimate specification of the dynamical behaviour of mechanical systems. However, the former is more usual; this is probably because the relative displacements of a system are immediately apparent from a visual inspection, and hence have a graphic appeal which momenta lack. From a practical viewpoint there are usually fewer force constraints in a mechanical system than there are velocity constraints. Although many of the velocity constraints are simple equalities, this nevertheless provides a strong motive to solution via force constraints. These points will be further clarified in the subsequent discussions of network analysis.

2. ELECTRICAL SYSTEMS

2.1. Interconnective laws for voltage and current

The interconnective constraints which result from joining electrical components together are embodied in the experimental observations of Kirchhoff. The current law of Kirchhoff is a continuity constraint upon electric circuit flow variables. It states that the sum of current flowing into a junction of conductors is zero. With reference to Fig. 5.10(a) the current law can be stated analytically:

$$\sum_{j=1}^{m} i_j = 0. \tag{11}$$

Kirchoff's voltage law is the complementary constraint upon voltage variables in a closed circuit or loop. It states that the sum of voltages around a loop is zero. The law is depicted in Fig. 5.10(b), and is stated analytically:

$$\sum_{j=1}^{m} v_j = 0. \tag{12}$$

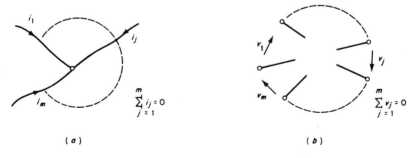

(a)   (b)

Fig. 5.10. Kirchhoff's current and voltage laws.

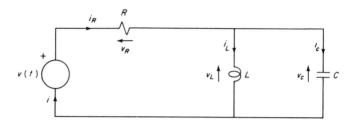

Fig. 5.11. A simple electrical system.

2.2. Application of the interconnective rules

Kirchhoff's laws of electric circuits are statements about the continuity of electric charge (current law) and compatibility of voltage measurements made between two points, but along differing paths. To solve a practical circuit problem involves the simultaneous application of three sets of relations: the interconnective relations (Kirchhoff's laws), the constitutive relations of the circuit elements and the dynamic relations of the circuit variables. The equations which result are then combined to obtain an internal (state) description of the circuit dynamical behaviour. The following simple example will serve to illustrate the procedure.

Consider the circuit shown in Fig. 5.11, which consists of linear resistive, inductive and capacitance components in a series, parallel circuit and driven by a voltage source $v(t)$. Application of Kirchhoff's current and voltage laws yield the following constraints on the circuit variables:

$$v(t) = v_R + v_c, \qquad v_L = v_c,$$

$$i_R = i_L + i_c, \qquad i = i_R. \tag{13}$$

The constitutive and dynamic relations for the circuit are

$$v_R = R i_R, \qquad \lambda_L = L i_L, \qquad q_c = C v_c, \tag{14}$$

$$i_c = dq_c/dt, \qquad v_L = d\lambda_L/dt. \tag{15}$$

By combining equations (13)–(15), the following internal system description arises:

$$\begin{bmatrix} \dot{q}_c \\ \dot{\lambda}_L \end{bmatrix} = \begin{bmatrix} -1/CR & -1/L \\ 1/C & 0 \end{bmatrix} \begin{bmatrix} q_c \\ \lambda_L \end{bmatrix} + \begin{bmatrix} 1/R \\ 0 \end{bmatrix} v(t). \tag{16}$$

Two complementary external descriptions of the system can be obtained from the circuit relations. The first, in terms of the charge variable q_c is

$$\dot{q}_c + \frac{1}{CR} q_c + \frac{1}{LC} \int q_c \, dt = \frac{1}{R} v(t). \tag{17}$$

The corresponding formulation in terms of the flux linkage variable λ_L is

$$\ddot{\lambda}_L + \frac{1}{CR}\dot{\lambda}_L + \frac{1}{CL}\lambda_L = \frac{1}{RC}v(t). \tag{18}$$

Both forms of the external formulation are widely used in electrical circuit analysis, since in general neither leads to a more rapid way of writing circuit dynamical equations. In specific cases it always pays to solve a circuit using the constraint (current or voltage) which involves the least number of equations and obtain a differential equation set in terms of the complementary variable (voltage or current, respectively). This point will be discussed further in subsequent chapters.

3. FLUID SYSTEMS

3.1. Interconnective laws for flow rate and pressure

The interconnective constraint on flow variables in a fluid system is a particular example of the fundamental law of conservation of matter. If the fluid flow is incompressible, the flow variable law states that the sum of all fluid flow rates at a junction is zero. In terms of the schematic pipe junction in Fig. 5.12(a) the constraint on fluid flow rates is

$$\sum_{j=1}^{m} Q_j = 0. \tag{19}$$

The corresponding flow variable constraint for compressible fluids must be in terms of mass flow rate in order to allow for variations in density. The law of conservation of matter then states that the sum of all mass flow rates at a junction is zero. With reference to Fig. 5.12(b) the interconnective constraint for compressible fluid flow is

$$\sum_{j=1}^{m} m_j = 0, \tag{20}$$

where m_j is the mass flow rate in the jth pipe.

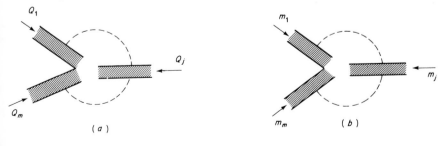

Fig. 5.12. Fluid continuity constraint.

The complementary constraint is upon the pressure variables in a fluid system. It states that the sum of pressures measured around a loop in a fluid system is zero. This is evidently a compatibility constraint which formalizes the notion that the pressure at any point in a fluid system, measured with respect to a datum pressure, is independent of the route taken in order to measure the pressure.

3.2. Application of the interconnective rules

The dynamical equations which govern the time variations in pressure and fluid flow rate in a fluid system are obtained by application of the three sets of relations which jointly specify the system. The fluid system is first put into a form whereby appropriate interconnective relations can be written, these are then combined with the component constitutive relations and the dynamic relations between system variables.

Consider the simple hydraulic system shown in Fig. 5.13, which consists of a positive displacement pump (ideal flow source) driving fluid into an open tank (flow store) the fluid then passes through a long pipe (pressure store) and discharges to atmospheric pressure through a dissipator. The interconnective relations for the pressure and flow variables are

$$P = P_c, \qquad P_c = P_L + P_R,$$

$$Q(t) = Q_c + Q_L, \qquad Q_L = Q_R. \tag{21}$$

The component constitutive relations are, in the linear case.

$$V_c = C_f P_c, \qquad \Gamma_L = L_f Q_L, \qquad P_R = R_f Q_R, \tag{22}$$

where the system state variables are defined by

$$Q_c = dV_c/dt, \qquad P_L = d\Gamma_L/dt. \tag{23}$$

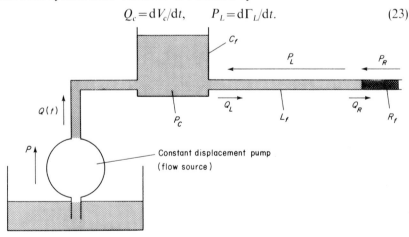

Fig. 5.13. A simple fluid system.

By combining equations (21), (22), (23) and eliminating redundant variables the following internal description of the system results:

$$\begin{bmatrix} \dot{V}_c \\ \dot{\Gamma}_L \end{bmatrix} = \begin{bmatrix} 0 & 1/L_f \\ 1/C_f & -R_f/L_f \end{bmatrix} \begin{bmatrix} V_c \\ \Gamma_L \end{bmatrix} + \begin{bmatrix} 1 \\ 0 \end{bmatrix} Q(t). \tag{24}$$

Manipulation of equation (24) yields the following differential equation description of the system:

$$\ddot{\Gamma}_L + \left(\frac{R_f}{L_f}\right)\dot{\Gamma}_L + \left(\frac{1}{C_f L_f}\right)\Gamma_L = \frac{1}{C_f}Q(t),$$

or

$$\left(\frac{L_f}{R_f}\right)\ddot{V}_c + \dot{V}_c + \left(\frac{1}{C_f R_f}\right)V_c = Q(t) + \left(\frac{L_f}{R_f}\right)\dot{Q}(t). \tag{25}$$

4. MAGNETIC SYSTEMS

4.1. Interconnective laws for magnetic flux and magnetomotive force

The distribution of magnetic flux and magnetomotive force in a magnetic system follow continuity and compatibility constraints which are usually given as magnetic versions of Kirchhoff's laws for electric circuits. In particular, the compatibility constraint for magnetomotive force is analogous to Kirchhoff's voltage law and states that "the net magnetomotive force measured around a closed magnetic loop is zero". By the same token, the continuity constraint for magnetic flux is the analogue of Kirchhoff's current law and states that "the net magnetic flux incident on a point in a magnetic circuit is zero".

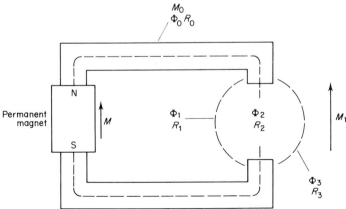

Fig. 5.14. A simple magnetic system.

4.2. Application of the interconnective rules

Figure 5.14 shows a simple magnetic circuit consisting of a permanent magnetic source which develops a magnetomotive force M. The resultant flux Φ_0 passes through an iron core with reluctance R_0 and then passes across an air gap thus closing the magnetic loop. The reluctance of the air gap is R_2 and supports a mean flux of Φ_2. The magnetic field leaks either side of the air gap such that two mean leakage paths can be discerned in Fig. 5.14 with reluctance R_1 and R_3, and supporting magnetic fluxes Φ_1, and Φ_3 respectively.

The continuity constraint on magnetic flux at the air gap gives the interconnective constraint:

$$\Phi_0 = \Phi_1 + \Phi_2 + \Phi_3. \tag{26}$$

If the magnetomotive forces developed across the iron core and the air gap respectively are M_0 and M_1, then the compatibility constraint on magnetomotive force gives

$$M = M_0 + M_1. \tag{27}$$

The constitutive relations for the various magnetic paths are

$$M_0 = \Phi_0 R_0, \qquad M_1 = \Phi_1 R_1,$$
$$M_2 = \Phi_2 R_2, \qquad M_3 = \Phi_3 R_3. \tag{28}$$

where $M_1 = M_2 = M_3$.

Combining the constitutive relations and the interconnective constraints, the magnetomotive force at the air gap is given as

$$M_1 = M[1 + R_0(1/R_1 + 1/R_2 + 1/R_3)]^{-1}. \tag{29}$$

5. THERMAL SYSTEMS

5.1. Interconnective laws for heat flow and temperature

The analysis of thermal systems presented here is distinct from other systems in that the flow variable is itself a power function. Thus the interconnective constraint on thermal flow is the first law of thermodynamics. In our visualization of lumped thermal systems it can be stated thus: The sum of heat flow rates into a thermal junction is zero. The complementary constraint is a compatibility restriction on temperature variables. It states that the sum of temperatures measured around a closed loop in a thermal system is zero. In common with the pressure constraint in fluid systems the interconnective rule for temperature is an affirmation of the observation that an object's temperature, measured with respect to a thermal reference, is independent of the spatial path traversed during the measurement.

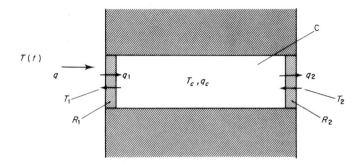

Fig. 5.15. A simple thermal system.

5.2. Application of the interconnective rules

The first law of thermodynamics and the compatibility of temperature measurements are the interconnective rules for thermal systems. When written in conjunction with the constitutive and dynamic relations they enable the time variations in thermal system variables to be determined. For example, consider the simple thermal conduction process of Fig. 5.15. An ideal temperature source $T(t)$ is in contact with a thermal flow store C, with dissipative properties which can be lumped as linear thermal dissipators R_1 and R_2 at either end of the store. The problem is to describe the time variation of heat H_c within the store.

The interconnective relations for the thermal variables heat flow rate q and temperature T are

$$T(t) = T_1 + T_2, \qquad T_c = T_2,$$
$$q_1 = q_c + q_2, \qquad q = q_1. \tag{30}$$

The constitutive relations are

$$H_c = CT_c, \qquad T_1 = R_1 q_1, \qquad T_2 = R_2 q_2, \tag{31}$$

and the dynamic relation is

$$dH_c/dt = q_c. \tag{32}$$

These equations are then combined to form the dynamic description of the system:

$$\frac{dH_c}{dt} = -\left(\frac{1}{R_1} + \frac{1}{R_2}\right)\frac{H_c}{C_c} + \frac{T(t)}{R_1}. \tag{33}$$

In this simple case, there is only one state variable and as a result internal and external description of the system are identical.

6. PROCESS SYSTEMS

The interconnective constraints as they occur in modelling of chemical processes deserve special treatment because the fluid flow stream is no longer homogeneous. In addition the possibility of reaction processes must be admitted. This results in additional terms in the continuity of flow constraint and since reactions either generate heat (exothermic) or absorb heat (endothermic), there is a continuity constraint on heat flow. The two continuity constraints are therefore cross-coupled. Compatibility constraints on pressure and temperature are determined in the usual way.

6.1. Continuity constraints on process flow variables

In general the fluid streams as they occur in the process industries have several components. Thus a continuity constraint upon a process flow stream involves a set of constraints, one for each component of the stream. The situation is further complicated when chemical reactions are involved, since the constraint set about a reaction process must be in terms of the material flow rates. Furthermore, the reaction rates must be taken into account. Consider the closed boundary of Fig. 5.16. The fluid flow stream into and out of the boundary consists of n different materials, for the jth material the input mass flow rate is m_{ij} and the output mass flow rate is m_{oj}. Within the boundary a reaction is taking place and the jth material component is being generated at a rate R_j, furthermore the total mass of component j in the boundary is M_j. Application of the law of conservation of material leads to the following n continuity constraints:

$$m_{ij} - m_{oj} + R_j = dM_j/dt, \qquad j = 1, \dots n, \qquad (34)$$

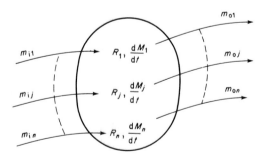

Fig. 5.16. Generalized continuity constraint.

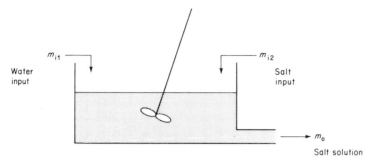

Fig. 5.17. A simple blending system.

along with the additional constraints:

$$\sum_{j=1}^{n} R_j = 0, \tag{35}$$

$$\sum_{j=1}^{n} m_{ij} - \sum_{j=1}^{n} m_{oj} = \sum_{j=1}^{n} \frac{dM_j}{dt}, \tag{36}$$

where equation (35) constrains the material generation by reaction, and equation (36) is the continuity constraint on the entire flow stream.

The following example of a two-component mixing process will illustrate the point. Figure 5.17 shows a system used in the formation of a salt solution by adding salt and water to a well stirred tank. Water is added at the rate m_{i1} and salt at rate m_{i2}, the solution is removed at rate m_o. The problem is to determine the concentration y of the salt solution as a function of time, assuming that the concentration within the tank is also y.

The continuity constraint on the salt component is

$$m_{i2} - ym_o = \frac{d}{dt}(M \cdot y) = M\frac{dy}{dt} + y\frac{dM}{dt}, \tag{37}$$

where M is the total mass of material in the tank. The continuity constraint on the entire stream is

$$(m_{i1} + m_{i2}) - m_o = \frac{dM}{dt}. \tag{38}$$

By combining equations (37) and (38) the differential equation governing fluctuations in concentration $y(t)$ is

$$M\dot{y}(t) + (m_{i1} + m_{i2})y(t) - m_{i2} = 0. \tag{39}$$

The total mass in the tank is obtained by integrating equation (38):

$$M = \int_0^t [(m_{i1} + m_{i2}) - m_o] \, dt, \tag{40}$$

so that the differential equation (39) is non-stationary, (i.e. $M = M(t)$).

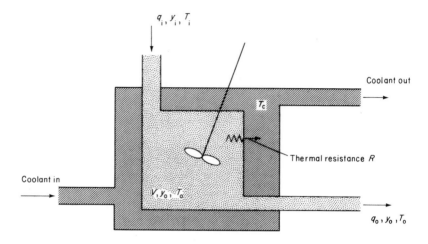

Fig. 5.18. A simple chemical reactor.

When the mixing of fluids is accompanied by a chemical reaction, there is usually a net variation in the thermodynamic state. The reaction either generates or absorbs heat according to its chemical nature. In this situation the reaction temperature will be moderated by some fluid medium, hence additional thermal flow constraints are placed up the reactor and the temperature moderating system. Moreover, the rate at which a reaction proceeds is dependent upon temperature, thus there is generally a cross-coupling of continuity constraints on materials and heat in the reactor.

A detailed study of reaction kinetics is beyond the scope of the present treatment; however the following grossly simplified example will serve to illustrate the form in which the dynamic equations for chemical reaction processes may be written. Figure 5.18 shows a continuous flow, stirred tank reactor. The tank is fed by a fluid stream at volumetric rate q_i and temperature T_i, the fluid stream leaves the reactor at a volumetric rate q_o and temperature T_o. The fluid stream contains a reactant A with concentration y_i (mass/unit volume) at the input and y_o at the output. The reactor itself has a fixed volume V, and the state of the reactant A inside the tank is assumed to be as for the output (e.g. concentration y_o, temperature T_o). The reaction generates heat and so must be cooled by a coolant stream which has output temperature T_c.

The continuity constraints are: (1) Material balance on reactant A (cf. equation (34)):

$$V\frac{dy_o}{dt} = q_i y_i - q_o y_o + R_A ; \qquad (41)$$

(2) Thermal balance on reactor:

$$MC_p \frac{\mathrm{d}T_o}{\mathrm{d}t} = Q_i - Q_o ; \tag{42}$$

where R_A = rate of generation of reactant A; M = total mass of reactants in the reactor; C_P = specific heat of the material in the reactor; Q_i = rate of heat generation due to reaction; Q_o = rate of heat abstraction by cooling fluid.

For a first-order reaction the rate at which the material is produced during a chemical reaction is the product of the amount of that material which is present and a factor which is a non-linear function of temperature. Suppose material A is consumed during the reaction, then

$$R_A = -Vy_o k(T_o). \tag{43}$$

The rate of heat generation q_i is proportional to the rate of consumption and is

$$Q_i = HVy_o k(T_o) \tag{44}$$

where H is the heat of reaction and is positive for an exothermic reaction.

Equations (43) and (44) define the coupling between the material and thermodynamic continuity constraints and can be thought of as the constitutive relations for the reaction process.

A third thermal balance is made on the coolant system in order to obtain the rate of heat abstraction:

$$Q_o = \rho_o C_p q_o T_o - \rho_i \tilde{C}_p q_i T_i + (T_o - T_c)/R, \tag{45}$$

where ρ_i = the density of the input stream; ρ_o = the density of the output stream and in the reactor; C_P = specific heat of the material in the reactor; $\tilde{C}_P$ = specific heat of the input stream; T_c = coolant temperature; R = net thermal resistance of the reactor walls.

These basic interconnective relations (equations (41), (42), (45)) are then combined with the constitutive relations for the thermochemical process (equations (43), (44)) and yield a set of dynamical equations which describe the reaction process. This gives the system state space equations:

$$V(\mathrm{d}y_o/\mathrm{d}t) = q_i y_i - q_o y_o - Vy_o k(T_o),$$
$$MC_p(\mathrm{d}T_o/\mathrm{d}t) = HVy_o k(T_o) - [(T_o - T_c)/R] - \rho_o C_p q_o T_o + \rho_o C_p q_i T_i. \tag{46}$$

7. SUMMARY

The interconnection of system components imposes a set of relationships upon system variables which involve continuity constraints upon the intensive (flow) variables and compatibility constraints upon the extensive (effort) variables.

A mathematical model of any system then follows by combining three sets of relationships (Fig. 5.4).

(1)   Interconnective relations which constrain the effort and flow to obey generalized continuity and compatibility laws.

(2)   Constitutive relations which define the physical properties of the system elements.

(3)   Dynamic relations which define the states of storage elements in terms of integrated effort and flow variables.

The combination of these sets may be done in two basic ways resulting in either:

(a)   A state space description of the system in the form of a set of coupled first-order differential equations in the stored energy variables.

(b)   A differential equation description in either the spatially extensive variables or the physically intensive variables, or a mixture of both. This external form of model can, for linear (or linearized) systems can be converted to transfer function form by taking Laplace transforms with zero initial conditions.

8. NOTES AND REFERENCES

[1]   The direct application of interconnective rules to the mathematical modelling of typical systems is given in the Case Studies of the overhead gantry crane; the paper machine flow box; and the coupled electric drives in part 3.

[2]   Sir Isaac Newton's laws of motion appeared in "Principia" (1687). See: "Newton's Principia". Translated by Motte, revised by Cajori. University of California Press, Berkeley (1960).

[3]   The mathematical modelling of process systems is a highly specialized area. For this reason the introductory discussion begun here is not continued in the text, except in as much as many fluid and hydraulic systems are classified as process systems (cf. the paper machine flow box case study).
Useful books on the modelling of process systems are
Campbell, D. P. (1960). "Process dynamics". Wiley, New York.
Buckley, P. (1964). "Techniques of process control". Wiley, New York.
Franks, R. (1972). "Modelling and simulation in chemical engineering". Wiley, New York.

9. PROBLEMS

9.1 An automobile suspension system can be modelled by the lumped linear system shown in Fig. 5.19, where b_1, k_1 are the suspension units; b_2, k_2 are the tyre dissipatance and stiffness. The effective motor mass is m_2 and the tyre mass is m_1. Take the displacements x_1 and x_2 as the system states and write the state space equations for the system.

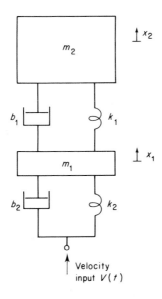

Fig. 5.19.

9.2. A two-stage turbine can be modelled, as shown in Fig. 5.20, by two inertias I_1 and I_2 representing the rotational mass of each stage. The stages are coupled by a shaft of stiffness k_1, and the effective load inertia I_3 is coupled to the turbine by a shaft of stiffness k_2. The bearings which support the turbine shaft have effective linear frictional coefficients b_1, b_2, b_3 as shown. Assume that the stiffness of the interstage shaft and the turbine load shaft can be split equally either side of the bearings. Write the system transfer functions between the torque inputs to the turbine stages τ_1, τ_2; and the angular velocity of the load ω.

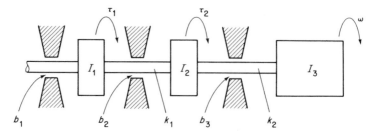

Fig. 5.20.

9.3. Find the state space description of the circuit shown in Fig. 5.21. Use flux linkages and capacitor charge as the state variables. Write the transfer function between the input current i and the voltage developed across the resistor R_2. Assume that all components are linear.

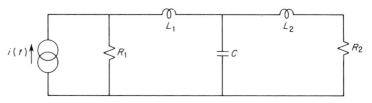

Fig. 5.21.

9.4. Write the state space description of the fluid system shown in Fig. 5.22, use the fluid volumes in the tanks as the states. Assume that the fluid energy dissipators are orifices and use the appropriate non-linear constitutive relations.

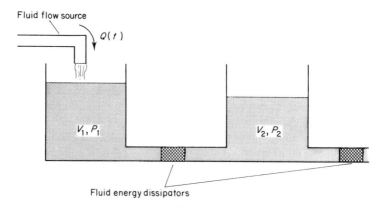

Fig. 5.22.

9.5. Write the transfer function relating the input mass flow rate $m(t)$ to the pressure P_3, for the pneumatic system shown in Fig. 5.23. Assume that the dissipators and tank capacitances have been linearized about a specific pressure point.

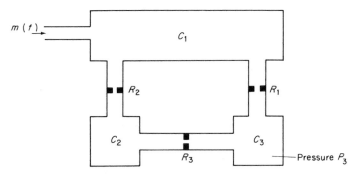

Fig. 5.23.

9.6. Write the state space description of the fluid system shown in Fig. 5.24, use the fluid volumes V_1, V_2, V_3, as states and assume that the dissipators are linear. The system inputs are pure fluid flow sources. $Q_1(t)$, $Q_2(t)$, $Q_3(t)$.

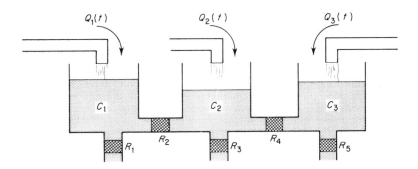

Fig. 5.24.

Part 2: Systematic Modelling Methods

In the sequel the interconnective relations are reviewed in three distinct ways. Each viewpoint leads to a systematic procedure for formulating a mathematical model of a physical system. The first method is the network analysis approach whereby the interconnective structure of a system is embedded into a linear graph. The second approach uses the interconnective constraints to construct a variational statement concerning the system energy distribution. The mathematical description of the system dynamics then follows from the rules of variational calculus.

Finally, a graphical method is developed which emphasizes the energetic interactions in a system by coupling components with energy bonds. The mathematical model of the system is then derived from the graph using techniques analogous to those of network analysis.

Network Methods

6

INTRODUCTION

The interconnective constraints on system variables can be formalized in a number of ways. Probably the most advanced method in terms of technical development is network analysis. As the name betrays, network methods have their historical roots in electrical circuit studies. In the electrical engineering context a circuit is drawn as a set of connected lines (or edges) to form a graph, from which Kirchoff's Laws can be stated in concise algebraic form. The constitutive properties of the edges then allow the dynamic equations of the circuit to be systematically written.

It should be clear from the discussion so far that any lumped parameter system with a pair of energy variables which have suitable interconnective constraints is amenable to network analysis. However, there is the initial task of drawing the system network; this problem is dealt with in section 1. The algebraic statements of the interconnective constraints are presented in sections 2 and 3. The transform representation of edge constitutive relations are discussed in section 4; the discussion then passes to the formulation of models for an entire system (sections 5 and 6). The chapter ends with a discussion of dual and analogue systems.

1. THE REPRESENTATION OF SYSTEMS BY LINEAR GRAPHS

1.1. System elements as oriented line segments

A linear graph is a set of connected lines. The lines represent symbolically the elements of the system, hence the primary task in constructing a linear graph of a system is to select a convention whereby one-port and two-port elements can be drawn as simple line segments. In addition, the line segments are *oriented* to

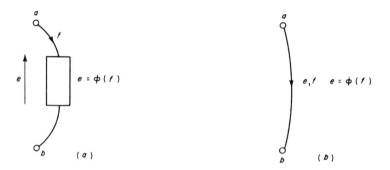

Fig. 6.1. Line segment representation of a general element.

indicate the reference directions of the element effort and flow variables. The convention adopted here is that a one-port with effort and flow variables e and f respectively, is drawn as a line segment oriented in the reference direction for positive flow and decreasing effort; that is in the direction of positive power flow. This convention is shown in Fig. 6.1(a) and (b) for a generalized element; in this example Fig. 6.1(b) states that effort e is positive when terminal a has a higher effort than terminal b. The flow variable f is positive when flow is in the direction of the arrow. Thus the significance of the orientation is to indicate the assumed positive convention for the across variable; the through variable has a corresponding convention which ensures positive signs in the one-port's constitutive relation.

The representation of mechanical systems requires special mention, since confusion can arise between the orientation convention for the line segment and the reference direction for positive velocities in the system. In describing the velocities in a mechanical system one talks of a positive or negative velocity of so many metres/second. Such statements suggest knowledge (often implicit) of the assumed direction of positive velocity. However, in order to make the oriented line segment meaningful, the positive velocity convention must be explicitly stated on each coordinate of translation. The conventions adopted here are depicted on Fig. 6.2 for all the one-port storage and dissipator devices mentioned so far.

The line segment representation of energy sources merits some explanation; the orientation of line segments is such that normally positive power flows into an element. However, with sources power normally flows out; this difference is accommodated within our convention by defining special source line segments as shown in Fig. 6.3. Notice that to maintain a compatible representation the line segment arrow convention for passive elements is used but the non-causal variable has its sign reversed. That is to say, for a flow source (Fig. 6.3(a)) the effort is negative indicating that the effort actually increases in the direction of

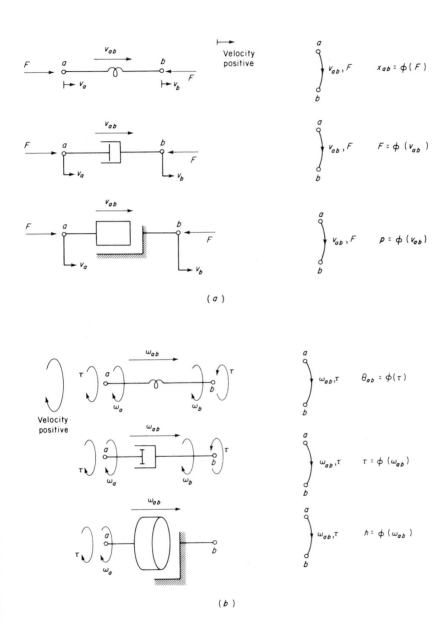

Fig. 6.2. Line segment representation of (*a*) translation mechanical elements, (*b*) rotational mechanical elements, (*c*) electrical elements, (*d*) fluid system elements, (*e*) thermal system elements.

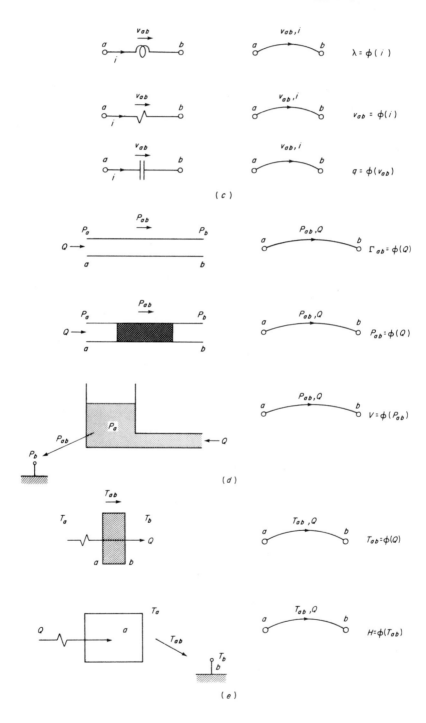

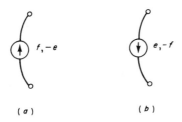

Fig. 6.3. Source element conventions.

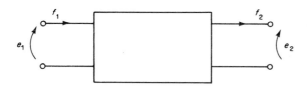

Fig. 6.4. Positive conventions for two-ports.

the arrow. Similarly, the effort source has a negative flow variable, this says that positive flow is in the opposite direction to the effort arrow (Fig. 6.3(b)).

In this treatment we will only be concerned with ideal power conserving two-ports which are either transformers or gyrators. Such devices are modelled as a pair of line segments with coupled efforts and flows. If the effort and flow reference directions are as shown in Fig. 6.4, then the coupled source representation leads to the line segment symbols of Fig. 6.5.

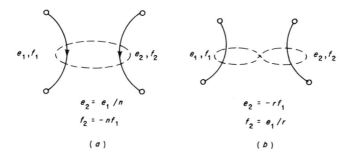

Fig. 6.5. Line segment representation of basic two-ports.

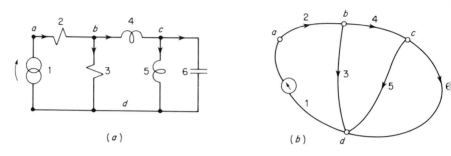

Fig. 6.6. Example of a system graph for an electrical system.

1.2. Examples of system graphs

It will clarify the conventions adopted here if some representative systems are put in linear graph form. The most straightforward system graphs to draw are those for electrical systems, since the conventions adopted for electrical

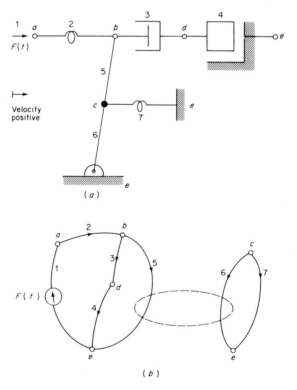

Fig. 6.7. Example of a system graph for a mechanical system.

voltage and current flow are identical to the line segment conventions; thus the electric circuit of Fig. 6.6(a) has the linear graph of 6.6(b). The following points should be noted concerning the graph and its construction.

(i) Each element is labelled to show the correspondence between elements in the physical system and line segments in the line graph. In this instance the elements are numbered.

(ii) Each junction at which two or more elements share a common terminal is labelled. In this case the junctions are indicated by letters.

(iii) With the exception of the source element, the graph in Fig. 6.6(b) contains no information about the physical nature of the electric circuit except its structure. Thus the graph itself specifies the interconnective constraints which exist in the system. The constitutive and dynamic relations must also be given in order to provide the extra information required to fully describe the system.

A typical mechanical translational system is shown in Fig. 6.7(a). The corresponding linear graphs are shown in Fig. 6.7(b). There are two parts of the

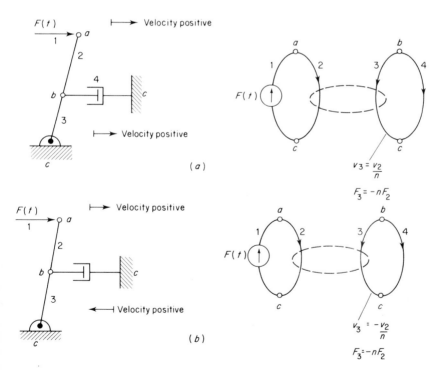

Fig. 6.8. Illustrating the effect of port velocity conventions on mechanical two-ports. (a) Velocity convention 1. (b) Velocity convention 2.

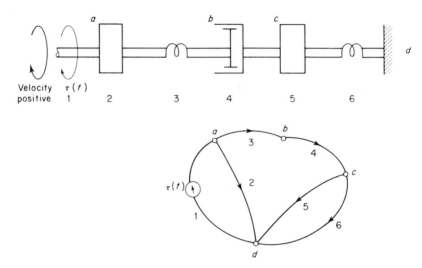

Fig. 6.9. Example of a mechanical system oriented line graph.

graph because of the transforming action of the lever. Note that the velocity reference direction is indicated. Actually for a mechanical system involving two-ports, the positive velocity reference direction must be indicated on all ports. This is in order that the different parts of the graph may be meaningfully oriented. Depending upon the relative reference direction for velocity the sign

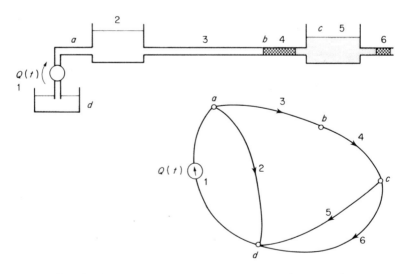

Fig. 6.10. Example of a fluid system oriented line graph.

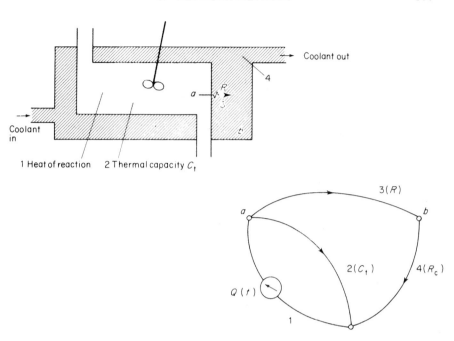

Fig. 6.11. Example of a thermal system oriented line graph.

of the velocity on (say) port 2 of a two-port will be either plus or minus. The simple example shown in Fig. 6.8 illustrates these differences.

Figures 6.9, 6.10 and 6.11 show typical rotational, fluid and thermal systems with their associated graphs. These figures are self-explanatory, except that one should note that Fig. 6.11 is the network model which corresponds to the cooling system of the chemical reactor mentioned in chapter 5. In this example the heat output of the reactor is modelled as a heat source $Q(t)$, the cooling fluid is assumed to be a thermal dissipator with dissipatance R_c controlled by the coolant flow rate.

2. LINEAR GRAPH DEFINITIONS

Before the interconnective constraints can be put in a form suitable for network methods, it is necessary to define and explain the notation used in network analysis. Firstly, a linear graph is defined as a set of interconnected line segments. The term linear is associated with the word line; it does not imply algebraic linearity of the constitutive relations which belong to the line segments. If the line segments are oriented, the graph is an oriented linear

INTRODUCTION TO PHYSICAL SYSTEM MODELLING

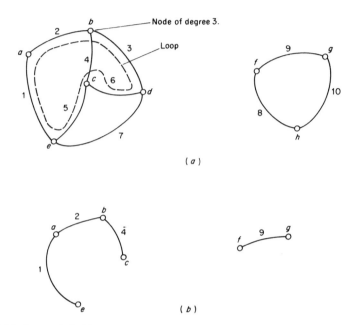

(a)

(b)

Fig. 6.12. Some definitions concerning linear graphs: (a) a graph with two parts; (b) a subgraph of graph (a).

graph. The line segments are conventionally called "edges", and the end of a set of edges is termed a "node" (or vertex). Nodes and edges are identified by an appropriate symbol; in our convention nodes are labelled with letters and edges are numbered.

Some of the examples in the previous section involved graphs with several parts. In general, a graph will consist of a number of connected graphs, and a "connected graph" is defined as one in which any node can be reached by tracing a path through edges. From time to time we need to refer to a "subgraph" which is defined as a sub-set of edges and nodes of the graph mutually incident exactly as in the original graph. It should be clear that a part of a graph and a sub-graph are distinct features of a graph. For example, Fig. 6.12(a) shows a graph with two parts; Fig. 6.12(b) is a sub-graph of this graph.

Other useful definitions are listed below:

Definition 1: The "degree" of a node is the number of edges connected to that node.

Definition 2: A "loopset" is a set of edges and nodes of a graph such that each node has degree 2. Note that linear graphs of physical systems always have nodes of degree two or more, since a node of degree one is equivalent to a disconnected terminal on an energy port.

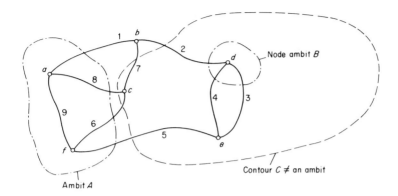

Fig. 6.13. Some properties of linear oriented graphs.

Definition 3: A "loop" is the simple closed path defined by a loopset.

These three definitions can be illustrated by reference to Fig. 6.12(a), in which node b has degree 3; the set of edges and nodes (1, 2, 3, 6, 5) (e, a, b, d, c) form a loopset and the dotted curve indicates the corresponding loop.

Definition 4: A "cutset" is a set of edges of a connected graph such that cutting these edges separates the graph in two connected graphs. If any edge from the cutset is omitted the graph should remain connected. If the edges in a cutset are all incident on the one node, the node is called a node cutset.

Definition 5: An "ambit" is the simple closed path intersecting all the edges of a cutset. If the cutset is a node cutset, the corresponding ambit is a node ambit.

These points are illustrated in Fig. 6.13, in which edges (1, 8, 6, 5) form a cutset but edges (2, 7, 8, 6, 5) do not. Edges (2, 4, 3) form a node cutset.

Definition 6: A "tree" of a graph is a connected sub-graph containing all the nodes of a graph, but no loops. The complement of a tree is called a "co-tree", and is that part of a graph which remains when the tree is removed. The edges in a tree are termed "branches" and those in a co-tree are called "chords".

Two possible trees for the graph of Fig. 6.13 are shown in Fig. 6.14(a) and (b). For the first tree the co-tree has chords (3, 5, 6, 7), and the second tree has co-tree with chords (1, 2, 4, 9).

Definition 7: A "basic cutset" is defined for a particular tree as the cutset consisting of one tree branch and some or all of the co-tree chords. Each basic cutset is oriented so as to assign a positive sign to its tree branch. A basic ambit is the ambit corresponding to a basic cutset. In Fig. 6.13 and with respect to the tree of Fig. 6.14(a), the edges (2, 5) form a basic cutset, as do edges (1, 7, 5) and (4, 3, 5). Notice that a basic cutset may or may not be a node cutset.

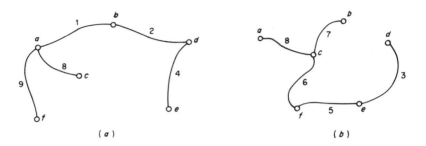

(a)   (b)

Fig. 6.14. Trees of the graph of Fig. 6.13.

Definition 8: A "basic loopset" is defined for a particular tree as a loopset consisting of one chord and some or all of the branches of the tree. A basic loop is the loop corresponding to a basic loopset. A basic loop therefore traverses a path including one chord and any number of branches.

Definition 9: A graph is "planar" if it can be deformed, without breaking an edge, to lie on a plane with no two edges crossing. A graph which cannot be put

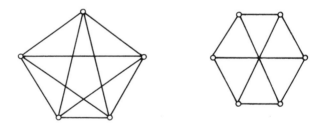

Fig. 6.15. Non-planar graphs.

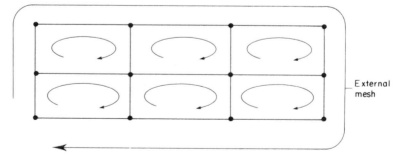

Fig. 6.16. The meshes of a planar graph.

in this form is "non-planar". The two basic forms of non-planar graphs are shown in Fig. 6.15.

For planar graphs we can define special loops which are known as "meshes".

Definition 10: The meshes of a planar graph are the set of empty loops; they comprise a set of interior meshes and one exterior mesh (Fig. 6.16). A loopset defined for a mesh is called a "mesh loopset".

3. ALGEBRAIC FORMS OF THE INTERCONNECTIVE CONSTRAINTS

The continuity and compatibility constraints on physical system energy variables can be given in a variety of concise forms when stated in terms of the corresponding oriented linear graph. Suppose that a physical system has been put in lumped parameter form and the oriented linear graph drawn; then the interconnective rules can be stated in terms of the generalized system variables.

(i)   Continuity constraint. In an oriented linear graph the total flow intersecting any ambit is zero.

(ii)   Compatibility constraint. In an oriented linear graph the total effort around any loop is zero.

Note that in both cases the flow and effort for a specific edge are directed variables with positive directions determined by the edge orientation. In the subsequent sections these generalized interconnective rules will be put in algebraic form.

3.1. Flow continuity constraint

The interconnective rule which assures continuity of flow in an oriented linear graph can be given a concise expression in terms of the cutset matrices of the graph. First we adopt the convention that a flow variable is positive if the associated edge is directed away from an ambit. The complete cutset matrix C_0 is constructed as follows:

(1)   Associate each column of C_0 with a specific edge flow; if the graph has b edges, C_0 has b columns.

(2)   Associate each row with a specific cutset, if the graph has r cutsets, C_0 has r rows.

(3)   If an edge is included in a cutset, then insert $+1$ in the appropriate matrix entry if the edge flow is oriented away from the ambit, and -1 if it is oriented towards the ambit. Otherwise put zero in the appropriate entry.

With the complete outset matrix constructed, the flow continuity constraint can be stated:

$$C_0 f_e = 0, \tag{1}$$

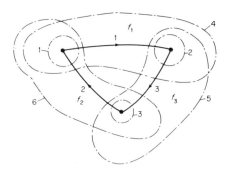

Fig. 6.17. The complete cutset of a graph.

where f_e is a b vector of the edge flows, and **0** is a zero vector. For the graph of Fig. 6.17, the statement of the flow variable constraints is in terms of the complete cutset matrix:

$$
\text{cutsets} \downarrow
\begin{array}{c}
1 \\ 2 \\ 3 \\ 4 \\ 5 \\ 6
\end{array}
\begin{bmatrix}
1 & -1 & 0 \\
-1 & 0 & 1 \\
0 & 1 & -1 \\
0 & -1 & 1 \\
-1 & 1 & 0 \\
1 & 0 & -1
\end{bmatrix}
\begin{bmatrix}
f_1 \\ f_2 \\ f_3
\end{bmatrix}
=
\begin{bmatrix}
0 \\ 0 \\ 0 \\ 0 \\ 0 \\ 0
\end{bmatrix}
\tag{2}
$$

The complete cutset matrix contains an explicit statement of every flow constraint in the system, and thus involves much redundant information. For example, the last three constraints in equation (2) are simply the negative of the first three constraints. It is important therefore to determine cutset matrices which are complete (in that they implicitly determine all constraint equations) yet are independent (i.e. they do not over-specify the constraints). A cutset matrix which is nearer this goal is the complete node cutset matrix C_{n0}, which is obtained by deleting from C_0 all rows, except those which refer to the node cutset. Thus, for a graph with b edges and n nodes the complete node cutset matrix has dimension (n, b). For the example of Fig. 6.17, the complete node cutset matrix is obtained by deleting the last three rows. Thus

$$
C_{n0} =
\begin{bmatrix}
1 & -1 & 0 \\
-1 & 0 & 1 \\
0 & 1 & -1
\end{bmatrix}.
\tag{3}
$$

However, the complete node cutset matrix still contains redundant information since there is linear dependence in the rows. Actually, there are just $(n-1)$ flow constraints in a connected graph with n nodes, or equivalently

"The rank of the complete node cutset matrix of a connected graph of n nodes is $(n-1)$."

This statement is readily justified by considering first a single-node cutset of a connected graph with more than one node, this cutset is clearly independent. Next consider a cutset whose ambit encloses the first cutset and just one additional node, this cutset will include at least one new edge flow and is hence independent of the first cutset. Continue in this way, each time adding a cutset which includes the previous cutset and one new node. This can be done until $(n-1)$ independent cutsets have been formed and just one node remains; a new cutset involving this final node would involve no new edges and hence the existing $(n-1)$ cutsets completely specify the flow constraints. The extension to this theorem states that the rank of the complete node cutset matrix of a graph of n nodes consisting of k separate parts has rank $(n-k)$.

A reduced node cutset matrix can be obtained by discarding any row of $\boldsymbol{C}_{n0}$. The resulting matrix $\boldsymbol{C}_n$ has rank $(n-1)$ and $(n-1)$ rows; it therefore specifies completely and independently the flow constraints in the graph. A more systematic way in which to write the flow constraints is in terms of the basic cutsets of a tree (cf. Definitions 6 and 7). First observe that a tree of a connected graph of n nodes has $(n-1)$ branches. Therefore if the flow constraints are written for the basic cutsets corresponding to a tree one gets

$$C_b f_e = 0 \qquad (4)$$

where $\boldsymbol{C}_b$ is an $(n-1)$ by b matrix termed the basic cutset matrix. If the edge flow vector is ordered such that the tree branch flows come first and the ordering of the rows of $\boldsymbol{C}_b$ corresponds with the branches in the edge flow vector, then equation (4) can be written thus:

$$C_b f_e = [I \quad H]\begin{bmatrix} f_t \\ f_c \end{bmatrix} = 0, \qquad (5)$$

where I is a unit matrix of dimension $(n-1)$ and H is a matrix of dimension $(n-1, b-n+1)$. The vectors f_t and f_c are respectively the tree branch flow vector and the co-tree chord flow vector which are obtained by appropriate reordering of the edge flow vector.

Consider the graph with its associated tree shown in Fig. 6.18. The basic cutset matrix for this graph and tree is

$$
C_b = \begin{bmatrix}
1 & 0 & 0 & 0 & 0 & 0 & 1 & -1 \\
0 & 1 & 0 & 0 & 1 & 1 & 0 & 1 \\
0 & 0 & 1 & 0 & 1 & 1 & 1 & 0 \\
0 & 0 & 0 & 1 & 0 & -1 & 0 & 0
\end{bmatrix}.
$$

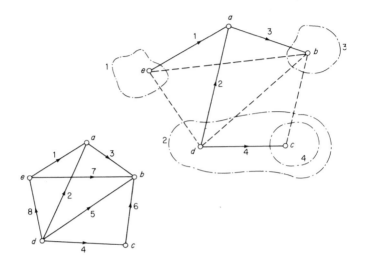

Fig. 6.18. The basic cutset of a graph tree.

Because the basic cutset matrix C_b has a unit matrix of dimension $(n-1)$ imbedded in it, the basic cutset matrix evidently has rank $(n-1)$. Thus the flow constraints on a connected matrix of n nodes are completely and independently specified by a basic cutset matrix.

3.2. Effort compatibility constraint

The interconnective rule which assures compatibility of effort in an oriented linear graph can be written in a concise way by employing loopset matrices. A set of effort constraints formed for all the loopsets in a graph is of the form:

$$B_0 e_e = 0, \tag{6}$$

where e_e is the b vector of edge efforts and $\mathbf{0}$ the zero vector of dimension l, where there are l possible loop sets. The complete loopset matrix B_0 is of dimension (l, b) and is assembled according to the rule:

The ijth entry of B_0 is $+1$ if edge j is contained in the ith loop and both have the same orientation.

The ijth entry of B_0 is -1 if edge j is contained in the ith loop and they have opposing orientations.

If the jth edge is not contained in the ith loop the ijth entry of B_0 is zero.

The complete loopset matrix specifies all the possible compatibility constraints which can be formulated for a graph, and clearly there will generally be redundancy in the specification. A more compact and systematic way of formulating the effort constraints is in terms of the basic loops of a graph and an associated tree. The basic loopset matrix $\boldsymbol{B}_0$ is obtained by writing the basic loopset effort constraints which are associated with each co-tree chord and orienting the basic loops to be compatible with the chord orientations. In this way a set of $(b-n+1)$ effort constraints are determined. Thus

$$\boldsymbol{B}_b\boldsymbol{e}_e = \boldsymbol{0}. \tag{7}$$

The basic loopset constraints each involve one new effort variable, they are therefore independent. Furthermore, all other effort constraints can be found as linear combinations of the basic loopset constraints. Hence the basic loopset matrix is a complete description of the effort constraints. Therefore there are $(b-n+1)$ unique effort constraints in a connected graph of n nodes and b edges.

The basic loopset equations (equation (7)) can be ordered such that the chord efforts are last in both the edge effort vector and the rows of $\boldsymbol{B}_b$, and have the same ordering. The basic loopset constraints can therefore be written in the form:

$$\boldsymbol{B}_b\boldsymbol{e}_e = [\boldsymbol{F} \quad \boldsymbol{I}]\begin{bmatrix} \boldsymbol{e}_t \\ \boldsymbol{e}_c \end{bmatrix} = \boldsymbol{0}, \tag{8}$$

where $\boldsymbol{F}$ is a matrix of dimension $(b-n+1, n-1)$ and $\boldsymbol{I}$ is a unit matrix of dimension $(b-n+1)$. The vector $\boldsymbol{e}_t$ consists of the tree branch efforts and $\boldsymbol{e}_c$ is the vector of co-tree chord efforts.

A basic loopset matrix for the graph and tree of Fig. 6.18 is

$$\boldsymbol{B}_b = \begin{bmatrix} 0 & -1 & -1 & 0 & 1 & 0 & 0 & 0 \\ 0 & -1 & -1 & 1 & 0 & 1 & 0 & 0 \\ -1 & 0 & -1 & 0 & 0 & 0 & 1 & 0 \\ 1 & -1 & 0 & 0 & 0 & 0 & 0 & 1 \end{bmatrix}$$

The complete loopset matrix and the basic loopset matrix have natural analogues in the complete cutset matrix and the basic cutset matrix. However, there is, in general, no loop analogue of the node cutset matrix, *except* in the case of planar graphs when the mesh loop set matrix defined below is the complement of the node cutset matrix. The mesh loopset equations are obtained by defining consistently oriented mesh loops on the graph, noting that if the interior meshes are clockwise the exterior mesh must be anticlockwise for consistency. The mesh loopset matrix $\boldsymbol{B}_{m0}$ is then obtained by assembling the mesh loopset equations.

Note that there are $(b-n+2)$ mesh equations and the mesh loopset matrix has rank $(b-n+1)$. Thus any $(b-n+1)$ mesh loopset equations form a complete and independent set of effort constraints for a connected planar graph. The loopset constraints for the interior meshes form a convenient set of independent constraints; this reduced mesh loopset matrix is denoted by B_m.

3.3. Relationship between cutset and loopset matrices

Consider a connected linear graph of n nodes and b edges. If C_0 and B_0 are respectively the complete cutset and complete loopset matrices with columns arranged in like order, then the matrices satisfy the important relationship

$$C_0 B_0' = 0 \qquad (9)$$

where the prime indicates the matrix transpose. This relationship can be justified by considering the product of the complete node cutset matrix and the transposed complete loopset matrix. Let this matrix have ijth element m_{ij} given by

$$m_{ij} = \sum_{k=1}^{b} c_{ik} b_{jk}, \qquad (10)$$

where c_{ik} and b_{jk} are respectively the ikth and jkth elements of C_{n0} and B_0. The jth row of B_0 and the ith row of C_{n0} only contain non-zero elements in like positions if the jth loopset contains edges which are incident at the ith node. The loopset must contain two edges incident on the node in order to fulfill the definition of a loopset. Let the incident edges be labelled f and h respectively, as shown in Fig. 6.19. These edges contribute the following terms to the inner product:

$$c_{if} b_{jf} + c_{ih} b_{jh}.$$

In the figure, if edges incident on the node are positive, and positive if they are oriented in the same sense as the loop, then the contribution of the ith edge is $+1$ and of the hth edge -1; a net contribution of zero. It can be seen that this is true no matter what edge orientations or node loop conventions are adopted. Thus the matrix element m_{ij} is zero and we have shown

$$C_{n0} B_0' = 0. \qquad (11)$$

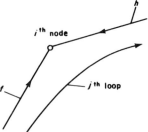

Fig. 6.19.

The complete cutset matrix is obtained from the complete node cutset matrix and thus we have justified equation (9).

If C and B are submatrices obtained by deleting rows from the complete matrices, then the following is clearly true:

$$CB' = 0. \tag{12}$$

This expression has especial significance when the submatrices are the basic cutset and loopset matrices, since it gives

$$C_bB_0' = [I \quad H]\begin{bmatrix} F' \\ I \end{bmatrix} = F' + H = 0, \tag{13}$$

that is

$$F' = -H. \tag{14}$$

Hence the basic cutset and loopset matrices can be written in the form:

$$C_b = [I \quad H], \qquad B_b = [-H' \quad I]. \tag{15}$$

3.4. Relationship between node efforts, loop flows, edge efforts and edge flows

The discussion in the previous sections was essentially concerned with the number of flow constraints and effort constraints required to specify the interconnective rules of a graph. It was shown that for a connected graph with n nodes and b edges, there are $(n-1)$ independent compatibility constraints on the effort variables and $(b-n+1)$ independent continuity constraints. However, in the cutset and loopset formulation, these constraints are in terms of edge energy variables. The question naturally arises as to whether these edge efforts and flows can be related to the node efforts and loop flows for a graph.

Consider first the transformation between edge efforts and node efforts. The node efforts of a graph are measured with respect to some datum point, and for connected graphs, a node is a convenient reference. For example, consider the connected graph of Fig. 6.20. Denote the efforts at a, b, c with respect to d by e_a,

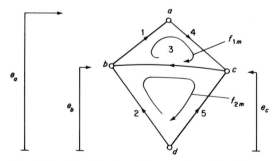

Fig. 6.20. Showing loop flows and node efforts.

e_b, e_c, then the edge efforts are related to the node efforts by the vector- matrix relation

$$
\begin{bmatrix} e_1 \\ e_2 \\ e_3 \\ e_4 \\ e_4 \end{bmatrix} = \begin{bmatrix} -1 & 1 & 0 \\ 0 & -1 & 0 \\ 0 & -1 & 1 \\ 1 & 0 & -1 \\ 0 & 0 & -1 \end{bmatrix} \begin{bmatrix} e_a \\ e_b \\ e_c \end{bmatrix}, \tag{16}
$$

where the convention is that the edge arrow is directed in the direction of decreasing effort.

The node cutset equations for nodes a, b, c are given by

$$
\begin{bmatrix} -1 & 0 & 0 & 1 & 0 \\ 1 & -1 & -1 & 0 & 0 \\ 0 & 0 & 1 & -1 & -1 \end{bmatrix} \begin{bmatrix} f_1 \\ f_2 \\ f_3 \\ f_4 \\ f_5 \end{bmatrix} = \begin{bmatrix} 0 \\ 0 \\ 0 \end{bmatrix} \tag{17}
$$

The reduced node cutset matrix in equation (17) is just the transpose of the matrix which transforms the node efforts into the edge efforts. This result is true in the general case, and is stated more formally thus:

Let C_n be the reduced node cutset matrix obtained by discarding a node. Let e_n be a vector of node efforts measured with respect to the discarded node, then the edge effort vector e_e is given by

$$
e_e = C_n' e_n. \tag{18}
$$

Note that equation (18) states that the edge efforts can be formed as a linear combination of $(n-1)$ node efforts.

A similar procedure can be followed to obtain the transformation between the edge flows and the (fictitious) flows which circulate in the loops of a graph. For the example in hand the interior mesh loops form a convenient set of $(b-n+1)$ independent loops. This choice is possible because the graph is planar. Define circulating flows f_{1m}, f_{2m} in the interior meshes of the graph in Fig. 6.20, and write the mesh effort constraint for the interior meshes:

$$
\begin{bmatrix} 1 & 0 & 1 & 1 & 0 \\ 0 & 1 & -1 & 0 & -1 \end{bmatrix} \begin{bmatrix} e_1 \\ e_2 \\ e_3 \\ e_4 \\ e_5 \end{bmatrix} = \begin{bmatrix} 0 \\ 0 \end{bmatrix} \tag{19}
$$

The edge flows can be written in terms of the mesh flows as follows:

$$\begin{bmatrix} f_1 \\ f_2 \\ f_3 \\ f_4 \\ f_5 \end{bmatrix} = \begin{bmatrix} 1 & 0 \\ 0 & 1 \\ 1 & -1 \\ 1 & 0 \\ 0 & -1 \end{bmatrix} \begin{bmatrix} f_{1m} \\ f_{2m} \end{bmatrix} \tag{20}$$

Thus, the transformation which relates the mesh flows to the edge flows is just the transposed reduced mesh loopset matrix. The general statement of this relationship is:

Let B be the loopset matrix for a set of $(b-n+1)$ independent loops of a connected graph. Let f_l be the vector of flows circulating in the specified loops, then the edge flow vector is related to the loop flow vector by the transformation:

$$f_e = B' f_l \tag{21}$$

Thus the b edge flows can be expressed as a linear combination of $(b-n+1)$ flows in a set of independent graph loops.

4. REPRESENTATION OF EDGE CONSTITUTIVE RELATIONS AND SOURCE EQUIVALENTS

The discussion so far has concerned the concise representation of interconnective constraints in terms of vector–matrix notation. The equations concerning cutset and loopset matrices, and the complementary constraints on node and loop variables are true, regardless of the physical components which form the graph edges. Thus in order to form the dynamical equations for a system the edge constitutive relations must be put in an algebraic form and combined with the interconnective constraints. The arguments in this section are for the most part a preparation for the node and loop analysis methods. These analysis techniques are for linear systems; therefore the discussion in this section is restricted to linear constitutive relations.

4.1. Source representations

When considering a graph driven by effort and flow sources, only two cases need be considered: (i) effort sources in series with a passive element (e.g. a store or dissipator); or (ii) flow sources in parallel with a passive element, or a combination of both. Any other source arrangement can be transformed to this basic form. Consider an effort source parallel connected across two nodes, any passive elements also connected across that node have the effort across them specified by the source and so they may be removed from the graph and

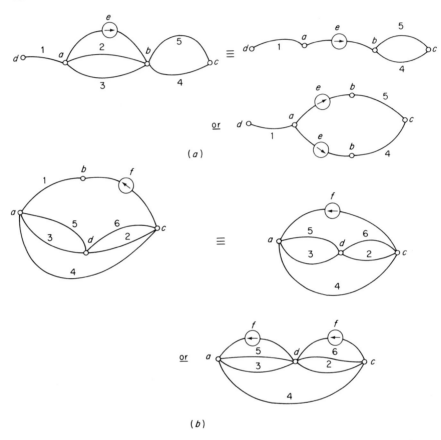

Fig. 6.21. Equivalent source positions: (*a*) effort source relocation; (*b*) flow source relocation.

considered separately. The source is then in series with two elements and may be tacitly grouped with either element. This procedure is depicted in Fig. 6.21(*a*).

Consider a flow source in series with an element or set of elements, these series elements have their flows imposed upon them by the source and so they may be removed from the graph and considered separately. The source will now be in parallel with a set of elements and may be tacitly associated with any of this set. This procedure is depicted in Fig. 6.21(*b*).

4.2. Source equivalents

The node and loop analysis methods described in the sequel are often more straightforward to apply when only flow and effort sources respectively are

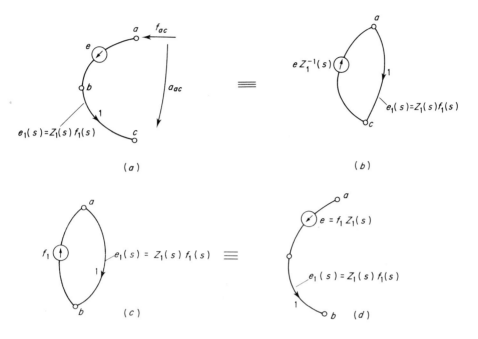

Fig. 6.22. Source replacements rules: (*a*) effort source; (*b*) flow source equivalent.

present. If a mix of both sources are driving a graph, it is sometimes convenient to replace one set of sources by their equivalent complementary sources. Consider the effort source in series with a passive element shown in Fig. 6.22(*a*), then considering the effort and flow e_{ac} and f_{ac} the performance of the circuit between *a* and *c* is identical if the series combination of Fig. 6.22(*a*) is replaced by the parallel combination of Fig. 6.22(*b*). Notice that the network elements are assumed linear and initial conditions are taken as zero so that the edge *bc* may be written with its constitutive relation in Laplace transform form. The transform relation for a generalized element is written

$$e(s) = Z(s)f(s), \tag{22}$$

where $Z(s)$ is the transform impedance of the edge component. Figures 6.22(*a*) and (*b*) therefore say that the series combination of an effort source $e(s)$ and impedance $Z(s)$ can be replaced by a flow source $f(s) = Z^{-1}(s)e(s)$ in parallel with an impedance $Z(s)$. To see this, consider a passive network with equivalent impedance $Z_i(s)$ connected across *ac* (representing the remainder of the circuit with sources set to zero) and compare the node effort e_{ac} and the flow f_{ac} which occur in either case. The equivalence when the remainder of the network contains source elements can be proved by the principle of superposition. Set the source in the edge ab to zero and compare the effort and flows which occur due to sources in the remainder of the network.

If the effort source in Fig. 6.22(a) is represented exactly by the flow source in Fig. 6.22(b), then the converse must be true, and the equivalence depicted in Figs. 6.22(c) and (d) is established.

4.3. Source equivalents for initial conditions

When the constitutive relations of flow stores and effort stores are Laplace transformed, the initial effort and flow respectively appear as additive terms in the transform equation. These additional terms can be absorbed into our scheme by replacing them by equivalent source elements. Consider a generalized flow store C with effort at time $t = 0$ written as $e(0-)$. The element has time domain relation:

$$f(t) = C \frac{de(t)}{dt} \tag{23}$$

and Laplace transform

$$f(s) = sCe(s) - Ce(0-). \tag{24}$$

The term $(sC)^{-1}$ is the generalized impedance of the flow store and the additional flow $Ce(0-)$ is the transform of the impulsive initial flow which is associated with the element. The general time domain flow store in Fig. 6.23(a) therefore has the transform equivalent shown in Fig. 6.23(b).

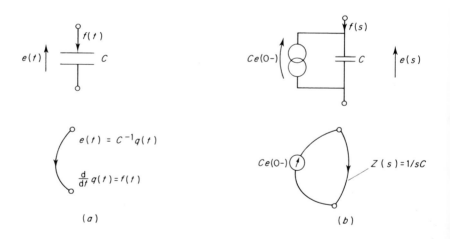

Fig. 6.23. Initial conditions on flow stores in transform form: (a) time domain; (b) complex frequency domain.

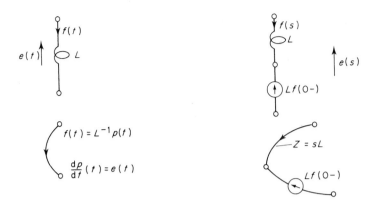

Fig. 6.24. Initial conditions on effort stores in transform form: (*a*) time domain; (*b*) complex frequency domain.

Consider a generalized effort store L with flow at time $t = 0$ written as $f(0-)$. The element has time domain relation

$$e(t) = L\frac{\mathrm{d}f(t)}{\mathrm{d}t} \tag{25}$$

and Laplace transform

$$e(s) = sLf(s) - Lf(0-). \tag{26}$$

The term sL is the generalized impedance of the element and the additional effort $Lf(0-)$ is the transform of the initial impulsive effort which is associated with the element. The general time domain effort store in Fig. 6.24(*a*) therefore has the transform equivalent shown in Fig. 6.24(*b*).

4.4. General edge: combining source and passive elements

For the development of node and loop analysis, each edge is thought of as consisting of a passive element with effort and flow variables e_{pk}, f_{pk}, a series effort source e_{sk} and parallel flow source f_{sk} where the index k is the edge identifier (Fig. 6.25). It is clear that each edge can be brought to this form. Moreover, the form accommodates initial conditions and if required one of the sources can be transformed to its complementary source. If the positive convention on source and passive element energy variables is as shown in Fig. 6.25, then the flow continuity constraint can be written as

$$\boldsymbol{Cf}_{ep} - \boldsymbol{Cf}_{es} = \boldsymbol{0}, \tag{27}$$

where $\boldsymbol{f}_{ep}$ is the edge passive element flow vector; $\boldsymbol{f}_{es}$ is the edge flow source

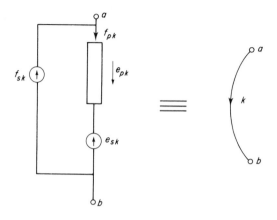

Fig. 6.25. Convention for a general edge with sources present.

vector; and C is an appropriate cutset matrix. The effort compatibility constraint can be similarly written,

$$Be_{ep} - Be_{es} = 0, \tag{28}$$

where e_{ep} is the edge passive element effort vector; e_{es} is the edge effort source vector; B is an appropriate loopset matrix.

The edge passive element flows and efforts are related by the generalized transform impedances. For an effort store L_k, the transform constitutive relation (neglecting initial conditions) is

$$e_{pk}(s) = sL_k f_{pk}(s). \tag{29}$$

For a flow store C_k, the transform constitutive relation (neglecting initial conditions) is

$$e_{pk}(s) = \frac{1}{sC_k} f_{pk}(s). \tag{30}$$

For a dissipator R_k, the transform constitutive relation is

$$e_{pk}(s) = R_k f_{pk}(s). \tag{31}$$

When assembled into matrix form, the edge passive flows and efforts are related by

$$e_{ep}(s) = Z(s) f_{ep}(s). \tag{32}$$

The matrix $Z(s)$ is the generalized impedance matrix for the graph. For a graph containing no two-ports the $Z(s)$ matrix is diagonal with entries composed of the generalized impedances of the stores and dissipators. The inverse of $Z(s)$

matrix is termed $Y(s)$, the generalized admittance matrix for the graph, and is defined by

$$f_{ep}(s) = Y(s)e_{ep}(s), \qquad (33)$$

$$Z(s) = Y(s)^{-1}.$$

5. TRANSFORM EQUATION FORMULATION

The cutset and loopset relations allow complete independent sets of continuity and compatibility constraints to be systematically written. These may be subsequently used, together with the source and impedance (admittance) relations, to form the Laplace transform equation set for the system. There are three basic methods available: (i) loop analysis, which starts with a basic statement of the compatibility constraints and results in an expression of the graph loop flows (as outputs) in terms of the system material properties and the source efforts (as inputs); (ii) nodal analysis, which starts with a basic statement of the continuity constraints and results in an expression of the graph node efforts (as outputs) in terms of the system material properties and the source flows (as inputs); (iii) mixed loop and nodal analysis, which uses a hybrid compatibility/continuity constraint method to obtain a mixed Laplace transform expression for the edge variables.

In the following we assume that only flow sources are present in a nodal analysis, and that only effort sources are present in a loop analysis. It is assumed that the source replacement method of section 4.2 can be used to bring systems into this form. The loop and nodal methods are formulated for graphs without two-ports, the more general case is dealt with in the mixed method of section 5.4.

5.1. Loop analysis

Consider a connected graph containing only effort sources. A set of $(b-n+1)$ independent loopset constraints may be written, thus

$$Be_{ep}(s) = Be_{es}(s), \qquad (34)$$

where B may be conveniently chosen as the basic loopset matrix B_b for a specific graph tree, or for a planar graph the loopset matrix for the interior meshes.

In the absence of flow sources, the vector of flows circulating in the loops defining the loopset is $f_l(s)$ and is related to the edge flow vector $f_e(s)$ by

$$f_e(s) = B'f_l(s). \qquad (35)$$

The edge effort and flows are themselves related by the graph impedance matrix $Z(s)$, thus

$$e_{ep}(s) = Z(s)f_e(s). \qquad (36)$$

Now the right-hand side of equation (34) is a column vector with entries which are the net source efforts in the individual loops. Denote this vector $E(s)$ and rewrite equation (34),

$$
\begin{aligned}
E(s) &= Be_{ep}(s) \\
&= BZ(s)f_e(s) \\
&= BZ(s)B'f_l(s) \\
&= Q(s)f_l(s),
\end{aligned}
\tag{37}
$$

where $Q(s) \equiv BZ(s)B'$ is termed the loop generalized impedance matrix. Notice that $Q(s)$ is a square matrix formed from the product of matrices of full rank, therefore it, too, has full rank. Hence the loop flows $f_l(s)$ are given by

$$
f_l(s) = Q^{-1}(s)E(s)
\tag{38}
$$

and the edge flows $f_e(s)$ are found by putting equation (38) in equation (35). The time behaviour of the system flow variables is obtained by Laplace transform inversion of the relevant equation.

The loop generalized impedance matrix $Q(s)$ is composed of entries $q_{ij}(s)$ given by

$$
q_{ij}(s) = \sum_{k=1}^{b} b_{ik}z_{kk}(s)b_{jk}, \qquad i, j = 1, 2, \ldots (b-n+1).
\tag{39}
$$

Thus the ijth entry of $Q(s)$ is composed of the impedances common to both loops i and j, entered as positive if the loops have the same orientation and negative if the loops have opposing orientations. The diagonal entries are the sum of all impedances in that particular loop. Notice also that $Q(s)$ is symmetric.

5.2. Nodal analysis

Consider a connected graph containing only flow sources. A set of $(n-1)$ independent cutset constraints may be written by considering the reduced node cutset:

$$
C_n f_{ep}(s) = C_n f_{es}(s).
\tag{40}
$$

In the absence of effort sources, the vector of node efforts measured with respect to the reference node is $e_n(s)$ and is related to the edge effort vector $e_e(s)$ by

$$
e_e(s) = C_n' e_n(s).
\tag{41}
$$

The edge efforts and flows are themselves related by the graph admittance matrix $Y(s)$, thus

$$
f_{ep}(s) = Y(s)e_e(s).
\tag{42}
$$

Now the right-hand side of equation (40) is a column vector with entries which are the net source flows incident on the individual nodes. Denote this vector $F(s)$ and rewrite equation (40) as

$$\begin{aligned}
F(s) &= C_n f_{ep}(s) \\
&= C_n Y(s) e_e(s) \\
&= C_n Y(s) C_n' e_n(s) \\
&= P(s) e_n(s),
\end{aligned} \tag{43}$$

where $P(s) = C_n Y(s) C_n'$ is termed the node generalized admittance matrix. Notice that $P(s)$ is a square matrix formed from the product of full rank matrices so that it too is of full rank. Hence the node efforts $e_n(s)$ are given by

$$e_n(s) = P^{-1}(s) F(s), \tag{44}$$

and the edge efforts $e_e(s)$ are found by putting equation (44) in equation (41). The time behaviour of the system effort variables is obtained by Laplace transform inversion of the relevant equation.

The node generalized admittance matrix $P(s)$ is composed of entries $p_{ij}(s)$ given by

$$p_{ij}(s) = \sum_{k=1}^{b} c_{ik} y_{kk}(s) c_{jk}, \qquad i, j = 1, 2, \ldots (n-1).$$

Thus the ijth element of $P(s)$ is composed of the negative sum of admittances incident on node i and j. The diagonal entries $p_{ii}(s)$ are the sum of all admittances incident on the ith node. Note that $P(s)$ is symmetric.

5.3. Examples

Consider the mechanical translational system shown in Fig. 6.26(a). The system graph is depicted in Fig. 6.26(b). Note that only velocity sources are present, so that loop analysis is appropriate. If the meshes a, b, c carry loop forces $F_a(s)$, $F_b(s)$ and $F_c(s)$, and the velocity source is associated with edge 1 (the spring k_1) then the loopset constraints yield the loopset matrix

$$B_m = \begin{bmatrix} 1 & 0 & 1 & 0 & 0 & 0 \\ 0 & 1 & -1 & 0 & 1 & 0 \\ 0 & 0 & 0 & 1 & -1 & 1 \end{bmatrix}.$$

The system impedance matrix is

$$Z(s) = \begin{bmatrix} k_1^{-1}s & 0 & 0 & 0 & 0 & 0 \\ 0 & b_2^{-1} & 0 & 0 & 0 & 0 \\ 0 & 0 & b_3^{-1} & 0 & 0 & 0 \\ 0 & 0 & 0 & k_4^{-1}s & 0 & 0 \\ 0 & 0 & 0 & 0 & (sM_5)^{-1} & 0 \\ 0 & 0 & 0 & 0 & 0 & (sM_6)^{-1} \end{bmatrix}$$

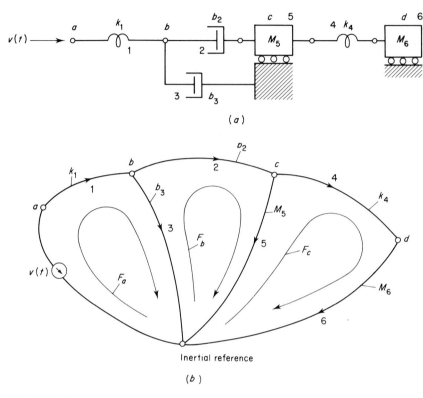

Fig. 6.26. An example of loop (or mesh) analysis: (a) the mechanical system; (b) the system graph.

The loop generalized impedance matrix $Q(s)$ is then obtained as

$$Q(s) = B_m Z(s) B'_m =$$

$$\begin{bmatrix} sk_1^{-1} + b_3^{-1} & -b_3^{-1} & 0 \\ -b_3^{-1} & b_2^{-1} + b_3^{-1} + (sM_5)^{-1} & -(sM_5)^{-1} \\ 0 & -(sM_5)^{-1} & sk_4^{-1} + (sM_5)^{-1} + (sM_6)^{-1} \end{bmatrix}.$$

The vector of mesh forces $F_l(s)$ is then given in terms of the vector of source velocities $V(s)$ by

$$F_l(s) = Q^{-1}(s) \cdot V(s) \qquad (45)$$

where

$$V'(s) = [v(s), 0, 0]$$
$$F'_l(s) = [F_a(s), F_b(s), F_c(s)].$$

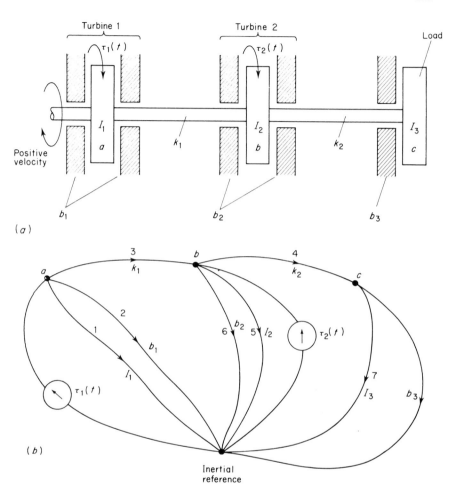

Fig. 6.27. An example of nodal analysis: (*a*) a two-stage turbine system; (*b*) the system graph.

The forces in the individual components may be found by applying equation (35).

Consider next the rotational system sketched in Fig. 6.27(*a*) which schematically depicts a two-stage turbine where the stages are modelled as inertias I_1 and I_2 which are subject to input torques $\tau_1(t)$ and $\tau_2(t)$ and which drive a load inertia I_3. The inter-turbine and load shafts are represented by pure rotational springs of stiffness k_1, k_2 respectively, and the shaft bearing frictions are represented by the coefficients b_1, b_2, b_3. The aim is to find the angular velocities of the turbine rotors ω_a, ω_b and the load ω_c as functions of the input torques.

Figure 6.27(b) shows the system graph. Since only torque sources are present, the nodal analysis procedure is appropriate. The nodes a, b, c will give directly the required output variables. Using the usual convention the reduced node cutset matrix is

$$
C_n = \begin{bmatrix} 1 & 1 & 1 & 0 & 0 & 0 & 0 & 0 \\ 0 & 0 & -1 & 1 & 1 & 1 & 0 & 0 \\ 0 & 0 & 0 & -1 & 0 & 0 & 1 & 1 \end{bmatrix}.
$$

The system admittance matrix is

$$
Y(s) = \mathrm{diag}\{sI_1, \, b_1, \, k_1 s^{-1}, \, k_2 s^{-1}, \, sI_2, \, b_2, \, sI_3, \, b_3\}.
$$

The node generalized admittance matrix $P(s)$ is then obtained as

$$
P(s) = C_n Y(s) C_n'
$$

$$
= \begin{bmatrix} sI_1 + b_1 + k_1 s^{-1} & -k_1 s^{-1} & 0 \\ -k_1 s^{-1} & sI_2 + b_2 + (k_1 + k_2)s^{-1} & -k_2 s^{-1} \\ 0 & -k_2 s^{-1} & sI_3 + b_3 + k_2 s^{-1} \end{bmatrix}.
$$

The vector of node angular velocities $\Omega_n(s)$ is then given in terms of the vector of source torques $\tau(s)$ by

$$
\Omega_n(s) = P^{-1}(s) \cdot \tau(s) \tag{46}
$$

where

$$
\Omega_n'(s) = [\omega_a(s), \, \omega_b(s), \, \omega_c(s)],
$$
$$
\tau(s) = [\tau_1(s), \, \tau_2(s), \, 0].
$$

5.4. Mixed loop and nodal analysis

The loop and nodal methods of transfer function matrix derivation work well when there are no two-ports in the system. In particular, unless the two-ports have a special form the graph edge constitutive relations will require modification prior to the equation formulation. Exceptions to this rule are systems containing mutual inductive coupling and gyrational two-ports. Such systems can be analysed by loop or nodal analysis in the normal way. However, difficulties arise when the two-ports concerned involve either modulated sources or ideal transformation. The problem concerns the construction of the impedance and admittance matrices since, in general, an arbitrary two-port device need not have an admittance or impedance

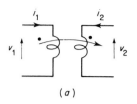

(a)

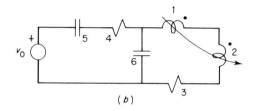

(b)

Fig. 6.28.

representation. Consider specifically a two-port involving mutual inductance as shown in Fig. 6.28(a) such that

$$\begin{bmatrix} v_1 \\ v_2 \end{bmatrix} = \begin{bmatrix} sL_{11} & sL_{12} \\ sL_{21} & sL_{22} \end{bmatrix} \begin{bmatrix} i_1 \\ i_2 \end{bmatrix}, \tag{47}$$

which is a proper impedance relationship and can be inverted to obtain a proper admittance relationship. For example, the circuit shown in Fig. 6.28(b) has impedance matrix:

$$Z = \begin{bmatrix} sL_{11} & sL_{12} & 0 & 0 & 0 & 0 \\ sL_{21} & sL_{22} & 0 & 0 & 0 & 0 \\ 0 & 0 & R_3 & 0 & 0 & 0 \\ 0 & 0 & 0 & R_4 & 0 & 0 \\ 0 & 0 & 0 & 0 & 1/sC_5 & 0 \\ 0 & 0 & 0 & 0 & 0 & 1/sC_6 \end{bmatrix},$$

where the ordering of columns and rows refer to the numbering used in the diagram. However, when the mutual coupling between the circuits approaches the ideal, then, as previously explained, the two-port equation becomes

$$\begin{bmatrix} v_1 \\ i_2 \end{bmatrix} = \begin{bmatrix} 0 & n \\ -n & 0 \end{bmatrix} \begin{bmatrix} i_1 \\ v_2 \end{bmatrix}, \tag{48}$$

which is a form known as the Hybrid h representation and cannot be put into admittance or impedance form, thus preventing direct application of loop or nodal analysis. Similar difficulties arise with modulated sources.

A practical way around this difficulty which is suitable for small systems is to rewrite the unsuitable two-ports as controlled sources. These can then be associated with passive components and the composite components given an admittance or impedance representation. For larger systems the following mixed transform analysis is more suitable.

Given a network representation of a system, select a tree and write mixed relations for the edges, thus:

$$\begin{bmatrix} e_e \\ f_t \end{bmatrix} = \begin{bmatrix} Y_c & J_{12} \\ J_{21} & Y_b \end{bmatrix} \begin{bmatrix} f_c \\ e_t \end{bmatrix}, \tag{49}$$

where e_c and f_c are respectively $(b - n)$ vectors of chord efforts and flows; e_t and f_t are respectively n vectors of tree branch efforts and flows; Z_c is an impedance matrix for the tree chords; Y_t is an admittance matrix for the tree branches; and J_{12} and J_{21} are hybrid matrices which quantify the coupling between tree branch and chord components.

The algebraic interconnective constraints can now be written for the basic loopsets and basic cutsets of the tree as follows:

$$B_b e_e = \begin{bmatrix} -H' & I \end{bmatrix} \begin{bmatrix} e_t \\ e_c \end{bmatrix} = B_b e_{es}, \tag{50}$$

$$C_b f_e = \begin{bmatrix} I & H \end{bmatrix} \begin{bmatrix} f_t \\ f_c \end{bmatrix} = C_b f_{es}. \tag{51}$$

Rearranging (50) and (51) and substituting in equation (49) gives

$$\begin{bmatrix} B_b e_{es} \\ C_b f_{es} \end{bmatrix} = \begin{bmatrix} Z_c & J_{12} - H' \\ J_{21} + H & Y_t \end{bmatrix} \begin{bmatrix} f_c \\ e_t \end{bmatrix}. \tag{52}$$

Equation (52) specifies in mixed form the transform relationship which can be solved for the chord flows and tree branch efforts in terms of the system sources and components.

The use of a mixed relation of this form is that it allows direct solution of the

TABLE 1.   Assignments for mixed loop and nodal analysis.

Component	Assignment in Tree	
	Modulating port	Modulated port
Modulated Sources		
Effort modulated effort source	branch	chord
Flow modulated flow source	chord	branch
Effort modulated flow source	branch	branch
Flow modulated effort source	chord	chord
Two-ports proper	*Port 1*	*Port 2*
Gyrator	branch	branch
	or chord	chord
Transformer	branch	chord
	or chord	branch

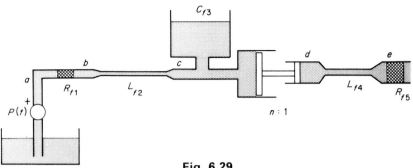

Fig. 6.29.

network equations when two-ports such as modulated sources and transformers are present. To be specific, these two-ports have constitutive relations which can only be written in certain hybrid or mixed forms. However almost all of these forms can be accommodated in the hybrid impedance/admittance matrix on the right-hand side of equation (49) by assigning the two-port edges to be branches or chords as laid out in Table 1.

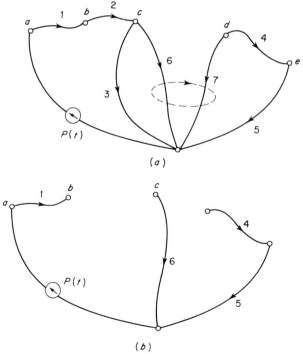

Fig. 6.30. System graph for the fluid system of Fig. 29: (*a*) graph; (*b*) tree.

It should be emphasized that the increased generality of the mixed nodal and loop analysis method is gained at the expense of an increase in the number of equations which must be solved. There are in fact six equations for a system graph with six edges. As an illustration of the use of mixed analysis, consider the fluid system shown in Fig. 6.29 which shows a fluid power supply driving a fluid inductance L_{f4} and dissipator R_{f5} through a fluid transformer.

The system has the network graph shown in Fig. 6.30, where the tree is selected to include edge 6 of the transformer and exclude edge 7. The basic cutset matrix for this graph is

$$\boldsymbol{C}_b = \begin{bmatrix} 1 & 0 & 0 & 0 & -1 & 0 & 0 \\ 0 & 1 & 0 & 0 & -1 & 1 & 0 \\ 0 & 0 & 1 & 0 & 0 & 0 & 1 \\ 0 & 0 & 0 & 1 & 0 & 0 & 1 \end{bmatrix} = [\boldsymbol{I} \quad \boldsymbol{H}]. \quad (53)$$

The relations of the form given in equation (49) become (in terms of fluid systems variables):

$$\begin{bmatrix} P_2 \\ P_3 \\ P_7 \\ Q_1 \\ Q_6 \\ Q_7 \\ Q_5 \end{bmatrix} = \begin{bmatrix} sL_{f2} & 0 & 0 & 0 & 0 & 0 & 0 \\ 0 & (sC_{f3})^{-1} & 0 & 0 & 0 & 0 & 0 \\ 0 & 0 & 0 & 0 & 1/n & 0 & 0 \\ 0 & 0 & 0 & R_{f1}^{-1} & 0 & 0 & 0 \\ 0 & 0 & -1/n & 0 & 0 & 0 & 0 \\ 0 & 0 & 0 & 0 & 0 & (sL_{f4})^{-1} & 0 \\ 0 & 0 & 0 & 0 & 0 & 0 & (R_{f5})^{-1} \end{bmatrix} \begin{bmatrix} Q_2 \\ Q_3 \\ Q_7 \\ P_1 \\ P_6 \\ P_7 \\ P_5 \end{bmatrix} \quad (54)$$

Using the relationship between $\boldsymbol{B}_b$ and $\boldsymbol{C}_b$ we have

$$\boldsymbol{B}_b = \begin{bmatrix} 1 & 1 & 0 & 0 & 1 & 0 & 0 \\ 0 & -1 & 0 & 0 & 0 & 1 & 0 \\ 0 & 0 & -1 & -1 & 0 & 0 & 1 \end{bmatrix} \quad (55)$$

and

$$\boldsymbol{e}'_{es} = [P(t) \quad 0 \quad 0 \quad 0 \quad 0 \quad 0 \quad 0], \quad (56)$$

from which

$$\boldsymbol{B}_b \boldsymbol{e}_{es} = \begin{bmatrix} P(t) \\ 0 \\ 0 \end{bmatrix}, \quad (57a)$$

whereas

$$\boldsymbol{C}_b \boldsymbol{f}_{es} = \begin{bmatrix} 0 \\ 0 \\ 0 \\ 0 \end{bmatrix}$$

(57*b*)

Substituting into equation (52) gives

$$\begin{bmatrix} P(t) \\ 0 \\ 0 \\ 0 \\ 0 \\ 0 \\ 0 \end{bmatrix} = \begin{bmatrix} L_{f2} & 0 & 0 & 1 & 1 & 0 & 0 \\ 0 & (sC_{f3})^{-1} & 0 & 0 & -1 & 0 & 0 \\ 0 & 0 & 0 & 0 & 1/n & -1 & -1 \\ -1 & 0 & 0 & R_{f1}^{-1} & 0 & 0 & 0 \\ -1 & 1 & 1/n & 0 & 0 & 0 & 0 \\ 0 & 0 & 1 & 0 & 0 & (sL_{f4})^{-1} & 0 \\ 0 & 0 & 1 & 0 & 0 & 0 & (R_{f5})^{-1} \end{bmatrix} \begin{bmatrix} Q_2 \\ Q_3 \\ Q_7 \\ P_1 \\ P_6 \\ P_7 \\ P_5 \end{bmatrix}, \quad (58)$$

which can be rearranged to express the fluid flows Q_2, Q_3, Q_7, and fluid pressures P_1, P_6, P_7, P_5 in terms of the input pressure and the system components.

6. STATE SPACE EQUATION FORMULATION

State space models of systems can be obtained by network methods in a number of well developed ways. However, the bond graph approach is in a sense a more natural way of formulating state descriptions. For this reason the network treatment given here is brief, a more complete discussion being provided in the bond graph chapter.

For many systems the best way to obtain a state space model is to follow the direct approach and simply combine the interconnective constraints, the constitutive relations and the dynamical relations. The reason for this is that systematic procedures tend to be cumbersome and cover generalities which rarely occur in practice. In this context the algorithm given in the following section is suited for computer implementation rather than hand calculation.

6.1. Redundancy: state and tree slection

In principle, the flow accumulations in the system flow stores and the effort accumulations in the system effort stores form a natural set of state variables. By the same token, since the constitutive relation relates accumulation variables to terminal variables it has become practice to use the terminal efforts of the flow stores and the terminal flows of the effort stores as the state

variables in network methods. If this convention is adopted, certain re-
dundancies which occur can be readily seen. In particular, if a loop containing
only flow stores and effort sources occurs, then the terminal efforts of the flow
stores will be linearly constrained by the effort compatibility constraint
around that loop. This gives rise to redundancy among the flow store state
variables. In a similar manner, if a node exists with only flow sources and effort
stores connected to it, then redundancy will occur amongst the effort store
state variables.

This question of redundant state variables is examined in a different light in
connection with bond graphs. For the moment it is only necessary to note that
the choice of state variables and the possibility of redundancy leads to the tree
for state equation formulation to be selected such that:

The tree contains: (1) all the effort sources;
                       (2) the maximum number of flow stores;
                       (3) dissipators;
                       (4) the minimum number of effort stores.

The co-tree contains: (1) all the flow sources;†
                      (2) the maximum number of effort stores;
                      (3) dissipators;
                      (4) the minimum number of flow stores.

The tree selected in this way is referred to as the normal tree. If this tree
contains any effort stores then redundancy-exists among the effort store
terminal flows and the flow sources. Likewise, if the co-tree contains any flow
stores then redundancy exists among the flow store terminal efforts and the
effort sources.

6.2 Systematic state space equation formulation

For a normal tree selected in the above manner, define the edge flow and effort
vectors as:

$$e = \begin{bmatrix} e_t \\ e_c \end{bmatrix} \quad \text{and} \quad f = \begin{bmatrix} f_t \\ f_c \end{bmatrix}, \tag{59}$$

where the tree branch vectors are partitioned to conform with the tree
selection procedure:

$$e_t = \begin{bmatrix} e_1 \\ e_{Ct} \\ e_{Rt} \\ e_{Lt} \end{bmatrix} \quad f_t = \begin{bmatrix} f_1 \\ f_{Ct} \\ f_{Rt} \\ f_{Lt} \end{bmatrix}. \tag{60}$$

N.B.   Sources are now assumed to constitute separate edges, they are not associated with passive
elements.

The co-tree edge vectors are correspondingly partitioned:

$$e_c = \begin{bmatrix} e_{Cc} \\ e_{Rc} \\ e_{Lc} \\ e_2 \end{bmatrix} \qquad f_c = \begin{bmatrix} f_{Cc} \\ f_{Rc} \\ f_{Lc} \\ f_2 \end{bmatrix}. \tag{61}$$

Now recall that the basic cutset and loopset relations for the tree are

$$e_c = H' e_t, \qquad f_t = -H f_c, \tag{62}$$

where H can be partitioned in the form:

$$H = \begin{bmatrix} H_{1c} & H_{1R} & H_{1L} & H_{12} \\ H_{CC} & H_{CR} & H_{CL} & H_{C2} \\ H_{RC} & H_{RR} & H_{RL} & H_{R2} \\ H_{LC} & H_{LR} & H_{LL} & H_{L2} \end{bmatrix} \tag{63}$$

and because of the manner in which the tree is constructed H_{RC}, H_{LC} and H_{LR} are zero matrices.

In addition to the interconnective relations embodied in equation (62) the following component relations exist:

$$\begin{bmatrix} f_{Ct} \\ f_{Cc} \end{bmatrix} = \begin{bmatrix} C_t & 0 \\ 0 & C_c \end{bmatrix} \frac{d}{dt} \begin{bmatrix} e_{Ct} \\ e_{Cc} \end{bmatrix}, \tag{64}$$

$$\begin{bmatrix} e_{Lc} \\ e_{Lt} \end{bmatrix} = \begin{bmatrix} L_c & 0 \\ 0 & L_t \end{bmatrix} \frac{d}{dt} \begin{bmatrix} f_{Lc} \\ f_{Lt} \end{bmatrix}, \tag{65}$$

$$\begin{aligned} f_{Rc} &= R_c^{-1} e_{Rc}, \\ f_{Rt} &= R_t^{-1} e_{Rt}, \end{aligned} \tag{66}$$

where if there are no redundant flow stores C_c is zero, and if there are no redundant effort stores L_t is zero.

Equations (62), (64), (65) and (66) can now be combined to eliminate all effort and flow variables *except* the system states (given by e_{Ct} and f_{Lc}) and the source variables (given by e_1 and f_2). The resulting equations are

$$\begin{bmatrix} C & 0 \\ 0 & L \end{bmatrix} \frac{d}{dt} \begin{bmatrix} e_{Ct} \\ f_{Lc} \end{bmatrix} = \begin{bmatrix} A_{11} & A_{12} \\ A_{21} & A_{22} \end{bmatrix} \begin{bmatrix} e_{Ct} \\ f_{Lc} \end{bmatrix}$$

$$+ \begin{bmatrix} B_{11} & B_{12} \\ B_{21} & B_{22} \end{bmatrix} \begin{bmatrix} e_1 \\ f_2 \end{bmatrix} + \begin{bmatrix} D_{11} & 0 \\ 0 & D_{22} \end{bmatrix} \frac{d}{dt} \begin{bmatrix} e_1 \\ f_2 \end{bmatrix}, \tag{67}$$

where

$$C = C_t + H_{CC}C_cH'_{CC},$$
$$L = L_c - H'_{LL}L_tH_{LL},$$
$$A_{11} = -H_{CR}(R_c + H'_{RR}R_tH_{CR})^{-1}H'_{CR},$$
$$A_{22} = -H'_{RL}(R_t^{-1} + H_{RR}R_c^{-1}H'_{RR})^{-1}H_{RL},$$
$$A_{12} = -H_{CL} + H_{CR}(R_c + H'_{RR}R_tH_{RR})^{-1}H'_{RR}R_tH_{RL},$$
$$A_{12} = -A'_{12},$$
$$B_{11} = -H_{CR}(R_c + H'_{RR}R_tH_{RR})^{-1}H_{1R},$$
$$B_{22} = -H'_{RL}(R_t^{-1} + H'_{RR}R_c^{-1}H'_{RR})^{-1}H_{RJ},$$
$$B_{12} = -H_{C2} + H_{CR}(R_c + H'_{RR}R_tH_{RR})^{-1}H'_{RR}R_tH_{R2},$$
$$B_{21} = H'_{1L} - H'_{RL}(R_t^{-1} + H_{RR}R_c^{-1}H'_{RR})^{-1}H_{RR}R_c^{-1},$$
$$D_{11} = -H_{CC}C_cH'_{1C},$$
$$D_{22} = -H'_{LL}L_tH_{L2}.$$

7. ANALOGUES AND DUALS

An essential advantage of a system graph is the structural knowledge which it conveys concerning the physical system which it portrays. The interconnective structure of a system is stripped of its physical context in the graph, and thus common interconnective features are revealed. If two different systems have the same system graph, then they obey identical interconnective constraints and are said to be structurally analogous. In algebraic terms, systems are analogous if their complete cutset and loopset matrices are identical. If two systems are structurally analogous and corresponding edges have identical constitutive relations, they are completely analogous. Figure 6.31 shows

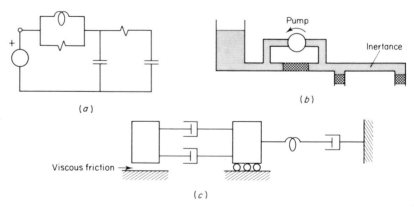

(a)

(b)

(c)

Viscous friction

Pump

Inertance

Fig. 6.31. Some structurally analogous systems.

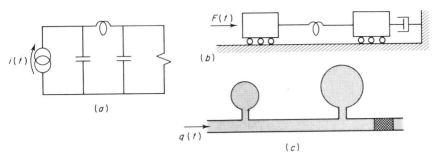

Fig. 6.32. Complete analogues.

examples of systems which are structural analogues, while the systems in Fig. 6.32 are complete analogues.

The complementary graph to an analogue is the dual graph. A pair of graphs drawn from systems with the same energy handling medium are structural duals if the compatibility (continuity) constraints in one graph are the continuity (compatibility) constraints in the other. This implies that the dual graph must have as many cutset (loopset) constraints as the original graph has loopset (cutset) constraints. For planar graphs a straightforward way of constructing the dual of a graph is to associate a dual node with every mesh, including the external mesh, and insert the appropriate number of edges. Figure 6.33 illustrates this procedure. This construction is not possible with non-planar graphs. Structural duals which also have dual constitutive relations on the corresponding edges are complete duals.

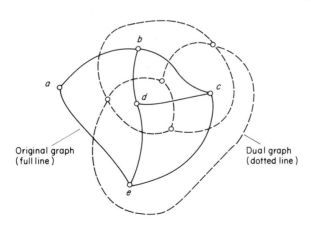

Fig. 6.33. The dual of a graph.

It is an outcome of the arbitrary assignment of effort and flow variables that the distinction between analogues and duals in dissimilar energy handling media is dubious, since a reversal of the effort/flow assignment results in a dual graph. Nevertheless, if this point is borne in mind, the idea of analogues and duals is a useful conceptual tool in assessing and comparing different physical systems. A problem which arises when constructing analogues of electrical circuits is that all other energy handling media dealt with here have one end of every flow store grounded to a common reference. This creates problems with analogues of electrical systems, but it is readily overcome by introducing ideal transformers.

An additional point concerns the modelling of non-planar mechanical systems. If analogy A.1 is adhered to, we can always construct a system graph of a non-planar mechanical system. However, if the complementary analogy (A.2) is used, we are essentially trying to construct a dual graph which does not exist.

8. NOTES AND REFERENCES

[1]   A good basic text on network methods is:
Shearer, J. L., Murphy, A. J. and Richardson, H. H. (1967). "Introduction to system dynamics". Addison-Wesley, Reading, Mass.
[2]   State space models are treated briefly in this chapter, since a fuller treatment is given by bond graph methods. Comprehensive treatments of state space network methods are available in:
Koenig, H. E., Tokad, Y. and Kesavan, H. K. (1967). "Analysis of discrete physical systems, McGraw-Hill, New York.
MacFarlane, A. G. J. (1970). "Dynamical system models". Harrap, London.
[3]   The use of analogue systems (particularly electrical circuits) to investigate physical phenomena has a long history. An excellent treatment of this topic is given in:
Olsen, H. F. (1958). "Dynamical analogies". Van Nostrand, New Jersey.

9. PROBLEMS

9.1.   Draw the system graphs for the problems used in problems 9.1 and 9.2 of chapter 5. Hence obtain (a) dual systems and (b) analogue fluid systems.

9.2.   Obtain analogue mechanical systems for the systems given in problems 9.4, 9.5, and 9.6 of chapter 5.

9.3. Draw the system graph for the system shown in Fig. 6.34; hence determine a linear external model of the system. Compare your results with Case Study 1 (see p. 239).

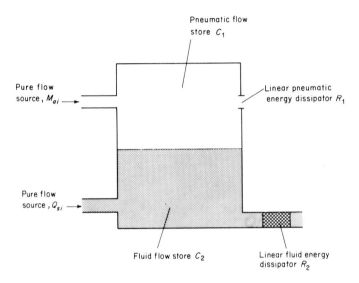

Pneumatic flow store C_1

Pure flow source, M_{ai}

Linear pneumatic energy dissipator R_1

Pure flow source, Q_{si}

Fluid flow store C_2

Linear fluid energy dissipator R_2

Fig. 6.34.

9.4. Determine the transfer function which relates the node voltages v_1, v_2 to the inputs v_a and i_b in the circuit shown in Fig. 6.35. Sketch an analogous rotational mechanical system.

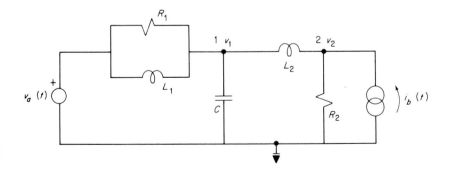

R_1

1 v_1 2 v_2

L_2

L_1

v_a (t)

C

R_2

i_b (t)

Fig. 6.35.

9.5. Figure 6.36 shows a steam distribution system in which two steam generating boilers deliver steam to a set of three steam storage reservoirs. Valves are included to allow steam to pass from one reservoir to another, and steam is withdrawn from the system by two loads. Assume, (1) the boilers can be modelled as controlled sources of steam flow rate, (2) the valves and loads have linear dissipative characteristics.

Neglecting thermal effects, use a network approach to determine the transfer function matrix relating the inputs (boiler steam flow rates $q_1(t)$, $q_2(t)$) and the outputs (load steam pressures $p_1(t)$, $p_2(t)$). Sketch an analogous hydraulic system.

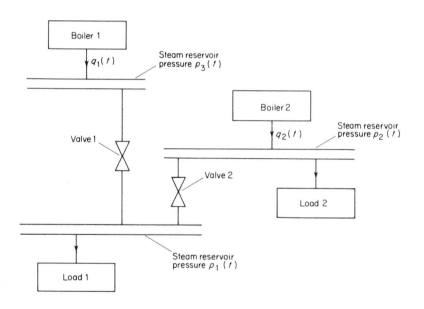

Fig. 6.36.

9.6. A particular process in the iron making industry involves the hardening of spherical balls of iron ore by heating them in an oven such that the internal temperature distribution of the balls follows a prescribed profile.

Figure 6.37 shows such a ball which is subject to a uniform temperature source $T(t)$. Draw a linear network graph model of the ball which will enable the approximate temperature profile along a radius AB to be determined by considering the regions P, Q and M to each have distinct temperatures T_1, T_2 and T_3 and thermal capacities C_1, C_2 and C_3 respectively.

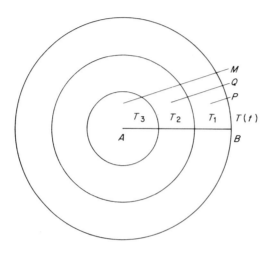

Fig. 6.37.

Sketch an analogous electrical network. Hence or otherwise write the nodal network analysis equations for the system. Assume that heat transfer takes place by conduction and that Fourier's law may be used to express the temperature drop due to conduction.

Variational Methods 7

INTRODUCTION

The strength of network analysis stems from the explicit interconnective information which is exposed in the system graph. This allows the interconnective constraints to be directly written in algebraic form, whence they are combined with dynamic and constitutive relations to form the dynamical description of the system. However, the interconnective constraints on system components are frequently rather complicated. Consequently the formulation of a full interconnective description is tedious and prone to error. In such cases the variational techniques of Hamilton and Lagrange are useful, since they avoid the explicit formulation of both sets of interconnective constraints. Only one set need be directly known, the complementary set is implicit in the variational solution procedure.

Variational methods and the associated extremum principles can be shown to be fundamental scientific techniques with widespread physical significance. However, this treatment will be restricted to variational methods of analysis for lumped physical systems which can be characterized by the energy variables effort and flow. In particular, systems which involve complex coupling of different energy handling media will be seen to be particularly susceptible to the variational approach.

1. THE BASIC IDEAS OF VARIATIONAL ANALYSIS OF PHYSICAL SYSTEMS

1.1. Admissible variations in effort and flow

The conventional starting point in variational analysis is the study of infinitesimal alterations in certain key system effort or flow accumulation variables, such that the appropriate compatibility or continuity constraint is

144

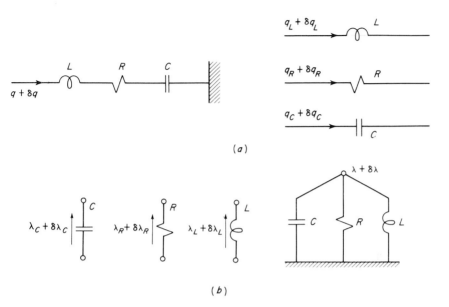

Fig. 7.1. Admissible variations in electrical systems. (*a*) An admissible variation δq in electrical charge q. (*b*) An admissible variation $\delta \lambda$ in flux linkages λ.

not transgressed. Such infinitesimal alterations are called "admissible variations".

The reason for considering admissible variations in the integrated effort and flow variables and not the effort or flow variables themselves will emerge later; for the moment it is sufficient to note that it is the variations in system *state* variables which attract our attention.

To establish the idea of an admissible variation, some examples from electrical, mechanical and fluid systems are discussed below. First consider Fig. 7.1(*a*) which shows a series combination of electrical circuit elements. Let the quantity of charge q flowing through the elements be subject to a small variation which is denoted δq. For this variation to be admissible, the principle of continuity of charge must still apply. For the circuit of Fig. 7.1(*a*) this means that the variations in the element charges must be equal to the variation δq. That is to say

$$\delta q = \delta q_R = \delta q_L = \delta q_C. \tag{1}$$

Notice that the transgression or otherwise of the voltage compatibility constraint in the circuit of Fig. 7.1(*a*) has no bearing upon the admissibility of the variation δq.

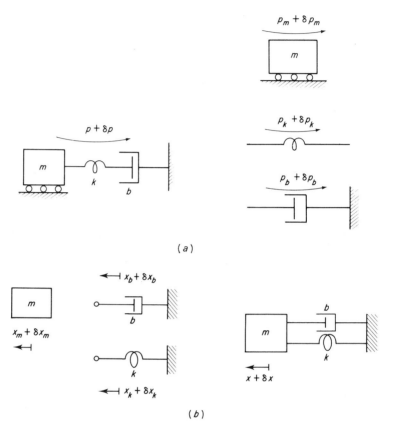

Fig. 7.2. Admissible variations in mechanical systems. (a) An admissible variation δp in momentum p. (b) An admissible variation δx in displacement x.

The complementary type of variation for electric circuits is shown in Fig. 7.1(b). Let the flux linkages λ be *formally defined* as the time integral of the voltage across the parallel circuit elements. Let the flux linkages λ be subject to a small variation which is denoted $\delta\lambda$. For this variation to be admissible, the principle of compatibility of the flux linkages must apply, which in this case means that the variations in the element flux linkages must be equal to the variation $\delta\lambda$. That is to say:

$$\delta\lambda = \delta\lambda_R = \delta\lambda_L = \delta\lambda_C. \tag{2}$$

Notice that the transgression or otherwise of the current continuity constraint in the circuit of Fig. 7.1(b) has no bearing upon the admissibility of the variation $\delta\lambda$.

The notion of an admissible variation is illustrated again in Fig. 7.2, this time in terms of simple mechanical translational systems. For the system of Fig. 7.2(a) the momentum p, *defined* here as the time integral of force, fixes the force through the combination of mass, spring, damper. An admissible variation δp in the momentum p is one which maintains the variation in the individual element momenta equal to δp. That is to say

$$\delta p = \delta p_m = \delta p_k = \delta p_b. \tag{3}$$

Figure 7.2(b) depicts the complementary situation, the position coordinate x determines the spatial compatibility constraint within the system. An admissible variation δx in the displacement x is one which maintains the variations in the individual element displacements equal to δx. That is to say

$$\delta x = \delta x_m = \delta x_k = \delta x_b. \tag{4}$$

A final demonstration of admissible variations is provided in terms of fluid systems (Fig. 7.3). The volumetric flow V through the fluid system of Fig. 7.3(a)

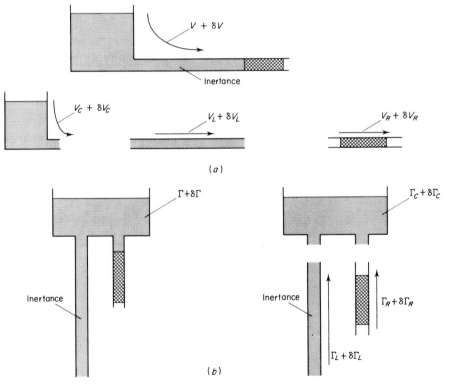

Fig. 7.3. Admissible variations in fluid systems. (a) An admissible variation δV in fluid volume V. (b) An admissible variation $\delta \Gamma$ in fluid momentum Γ.

fixes the flow through all the elements (open tank reservoir inertance and dissipator). An admissible variation δV in V is one which does not break the continuity constraint on flow variables. That is, an admissible variation δV is such that the following holds:

$$\delta V = \delta V_C = \delta V_L = \delta V_R \tag{5}$$

Figure 7.3(b) illustrates the complementary situation for fluid variations. The fluid pressure momentum Γ, here *defined* as the time integral of pressure, is sufficient to determine the pressure compatibility constraint in the system. An admissible variation $\delta \Gamma$ in the momentum Γ is thus one which ensures that variations in the element pressure momenta are equal to $\delta \Gamma$. That is to say

$$\delta \Gamma = \delta \Gamma_C = \delta \Gamma_L = \delta \Gamma_R. \tag{6}$$

To summarize, an admissible variation in an integrated effort and flow variable is one which does not transgress the appropriate interconnective constraint for the variable.

It is important to note that an infinitesimal variation δx is quite distinct from a differential dx. The latter implies a small change in the dependent variable as a result of a small change in the independent variable. A variation, on the other hand, is a deliberately introduced alteration in the variable x, and if x is dependent upon time as is normally the case in system modelling, the variation $x(t) + \delta x(t)$ actually defines a new function of time.

1.2. Generalized effort and flow accumulation coordinates

In order to investigate the consequence of infinitesimal variations in all the system states, it is essential to define a complete and independent set of effort accumulation or flow accumulation variables. This procedure is completely analogous to the selection of a complete independent set of compatibility or continuity constraints in network methods, with the important exception that in variational methods it is necessary to define a complete independent set of variables for infinitesimal variations *and* for large-scale changes of the system. Before discussing this point further, the meaning of completeness and independence must be clarified.

A set of variational variables is said to be *complete* if the values of the variational variables corresponding to an admissible variation in the state of a system is sufficient to determine the variations of all parts of the system. A set of variational variables is said to be *independent* if, when all but one of the variational variables are fixed, it is possible to vary the remaining variable in an admissible manner. The number of complete and independent variational variables in a system is termed the number of degrees of freedom of the system.

If the variables which characterize large-scale changes in the state of a system are termed "coordinates", then the notions of a complete independent

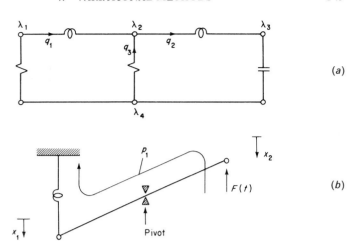

Fig. 7.4. (*a*) Generalized flux linkage and charge coordinates, (*b*) Generalized momentum and displacement coordinates.

set of system coordinates can be explained. A set of system coordinates is said to be *complete* if the values of the coordinates are, through the interconnective constraints, sufficient to fix the state of the entire system. A set of system coordinates is said to be *independent* if, when all except one coordinate are fixed, it is still possible to vary that coordinate over a continuous range of admissible values. Furthermore, since *any* complete, independent set of variables is sufficient to characterize the system state, such variables are called "generalized coordinates".

Some examples will serve to illustrate the ideas of completeness and independence of generalized coordinates. The electrical circuit of Fig. 7.4(*a*) has three charge coordinates defined on it. Any two of these charges form a complete set, since fixing two charges (say q_1, q_2) is sufficient to fix all the charges in the system. In addition, any two charges are independent since if one charge is fixed, the remaining charge can be continuously varied in an admissible manner. A complete independent set of variational charge variables for the electrical circuit of Fig. 7.4(*a*) would be any pair selected from the triple $(\delta q_1, \delta q_2, \delta q_3)$. The system has two degrees of freedom in charge. The electrical circuit also has four flux linkage coordinates defined as $(\lambda_1, \lambda_2, \lambda_3, \lambda_4)$, any three of these variables forms a complete, independent set of flux linkage coordinates. A complete independent set of variational variables is formed by picking any three of the variations $(\delta\lambda_1, \delta\lambda_2, \delta\lambda_3, \delta\lambda_4)$. The system has three degrees of freedom in flux linkages.

For the mechanical system of Fig. 7.4(*b*), the displacement coordinates (x_1, x_2) are a complete, but dependent, set of system coordinates. The transforming action of the level constrains the two displacements, thus either x_1 or x_2 forms a complete, independent coordinate set. A complete, independent set of variational displacement variables is formed by selecting either of the variations δx_1, δx_2; the system has one degree of freedom in displacement. The mechanical system has one momentum coordinate p_1, which constrains the momenta at either end of the lever. In the absence of an external force, the momentum p_1 would be a complete, independent set of momentum coordinates. The system would have one degree of freedon in momentum. However, the external force $F(t)$ places a constraint upon the momentum, thus the momentum state is completely fixed. There is no admissible variation in p_1, and the system has no degree of freedom in momentum.

For a wide variety of systems the number of complete independent coordinates is equal to the number of complete independent variational variables, and in such cases it is normal to define variational variables corresponding to the system coordinates. It frequently occurs, however, that the generalized coordinates are constrained such that this choice is not possible. For a system to be directly handled by variational methods the constraints must be holonomic. A holonomic constraint upon a complete independent set of system coordinates $(q_1, q_2, \ldots, q_r)$ is one which can be written

$$g(q_1, q_2, \ldots, q_r) = \text{const.}, \tag{7}$$

since in this form the variations of the system coordinates can be written

$$\delta q_1 \varphi_1 + \delta q_2 \varphi_2 + \ldots + \delta q_r \varphi_r = 0, \tag{8}$$

where

$$\varphi_i = \partial g / \partial q_i. \tag{9}$$

If the variations in equation (8) are replaced by differentials, then equation (8) is the complete differential of $g(q_1, \ldots, q_r)$, and as such is integrable (holonomic) provided the φ_i have the form of equation (9). Otherwise the constraint is non-integrable (non-holonomic). The simplest example of a non-holonomic constraint appears in the motion of a sledge moving on firm snow (Fig. 7.5). The action of the runners on the snow prevents lateral motion of the sledge, thus for infinitesimal motions it is constrained such that variations in the x and y coordinates are related

$$\delta y = \delta x \tan \theta. \tag{10}$$

The system has two degrees of freedom in displacement. However, for large-scale motions the system has three coordinates, since all three coordinates, x, y, θ are required to specify the system state. The constraint on infinitesimal motions is non-holonomic since the constraint equation (10) does not satisfy conditions implied by equations (8) and (9).

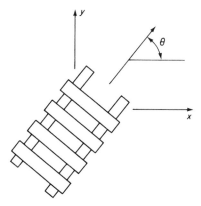

Fig. 7.5. A sledge as an example of a non-holonomic constraint. The coordinates y, x, θ specify the system configuration, but for infinitesimal motions they are constrained by $\tan \theta = \delta y / \delta x$.

The systems considered here are those involving only holonomic constraints introduced by external agencies (such as the force $F(t)$ in Fig. 7.4(b)), and simple multi-ports (such as the mechanical lever in Fig. 7.4(b)).

2. THE CONSTRUCTION OF A VARIATIONAL INDICATOR

The purpose of variational methods is to construct a scalar function termed a "variational indicator" from a study of admissible variations in the system configuration. If the system configuration is "natural", that is to say all interconnective constraints are satisfied, then the variational indicator vanishes.

Two distinct types of variational indicators can be formulated, these are termed differential indicators and integral indicators. The former are essentially static equilibrium principles, and include the principle of virtual work. In addition, it is interesting to note that a form of D'Alembert's principle is cast as a differential variational principle. Although differential variational methods are historically interesting and of wide practical use, particularly in determining the constitutive properties of power conserving multiports, they will not be pursued here, since they relate to static equilibrium behaviour and give no direct insight into dynamic phenomena.

The variational analysis of dynamic behaviour is made possible by integral variational methods, in which natural system configurations over a continuous period of time are studied. Because either admissible variations in effort accumulation *or* flow accumulation can be considered, there are two complementary procedures for developing variational indicators. The two methods lead to dual variational analysis tools in the same sense that loop and node analysis can be considered dual network analysis techniques.

In what follows the dual variational methods will be referred to as nodal and loop variational indicators respectively. Also, because variational methods employ effort and flow accumulation variables it will be convenient to change the symbols used. Specifically, let

$$q \equiv \text{effort accumulation} = \int_0^t e(t)\,\mathrm{d}t,$$

$$\tag{11}$$

$$p \equiv \text{flow accumulation} = \int_0^t f(t)\,\mathrm{d}t,$$

so that

$$e = \dot{q} = \mathrm{d}q/\mathrm{d}t, \qquad f = \dot{p} = \mathrm{d}p/\mathrm{d}t. \tag{12}$$

3. NODAL VARIATIONAL ANALYSIS

In this section the nodal variational approach is introduced by considering the simple case of a system with one generalized coordinate of effort accumulation to which is attached a flow source, an effort store, a flow store and a dissipator (Fig. 7.6). Such a system would correspond to a network with one node or the electrical, mechanical and fluid systems shown in Figs. 7.1(b), 7.2(b), and 7.3(b) respectively.

The system in Fig. 7.6 has generalized coordinate q. The coordinate is not constrained externally hence δq is a generalized variational coordinate. If q were constrained, then $\delta q = 0$ and the problem can be solved by considering each component and the externally controlled effort separately.

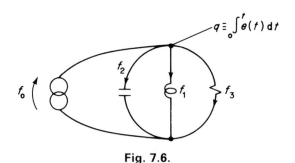

Fig. 7.6.

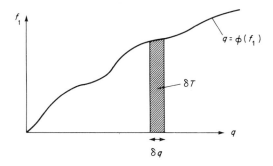

Fig. 7.7. Effort store constitutive relation.

As a first step in constructing a nodal variational indicator, an admissible variation δq is made. Consider the work increment δI which accompanies this variation:

$$\delta I = [f_0 - f_1 - f_2 - f_3]\delta q, \tag{13}$$

where the flows f_0, f_1, f_2, f_3, are defined in Fig. 7.6. By assumption, the variation δq does not infringe the effort compatibility constraints, and if the continuity constraints on the flow variables are satisfied:

$$\delta I = 0. \tag{14}$$

That is to say, if the system configuration is "natural", the work increment δI associated with the admissible variation δq is zero. The term "natural" means in this connection that the continuity of flow constraint is obeyed. Equation (13) is now put in a form which shows the work increment associated with each component. Specifically,

$$\delta I = [\delta q f_0 - \delta q f_1 - \delta q f_2 - \delta q f_3] \tag{15}$$

$= +$ work increment for the source

$-$ work increment for the effort store

$-$ work increment for the flow store

$-$ work increment for the dissipator.

However, it is clear from the constitutive relation (Fig. 7.7) for the effort store that

$$-\delta q f_1 = -\delta T, \tag{16}$$

where δT is the variation in the stored energy in the effort store. The work increment for the flow store can be written as

$$-f_2 \delta q = p_2 \delta \dot{q} - \frac{d}{dt}(p_2 \delta q). \tag{17}$$

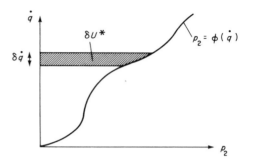

Fig. 7.8. Flow store constitutive relation.

From the constitutive relation for the flow store (Fig. 7.8) the first term on the right-hand side is the variation in co-energy stored in the flow store, δU^*. Thus

$$-f_2\delta q = \delta U^* - \frac{\mathrm{d}}{\mathrm{d}t}(p_2\delta q). \tag{18}$$

From the constitutive relation for the dissipator (Fig. 7.9) the work increment for the dissipator is

$$-f_3\delta q = -\frac{\partial J}{\partial \dot{q}}\,\delta q. \tag{19}$$

The various energy, co-energy, co-content and flow source terms can now be assembled and inserted in equation (1) as follows:

$$\delta I = \delta U^* - \delta T - \left[\frac{\partial J}{\partial \dot{q}} - f_0\right]\delta q - \frac{\mathrm{d}}{\mathrm{d}t}[p_2\delta q]. \tag{20}$$

Equation (20) is in effect a static variational indicator which vanishes for "natural" system configurations. However, the aim is to determine the

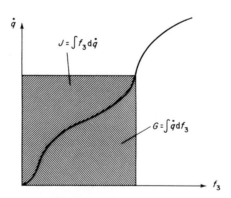

Fig. 7.9. Dissipator constitutive relation.

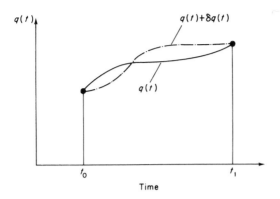

Fig. 7.10. Admissible effort accumulation trajectory.

dynamic behaviour of a system and to this end we consider arbitary admissible variations in the effort accumulation coordinate, as the system changes from one known configuration at time t_0 to another known configuration at time t_1. Figure 7.10 depicts a hypothetical trajectory for the effort accumulation $q(t)$, together with a varied trajectory $q(t) + \delta q(t)$. Note that since the configurations at the starting and end points are known the only admissible variations at these points are zero.

An integral (or dynamic) nodal variational indicator can now be constructed using the following reasoning. If the system motion between two known configuration is natural, the work increment δI must vanish at all points along the trajectory t_0 to t_1. It follows that a dynamic variational indicator which vanishes for a natural system motion is

$$\delta V = \int_{t_0}^{t_1} \delta I \, \mathrm{d}t, \tag{21}$$

$$\delta V = \int_{t_0}^{t_1} \left[\delta U^* - \delta T - \left(\frac{\partial J}{\partial \dot{q}} - f_0 \right) \delta q - \frac{\mathrm{d}}{\mathrm{d}t} (p_2 \delta q) \right] \mathrm{d}t,$$

$$V = \int_{t_0}^{t_1} \left[\delta U^* - \delta T - \left(\frac{\partial J}{\partial \dot{q}} - f_0 \right) \delta q \right] \mathrm{d}t, \tag{22}$$

where the terms in $\delta q(t_1)$ and $\delta q(t_0)$ vanish because the only admissible variation at these boundary points is zero.

Equation (22) is the nodal variational indicator which must vanish for any dynamical transition which does not break continuity of flow at the generalized coordinate. As it stands the indicator is of limited use; however, it can be shown using the calculus of variations that if the variation of V is zero for a natural dynamical transition between known configurations of effort accumulation, then the system must satisfy the extended Lagranges' equations:

$$\frac{\mathrm{d}}{\mathrm{d}t}\left[\frac{\partial L}{\partial \dot{q}}\right] - \frac{\partial L}{\partial q} + \frac{\partial J}{\partial \dot{q}} = f_0, \tag{23}$$

where $L(q, \dot{q})$ is the system Lagrangian and is defined as

$$L(q, \dot{q}) = U^*(\dot{q}) - T(q). \tag{24}$$

The preceeding discussion introduced the nodal variational indication in terms of a system with a single effort accumulation coordinate. By applying the foregoing procedure to a system with m generalized effort accumulation coordinates and l generalized variational coordinates, it can be shown that the following indicator vanishes for a natural movement between known configurations of effort at time t_0 and t_1:

$$\delta V = \int_{t_0}^{t_1} \left[\delta U^* - \delta T - \sum_{j=1}^{l} \left(\frac{\partial J}{\partial \dot{q}_j} - F_j \right) \delta q_j \right] \mathrm{d}t = 0, \tag{25}$$

where the generalized coordinates are $(q_1, q_2, \ldots, q_m)$ and the generalized variational coordinates are $(\delta q_1, \delta q_2, \ldots, \delta q_l)$. In addition:

$U^* =$ the total co-energy in the system flow stores expressed as a function of the generalized effort coordinates.

$T =$ the total energy in the system effort stores expressed as a function of the generalized effort accumulation coordinates.

$J =$ the total co-content in the system dissipators expressed as a function of the generalized effort co-ordinates.

$F_j =$ the effective flow applied to the jth generalized coordinate.

Variational solutions to dynamical modelling problems have their roots in the work of Hamilton and Lagrange. In fact equation (25) is an extended form of *Hamilton's Principle* which states that

"For natural motion between two fixed configurations of effort accumulation at times t_0 and t_1, the indicator δV must vanish".

Again by the calculus of variations, for Hamilton's Principle to be satisfied the system must obey the extended set of Lagrange's equations:

$$\frac{\mathrm{d}}{\mathrm{d}t}\left[\frac{\partial L}{\partial \dot{q}_j}\right] - \frac{\partial L}{\partial q_j} + \frac{\partial J}{\partial \dot{q}_j} = F_j, \qquad j = 1, 2, \ldots, l, \tag{26}$$

where the Lagrangian is now defined as

$$L(q_1, \ldots, \ldots, q_m, \dot{q}_1, \ldots, \dot{q}_m) = U^*(\dot{q}_1, \ldots, \dot{q}_m) - T(q_1, \ldots, q_m). \quad (27)$$

The nodal variational approach leads to the extended set of Lagrange's equations which are solved to obtain a mathematical model of the system as a set of non-linear coupled second-order differential equations in terms of the generalized effort accumulation coordinates. Note that in formulating these equations the analyst must be able to write down the effort compatibility constraints for the system. The continuity of flow constraints are not explicitly required. They are automatically obeyed by systems which have Lagrange's equations as their solution. In fact it is the simultaneous adherence to the continuity constraint at all times across the system which makes the indicator δV vanish.

4. LOOP VARIATIONAL ANALYSIS

The complementary form of variational method depends upon sets of generalized flow accumulation coordinates, which intuitively can be as-sociated with closed flow loops in the system. Consider the simple case of a system with one generalized coordinate of flow accumulation which contains an effort source, an effort store, a flow store and a dissipator (Fig. 7.11). Such a system would correspond to a network with one loop, or the electrical, mechanical and fluid system shown in Figs. 7.1(a), 7.2(a), and 7.3(a) respectively.

The system in Fig. 7.11 has generalized coordinate p. The coordinate is not constrained externally, hence δp is a generalized variational coordinate. If p were constrained then $\delta p = 0$ and the problem can be solved by considering each component and the externally controlled flow separately.

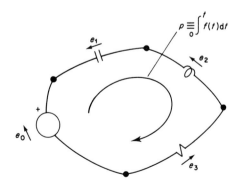

Fig. 7.11.

As a first step in constructing a loop variational indicator, an admissible variation δp is made. Consider the work increment δK which accompanies this variation:

$$\delta K = [e_0 - e_- - e_2 - e_3]\delta p, \tag{28}$$

where the efforts e_0, e_1, e_2, e_3, are defined in Fig. 7.11.

By assumption, the variation δp does not infringe the flow continuity constraints, and if the compatibility constraints on the effort variables are satisfied:

$$\delta K = 0. \tag{29}$$

That is to say, if the system configuration is "natural", the work δK associated with the admissible variation δp is zero. The term "natural" means in this connection that the compatibility of effort constraint is obeyed. Equation (28) is now put in a form which shows the work increment associated with each component. Specifically,

$$\delta K = [\delta pe_0 - \delta pe_1 - \delta pe_2 - \delta pe_3] \tag{30}$$

$= +$ work increment for the store

$\quad -$ work increment for the flow store

$\quad -$ work increment for the effort store

$\quad -$ work increment for the dissipator.

By following an analogous procedure to that used in the nodal variational approach, the constitutive relations of the elements in the loop can be used to re-express the loop work increment as

$$\delta K = \delta T^* - \delta U - \left[\frac{\partial G}{\partial \dot{p}} - e_0\right] - \frac{d}{dt}\,[q\delta p], \tag{31}$$

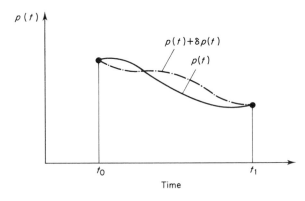

Fig. 7.12. Admissible flow accumulation trajectory.

where δT^* is the variation in the co-energy stored in the loop effort store, δU is the variation in the energy stored in the loop flow store, and G is the content of the dissipator in the loop.

Equation (31) is a static loop variational indicator which vanishes for "natural" system configurations. The equivalent dynamical loop variational indicator is obtained by considering arbitrary admissible variations in the flow accumulation coordinate as the system changes from one known configuration at time t_0 to another known configuration at time t_1. Figure 7.12 depicts a hypothetical trajectory for the flow accumulation $p(t)$, together with a varied trajectory $p(t) + \delta p(t)$. The configurations at the starting and end points are known and are hence zero. An integral (or dynamic) loop variational indicator can be constructed by demanding that the integral δK over the time t_0 to t_1 vanish for a natural motion, where

$$\delta Y = \int_{t_0}^{t_1} \delta K \, dt, \tag{32}$$

we have

$$\delta Y = \int_{t_0}^{t_1} \left(\delta T^* - \delta U - \left(\frac{\partial G}{\partial \dot{p}} - e_0 \right) \delta p \right) dt, \tag{33}$$

where the terms in $\delta p(t_0)$ and $\delta p(t_1)$ vanish because of the fixed start and end configurations. The loop variational indicator δY must be zero for any dynamical transition which does not break compatibility of effort around the generalized coordinate. It follows from variational calculus that if the variation of Y is zero for a natural dynamical transition between known configurations of flow accumulation, then the system must obey the complementary form of Lagrange's equation:

$$\frac{d}{dt} \left[\frac{\partial L^*}{\partial \dot{p}} \right] - \frac{\partial L^*}{\partial p} + \frac{\partial G}{\partial \dot{p}} = e_0, \tag{34}$$

where $L(p, \dot{p})$ is the system co-Lagrangian, defined as

$$L(p, \dot{p}) = T^*(\dot{p}) - U(p). \tag{35}$$

The foregoing single loop example may be generalized to a system with r generalized flow accumulation coordinates and g generalized variational flow accumulation coordinates. It can be shown that the following indicator vanishes for a natural motion between known configurations of flow at time t_0 and t_1:

$$\delta Y = \int_{t_0}^{t_1} \left[\delta T^* - \delta U - \sum_{j=1}^{g} \left(\frac{\partial G}{\partial \dot{p}_j} - E_j \right) \delta p_j \right] dt, \tag{36}$$

where the generalized coordinates are $(p_1, \ldots, p_r)$ and the generalized variational coordinates are $(\delta p_1, \ldots, \delta p_g)$. In addition:

T^* = the total co-energy in the system effort stores expressed as a function of the generalized flow coordinates.

U = the total energy in the system flow stores expressed as a function of the generalized flow accumulation coordinates.

G = the total content in the system dissipators expressed as a function of the generalized effort coordinates.

E_j = the effective external effort occurring in the jth generalized flow coordinate.

The requirement that δY vanish constitutes a *complementary* form of the extended *Hamilton's Principle*:

"For natural motion between two fixed configurations of flow accumulation at time t_0 and t_1, the indicator δY must vanish".

By variational calculus for the complementary form of Hamilton's Principle to be satisfied the system must obey the extended set of co-Lagrangian equations:

$$\frac{\mathrm{d}}{\mathrm{d}t}\left(\frac{\partial L^*}{\partial \dot{p}_j}\right) - \frac{\partial L^*}{\partial p_j} + \frac{\partial G}{\partial \dot{p}_j} = E_j, \qquad j = 1, \ldots, g, \tag{37}$$

where the co-Lagrangian is now defined as

$$L^*(p_1, \ldots, p_r, \dot{p}_1, \ldots, \dot{p}_r) = T^*(\dot{p}_1, \ldots, \dot{p}_r) + U(p_1, \ldots, p_r), \tag{38}$$

The loop variational approach leads to the extended set of co-Lagrangian equations which are solved to obtain a mathematical model of the system as a set of non-linear coupled second-order differential equations in terms of the generalized flow accumulation coordinates. In formulating these equations the analyst must be able to write down the flow continuity constraints for the system. The compatibility of effort constraints are not explicitly required. They are automatically obeyed by systems which have the complementary set of Lagrange's equations as their solution. It is the simultaneous adherence to the compatibility constraint at all times across the system which makes the indicator δY vanish.

5. VARIATIONAL ANALYSIS OF MECHANICAL SYSTEMS

Variational methods are historically derived from the studies of Lagrange, Hamilton and Euler concerning the dynamic behaviour of mechanical systems. It is not surprising therefore that variational methods are highly developed tools for the analysis of mechanical systems, in particular they are extremely useful in the study of systems involving coupled translation and rotation. From a practical viewpoint, variational methods avoid the explicit formulation of either velocity compatibility constraints or force continuity constraints. As a rule it is the latter which are most tedious to formulate, and accordingly it is the variational method which avoids this tedium that is most frequently used. If the analogy A.1 is applied the following effort/flow assignment results:

$$\text{flow} \rightarrow \text{force}$$
$$\text{flow accumulation} \rightarrow \text{momentum}$$
$$\text{effort} \rightarrow \text{velocity}$$
$$\text{effort accumulation} \rightarrow \text{displacement.}$$

Thus it is the method which we have called nodal variational analysis which avoids explicit formulation of force constraints, and is therefore the most fruitful technique for mechanical system analysis.

5.1. Generalized displacement coordinates

For a mechanical system obeying only holonomic constraints, nodal variational analysis requires that a complete independent set of generalized displacement coordinates be selected such that the system configuration is unambiguously, and without redundancy, defined by the m generalized coordinates $(q_1, q_2, \ldots, q_m)$. If f generalized coordinates are constrained holonomically by external velocity or displacement sources, then the only admissible variation of these coordinates is zero. The variational coordinate set $(\delta q_1, \delta q_2, \ldots, \delta q_l)$ is therefore obtained by considering variations in the unconstrained generalized coordinates. The system has $l = m - f$ degrees of freedom in displacement. For example, the mechanical system depicted in Fig. 7.13 has generalized coordinates (q_1, q_2, q_3); however, the third coordinate is holonomically constrained by the velocity source $v(t)$ such that

$$v(t) = \dot{q}_3 \quad \text{and} \quad \delta q_3 = 0.$$

The system has the variational coordinate set $(\delta q_1, \delta q_2)$ and has two degrees of freedom in displacement.

The vital feature of a set of generalized coordinates is that *any* displacement

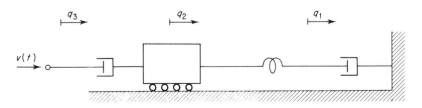

Fig. 7.13. A mechanical system with constrained coordinates.

in the system can be expressed as a function of the generalized displacements. Denoting a displacement within the system by x, then

$$x = x(q_1, q_2, \ldots, q_m).$$

The velocity $\dot{x}$ of a point in the system is given by

$$\dot{x} = \frac{dx}{dt} = \sum_{i=1}^{m} \frac{\partial x}{\partial q_i} \dot{q}_i. \tag{39}$$

The variables $\dot{q}_i$, $(i = 1, 2, \ldots, m)$, are termed the generalized velocity coordinates. Equation (39) indicates that the velocity at any point in the system can be expressed as a function of the generalized velocity coordinates

5.2. Generalized forces sources

The nodal variational method requires that the actual external forces applied to the mechanical system be referred to the generalized coordinate set to form a set of generalized forces. In many cases this can be done by resolving applied forces along appropriate directions. In the general case it is achieved using a form of the differential variational principle known as the "principle of virtual work". Suppose that the actual applied forces f_i $(i = 1, 2, \ldots, \Gamma)$ are applied along system coordinates x_i $(i = 1, 2, \ldots, \Gamma)$, then the work increment δW associated with arbitrary admissible variations δx_i $(i = 1, 2, \ldots, \Gamma)$ can be equivalently represented by generalized forces $F_i (i = 1, \ldots, l)$ and geometrically compatible variations in the variational coordinates $(\delta q_1, \delta q_2, \ldots, \delta q_l)$. That is

$$\delta W = \sum_{i=1}^{\Gamma} f_i \delta x_i = \sum_{i=1}^{l} F_i \delta q_i. \tag{40}$$

Since the coordinates x_i can be written as a function of the generalized coordinates, it follows that for a holonomic system the variations δx_i can be expressed as a function of the variational coordinates. That is

$$\delta x_i = \sum_{j=1}^{l} \frac{\partial x_i}{\partial q_j} \delta q_j \tag{41}$$

By substituting equation (41) into (40), the generalized forces can be found as a function of the actual external forces.

5.3. Nodal variational analysis for conservative mechanical systems

For mechanical systems moving without dissipation and externally applied forces, the nodal variational indicator of equation (25) takes the particularly simple form:

$$\delta V = \int_{t_0}^{t_1} \delta L dt = \delta \int_{t_0}^{t_1} L dt, \tag{42}$$

where the system Lagrangian L is defined by

$$L = U^* - T.$$

$U^*(\dot{q}_1, \dot{q}_2, \ldots, \dot{q}_m)$ is the system co-kinetic energy and $T(q_1, q_2, \ldots, q_m)$ is the system potential energy.

In this form equation (42) constitutes the basis for Hamilton's principle for a conservative† mechanical system under holonomic constraints and with l degrees of freedom in displacement. Hamilton's principle is

"An admissible motion of the system between specified configuration at t_0 and t_1 is a natural motion if, and only if, the variational indicator δV [equation (42)] vanishes for arbitrary admissible variations."

For a conservative mechanical system with a Lagrangian L, Lagrange's equations take the particularly simple form:

$$\frac{\mathrm{d}}{\mathrm{d}t}\left(\frac{\partial L}{\partial \dot{q}_j}\right) - \frac{\partial L}{\partial q_j} = 0, \qquad j = 1, \ldots, l. \tag{43}$$

In this form Hamilton's principle is of limited direct use since most systems of interest contain dissipative elements and are subject to external forces as well as external velocity inputs. However, the principle of conservation of energy for conservation mechanical systems can be readily deduced from equation (43), as can a form of D'Alembert's principle.

D'Alembert's Principle

First, note that the system co-kinetic energy U^* can be written as

$$U^*(\dot{q}_1, \dot{q}_2, \ldots, \dot{q}_m) = \sum_{j=1}^{m} U_j^*(\dot{q}_j), \tag{44}$$

in which the terms U_j^* are the co-kinetic energies stored in the generalized mass associated with the jth displacement coordinate. The generalized momentum p_j, which is associated with this fictitious generalized mass, is given by

$$p_j = \partial U_j^*/\partial \dot{q}_j = \partial U^*/\partial \dot{q}_j = \partial L/\partial \dot{q}_j. \tag{45}$$

Now Lagrange's equations can be put in the form:

$$\frac{\mathrm{d}}{\mathrm{d}t}\left(\frac{\partial U^*}{\partial \dot{q}_j}\right) + \frac{\partial T}{\partial q_j} = 0, \qquad \frac{\mathrm{d}}{\mathrm{d}t}(\dot{p}_j) + \frac{\partial T}{\partial q_j} = 0. \tag{46}$$

The second term of the left-hand side of equation (46) can be visualized as the generalized force associated with a generalized spring referred to the jth

---

† In this context conservative means free of dissipation and external force inputs; any velocity source is treated as a *constraint* on the system, not an input.

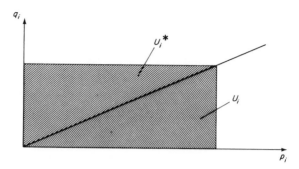

Fig. 7.14. Constitutive relation of the fictitious mass associated with the ith generalized coordinate.

generalized coordinate. The Lagrange equations (equation (46)) can be expressed in words thus:

(inertial force of jth generalized mass)

$-$(force of jth generalized spring)$=0$.

In this way Lagrange's equations can be thought of as an abstraction in terms of generalized coordinates of D'Alembert's principle.

Conservation of Energy

The principle of conservation of energy can be established for conservative mechanical systems without external velocity sources by considering the time derivative of the Lagrangian:

$$\frac{dL}{dt}=\sum_{i=1}^{m}\left(\frac{\partial L}{\partial q_i}\dot{q}_i+\frac{\partial L}{\partial \dot{q}_i}\ddot{q}_i\right). \tag{47}$$

Now the sum of all Lagrange's equations give

$$\sum_{i=1}^{m}\left[\frac{d}{dt}\left(\frac{\partial L}{\partial \dot{q}_i}\right)-\frac{\partial L}{\partial q_i}\right]=0. \tag{48}$$

By the rules for differentiation of a product:

$$\frac{d}{dt}\left(\dot{q}_i\frac{\partial L}{\partial \dot{q}_i}\right)=\ddot{q}_i\frac{\partial L}{\partial \dot{q}_i}+\dot{q}_i\frac{d}{dt}\left(\frac{\partial L}{\partial \dot{q}_i}\right). \tag{49}$$

Therefore, multiplying each term in equation (48) by $\dot{q}_i$ and substituting from equation (49) gives

$$\sum_{i=1}^{m}\left[\frac{d}{dt}\left(\dot{q}_i\frac{\partial L}{\partial \dot{q}_i}\right)\right]=\left(\ddot{q}_i\frac{\partial L}{\partial \dot{q}_i}+\dot{q}_i\frac{\partial L}{\partial q_i}\right).$$

This expression can be substituted into equation (47) to yield:

$$\sum_{i=1}^{m} \frac{d}{dt}\left(\dot{q}_i \frac{\partial L}{\partial \dot{q}_i}\right) - \frac{dL}{dt} = 0.$$

This expression can be integrated, and the term $\partial L / \partial \dot{q}_i$ identified as the generalized momentum p_i associated with the ith coordinate of displacement:

$$\sum_{i=1}^{m} p_i \dot{q}_i - L = \text{const.} \tag{50}$$

Now from the constitutive relation of the fictitious mass associated with the ith generalized coordinate, each term $p_i \dot{q}_i$ is the sum of generalized co-kinetic and kinetic energies for the ith coordinate. The summation over m in equation (50) is therefore the sum of the total system co-kinetic energy U^* and the total system kinetic energy U. Therefore

$$U^* + U - L = U^* + U - (U^* - T) = \text{const.}$$

Hence,

$$U + T = \text{const.} \tag{51}$$

The principle of conservation of energy for conservative systems has therefore been established as a consequence of the variational indicator (equation (42)) vanishing.

Hamilton's Equations

Lagrange's equations of motion can be obtained in two complementary forms. The nodal form discussed here provides a set of second-order equations in terms of generalized displacement coordinates. The less well used loop formulation gives a set of second-order equations in terms of generalized momentum coordinates. It is clear, therefore, that variational procedures such as these yield external descriptions of a mechanical system. An internal description in terms of *both* displacement and momentum coordinates is provided by Hamilton's equations. Consider a dissipation-less mechanical system with no external applied force or velocity constraints. The system Hamiltonian H is defined by the Legendre transformation:

$$H(p_1, \ldots, p_m, q_1, \ldots, q_m) = \sum_{i=1}^{m} p_i \dot{q}_i - L(\dot{q}_1, \ldots, \dot{q}_m, q_1, \ldots, q_m). \tag{52}$$

In this conservative case the Hamiltonian H is identified via equation (51) as the total system energy. From the definition it follows that

$$\partial H / \partial p_i = \dot{q}_i, \qquad i = 1, \ldots, m. \tag{53}$$

Also,

$$\frac{\partial H}{\partial q_i} = \frac{-\partial L}{\partial q_i} = -\dot{p}_i, \qquad i = 1, \ldots, m, \tag{54}$$

where the last equation is a consequence of Lagrange's equations.

The equation pair (equations (53, 54)) are Hamilton's equations for a conservative system. They define a set of $2m$ first-order differential equations which constitute an internal or state description of the system.

5.4. Nodal variational analysis for non-conservative mechanical systems

For mechanical systems containing dissipative elements and moving under the influence of external force and velocity sources, the nodal variational indicator of equation (25) retains its form and is written as

$$\delta V = \int_{t_0}^{t_1} \left[\delta L - \sum_{j=1}^{l} \left(\frac{\partial J}{\partial \dot{q}_j} - F_j \right) \delta q_j \right] \mathrm{d}t, \tag{55a}$$

where L is the system Lagrangian; J is the total co-content of the system dissipators; and the (F_j) are the generalized forces applied to the system.

The extended statement of Hamilton's principle for a non-conservative mechanical system under holonomic constraints and with l degrees of freedom in displacement is:

"An admissible motion of the system between specified configurations at t_0 and t_1 is a natural motion if, and only if, the variational indicator δV [equation (55a)] vanishes for arbitrary admissible variations."

For a non-conservative system, Lagrange's equations of motion take the form:

$$\frac{\mathrm{d}}{\mathrm{d}t} \left(\frac{\partial L}{\partial \dot{q}_j} \right) - \frac{\partial L}{\partial q_j} + \frac{\partial J}{\partial \dot{q}_j} = F_j, \qquad j = 1, \ldots, l. \tag{55b}$$

Some examples are now given which illustrate the use of nodal variational analysis of mechanical systems.

Consider the combined mechanical rotational and translational system of Fig. 7.15. It consists of a linear translational spring of stiffness k which is constrained to move vertically by a guideway. If a simple pendulum is attached to the free end of the spring, and the motion in the guideway is subject to viscous friction with linear coefficient b, determine the equations of motion in terms of suitable displacement coordinates.

The generalized coordinates (q_1, q_2) form a complete, independent set, where q_1 = the displacement of the spring from its rest position, q_2 = the angle made by the pendulum arm with the vertical. The system is not constrained by external velocity sources, but is subject to gravitational force of attraction on the mass m; this can be considered as an external force mg. The generalized forces F_1 and F_2 are obtained by referring the force mg to the generalized coordinates q_1, q_2. The gravitational force resolved in the direction of q_1 is just mg. The gravitational force has a component $-mg \sin q_2$ tangential to the

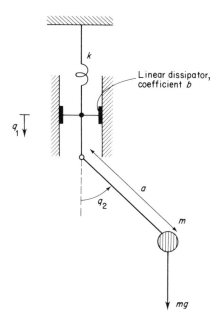

Fig. 7.15. Spring–pendulum system.

direction of rotation, the generalized torque† τ_2 in the direction of the coordinate q_2 is therefore $-mga \sin q_2$. The generalized forces are

$$F_1 = mg, \qquad \tau_2 = -mga \sin q_2.$$

The system co-kinetic energy is given by

$$U^* = \tfrac{1}{2}mv^2 = \tfrac{1}{2}m[\dot{q}_1^2 + (a\dot{q}_2)^2 - 2\dot{q}_1\dot{q}_2 a \sin q_2],$$

where the instantaneous velocity of the mass is obtained by applying the law of cosines to the shaded triangle in Fig. 7.16.

The system potential energy is given by

$$T = \tfrac{1}{2}kq_1^2.$$

The system Lagrangian is thus

$$L = U^* - T$$
$$= \tfrac{1}{2}m(\dot{q}_1^2 + a^2\dot{q}_2^2 - 2\dot{q}_1\dot{q}_2 a \sin q_2) - \tfrac{1}{2}kq_1^2.$$

The system co-content is given by

$$J = \tfrac{1}{2}b\dot{q}_1^2.$$

† Forces referred to generalized coordinates which are *angular* displacements become generalized torque inputs.

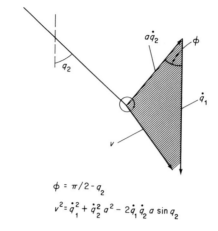

$$\phi = \pi/2 - q_2$$
$$v^2 = \dot{q}_1^2 + \dot{q}_2^2 a^2 - 2\dot{q}_1 \dot{q}_2 a \sin q_2$$

Fig. 7.16. Velocity diagram for the spring–pendulum system.

For the coordinate q_1, Lagrange's equation is

$$\frac{\mathrm{d}}{\mathrm{d}t}\left(\frac{\partial L}{\partial \dot{q}_1}\right) - \frac{\partial L}{\partial q_1} + \frac{\partial J}{\partial \dot{q}_1} = mg,$$

$$m\ddot{q}_1 - ma\ddot{q}_2 \sin q_2 - ma\dot{q}_2^2 \cos q_2 + kq_1 + b\dot{q}_1 = mg. \qquad (56)$$

For the coordinate q_2, Lagrange's equation is

$$\frac{\mathrm{d}}{\mathrm{d}t}\left(\frac{\partial L}{\partial \dot{q}_2}\right) - \frac{\partial L}{\partial q_2} + \frac{\partial J}{\partial \dot{q}_2} = -mga \sin q_2,$$

$$m(a^2\ddot{q}_2 - \dot{q}_1\dot{q}_2 a \cos q_2 - \ddot{q}_1 a \sin q_2) + m\dot{q}_1\dot{q}_2 a \cos q_2 = -mga \sin q_2$$

$$a\ddot{q}_2 - \ddot{q}_1 \sin q_2 + g \sin q_2 = 0. \qquad (57)$$

The non-linear coupled differential equations (56) and (57) constitute the equations of motion for the spring/pendulum system. An alternative way to formulate this problem is to consider the potential energy associated with the mass m, by virtue of gravitational attraction. This approach has the advantage that the system can then be considered to have no external forces, and the labour of determining the generalized forces is removed.

Another example in which a variational approach is worthwhile is the analysis of a mechanical arm, such as is used in industrial robots. Figure 7.17 depicts a simplified arm which is assumed to move in a horizontal plane so that gravity can be neglected. The arm consists of two light rods, the first is pivoted on an inertial reference at point 1 and the rods are joined at a pivot 2. The arm is driven by two motors which are represented by torque sources τ_1 and τ_2. The arm is carrying a load m_2, and the second motor can be assumed to be a point mass m_1 at the second pivot.

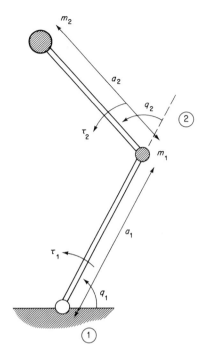

Fig. 7.17. A mechanical arm system.

As a set of generalized coordinates the angles q_1, q_2 shown in the figure may be taken, since they form a complete independent set. The torque sources are already acting on the generalized coordinates so that they are generalized torques. The system moves in a horizontal plane and there are no compliant members, therefore the system potential energy is zero. That is

$$T = 0.$$

The system co-kinetic energy is the sum of the kinetic energies of the masses m_1, m_2, and so is

$$U^* = \tfrac{1}{2} m_1 (v_1)^2 + \tfrac{1}{2} m_2 (v_2)^2,$$

where v_1 and v_2 are the instantaneous velocities of m_1 and m_2 respectively. Applying the cosine rule of triangles to the triangle indicated in Fig. 7.18, yields

$$U^* = \tfrac{1}{2} m_1 (a_1 \dot{q}_1)^2 + \tfrac{1}{2} m_2 [(a_1 \dot{q}_1)^2 + (a_2 \dot{q}_2)^2 + 2 a_1 a_2 \dot{q}_1 \dot{q}_2 \cos q_2].$$

The system Lagrangian is

$$L = U^*.$$

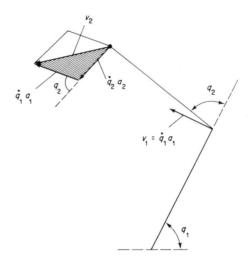

Fig. 7.18. Velocity diagram for the mechanical arm system.

For the coordinate q_1, Lagrange's equation is

$$\frac{d}{dt}\left(\frac{\partial U^*}{\partial \dot{q}_1}\right) - \frac{\partial U^*}{\partial q_1} = \tau_1,$$

$$(m_1 + m_2)a_1^2\ddot{q}_1 + m_2 a_1 a_2(\ddot{q}_2 \cos q_2 - \dot{q}_2 \sin q_2) = \tau_1. \tag{58}$$

For the coordinate q_2, Lagrange's equation is

$$\frac{d}{dt}\left(\frac{\partial U^*}{\partial \dot{q}_2}\right) - \frac{\partial U^*}{\partial q_2} = \tau_2,$$

$$m_2 a_2^2\ddot{q}_2 + m_2 a_1 a_2(\ddot{q}_1 \cos q_2 - 2\dot{q}_2\dot{q}_1 \sin q_2) = \tau_2. \tag{59}$$

Equations (58) and (59) are the equations of motion of the mechanical arm in terms of the displacement coordinates (q_1, q_2).

5.5. Loop variational analysis for mechanical systems

For mechanical systems containing dissipative elements and moving under the influence of external velocity and force sources, the loop variational indicator (equation (36)) can be used to obtain the system equations of motion in terms of generalized *momentum* coordinates. If a mechanical system's force configuration is completely and independently specified by r generalized momentum coordinates $(p_1, p_2, \ldots, p_r)$, and is constrained holonomically by external force sources and multiports such that the variational coordinates

$(\delta p_1, \delta p_2, \ldots \delta p_g)$ completely and independently specify infinitesimal variations in momentum, then the loop variational indicator takes the form:

$$\delta Y = \int_{t_0}^{t_1} \left[\delta L^* - \sum_{j=1}^{g} \left(\frac{\partial G}{\partial \dot{p}_j} - V_j \right) \delta p_j \right] \mathrm{d}t, \tag{60}$$

where L^* is the system co-Lagrangian defined by $L^* = T^* - U$ and $T^* =$ the
system co-potential energy; $U =$ the system kinetic energy. The total content of
the system dissipators is G and the V_j $(j = 1, \ldots, g)$ are a set of generalized
velocity sources representing the actual velocity sources referred to the
generalized momentum coordinates.

The complementary form of Hamilton's principle for mechanical systems is:

"An admissible motion of a mechanical system between specified
momentum configurations at time t_0 to another at time t_1 is a natural
motion if, and only if, the variational indicator δY [equation (60)]
vanishes for arbitrary admissible variations of momenta."

For a loop variational technique, Lagrange's equations take the complementary form:

$$\frac{\mathrm{d}}{\mathrm{d}t} \left(\frac{\partial L^*}{\partial \dot{p}_j} \right) - \frac{\partial L^*}{\partial p_j} + \frac{\partial G}{\partial \dot{p}_j} = V_j, \qquad j = 1, 2, \ldots, g. \tag{61}$$

The loop variational method requires the specification of a generalized
momentum coordinate set, and the explicit formulation of force continuity
constraints in a system. Momentum coordinates lack the immediate graphic
interpretation of displacement coordinates, and in certain systems the
force/momenta constraints are not independent of the system geometric
configuration as required. For these reasons loop variational analysis of
mechanical systems is generally less useful than the nodal approach. An
important exception is the analysis of redundant structures, where the number
of independent geometric constraints is much greater than the number of
momentum constraints.

6. VARIATIONAL ANALYSIS OF ELECTRICAL CIRCUITS

For electrical systems the tools of network analysis are so well developed that
the need rarely arises to seek another analysis method. Nevertheless, instances
may occur in the study of non-linear electrical systems where transform
methods are inapplicable, or where the electrical components form part of a
mixed energy handling system. It is in cases of this type that variational
methods may well prove fruitful. The choice between loop and nodal
variational analysis is, in the case of electrical systems, largely subjective,

although as a rule the method which requires the explicit formulation of the least number of interconnective constraints is used.

6.1. Nodal varational analysis of electrical circuits

Nodal variational analysis of electrical circuits requires that a complete independent set of generalized flux linkage coordinates be selected that specify the configuration of the system. It is not necessary that the coordinates correspond to actual stored flux linkage variables in the circuit inductors since, in general, a flux linkage coordinate can be *defined* as the time integral of the voltage measured across any two points in the circuit. For many circuits the flux linkages defined as the time integral of the node voltages will form a natural complete and independent set of generalized coordinates.

Consider an electrical circuit with generalized flux linkage coordinates $(\lambda_1, \lambda_2, \ldots, \lambda_m)$. If the flux linkage configuration is holonomically constrained by voltage sources and multiports such that the variational variables $(\delta\lambda_1, \delta\lambda_2, \ldots, \delta\lambda_l)$ form a complete independent set, the nodal variational indicator (equation (25)) becomes:

$$\delta V = \int_{t_0}^{t_1} \left[\delta L - \sum_{j=1}^{l} \left(\frac{\partial J}{\partial \dot{\lambda}_j} - I_j \right) \delta\lambda_j \right] dt, \tag{62}$$

where the circuit Lagrangian L is defined by

$$L = U^* - T$$

and $U^* =$ the total co-capacitative energy of the circuit; $T =$ the total inductive energy of the circuit; also $J =$ the total co-content of the circuit resistors; $I_j =$ the generalized current source associated with the jth generalized flux linkage coordinate.

Hamilton's principle for electrical circuits is stated:

"An admissible motion of an electrical circuit between a fixed flux-linkage configuration at t_0 and another fixed configuration at t_1 is a natural motion if, and only if, the variational indicator [equation (62)] vanishes for arbitrary admissible variations in flux linkage."

It is appropriate to recall that an admissible variation in flux linkage $\delta\lambda_j$ is one which does not infringe the voltage compatibility constraint (Kirchhoff's Voltage Law). Similarly, a "natural" motion of the circuit is one for which Kirchhoff's Current Law holds.

Lagrange's equations of motion which follow from Hamilton's principle for electrical circuits are

$$\frac{d}{dt}\left(\frac{\partial L}{\partial \dot{\lambda}_j} \right) - \frac{\partial L}{\partial \lambda_j} + \frac{\partial J}{\partial \dot{\lambda}_j} = I_j, \qquad j = 1, 2, \ldots, l. \tag{63}$$

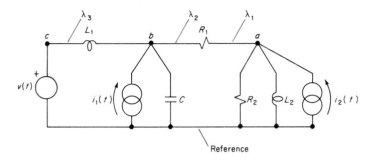

Fig. 7.19.

An example of nodal variational analysis for an electrical circuit will serve to demonstrate the salient features of the technique. The electrical circuit shown in Fig. 7.19 has four nodes. From elementary network analysis any three node voltages are sufficient to specify the voltages in the circuit. Hence, the flux linkages $(\lambda_1, \lambda_1, \lambda_3)$ defined as the time integrals of the voltages at a, b, c respectively, measured with respect to the reference, are a complete independent set of coordinates. However, the flux linkage configuration is constrained by a voltage source $v(t)$ acting on the node c, thus the only admissible variation in λ_3 is zero. That is

$$\lambda_3 = \int_0^t v(t)\mathrm{d}t, \qquad \delta\lambda_3 = 0.$$

The variational coordinates $\delta\lambda_1, \delta\lambda_2$ are therefore a complete independent set. The system co-capacitative energy is

$$U^* = \tfrac{1}{2}C\dot\lambda_2^2.$$

The system inductive energy is

$$T = \frac{1}{2L_1}(\lambda_3 - \lambda_2)^2 + \frac{1}{2L_2}\lambda_1^2.$$

The Lagrangian of the circuit is

$$L = \frac{1}{2}\left(C\dot\lambda_2^2 - \frac{1}{L_1}(\lambda_3 - \lambda_2)^2 - \frac{1}{L_2}\lambda_1^2\right).$$

The co-content of the system is

$$J = \frac{1}{2R_1}(\dot\lambda_2 - \dot\lambda_1)^2 + \frac{1}{2R_2}\dot\lambda_1^2.$$

Lagrange's equation for the λ_1 coordinate is

$$\frac{d}{dt}\left(\frac{\partial L}{\partial \dot\lambda_1}\right) - \frac{\partial L}{\partial \lambda_1} + \frac{\partial J}{\partial \dot\lambda_1} = i_2(t),$$

$$\frac{1}{L_2}\lambda_1 + \left(\frac{1}{R_1} + \frac{1}{R_2}\right)\dot\lambda_1 - \frac{1}{R_1}\dot\lambda_2 = i_2(t). \tag{64}$$

Lagrange's equation for the λ_2 coordinate is

$$\frac{d}{dt}\left(\frac{\partial L}{\partial \dot\lambda_2}\right) - \frac{\partial L}{\partial \lambda_2} + \frac{\partial J}{\partial \dot\lambda_2} = i_1(t),$$

$$C\ddot\lambda_2 + \frac{1}{R_1}\dot\lambda_2 + \frac{1}{L_1}\lambda_2 - \frac{1}{R_1}\dot\lambda_1 - \frac{1}{L_1}\lambda_3 = i_1(t). \tag{65}$$

The λ_3 coordinate is constrained by the voltage source $v(t)$ to be

$$\lambda_3 = v(t). \tag{66}$$

Equations (64), (65), (66) constitute the equations of motion of the electrical circuit.

6.2. Loop variational analysis of electrical circuits

Loop variational analysis of electrical circuits requires that a complete independent set of generalized charge coordinates be selected that specify the configuration of the system. It is not essential that the charge coordinates correspond to actual stored charge variables in the circuit capacitors since in general a charge coordinate can be *defined* as the time integral of any convenient current in the circuit. For a wide class of circuits the charges defined as the time integral of the interior mesh currents will form a natural complete and independent set of generalized coordinates.

Consider an electrical circuit with generalized charge coordinates $(q_1, q_2, \ldots, q_r)$. If the charge configuration is holonomically constrained by current sources and multi-ports such that the variational variables $(\delta q_1, \delta q_2, \ldots, \delta q_g)$ form a complete independent set, the loop variational indicator (equation (36)) becomes:

$$\delta Y = \int_{t_0}^{t_1} \left(\delta L^* - \sum_{j=1}^{g}\left(\frac{\partial G}{\partial \dot q_j} - V_j\right)\delta q_j\right) dt, \tag{67}$$

where the circuit co-Lagrangian L^* is defined by

$$L^* = T^* - U$$

and $T^* =$ the total co-inductive energy of the circuit; $U =$ the total capacitative energy of the circuit; also $G =$ the total content of the circuit resistors; $V_j =$ the generalized voltage source associated with the jth generalized charge coordinate.

The complementary form of Hamilton's principle for electrical circuits is stated as:

"An admissible motion of an electrical circuit between a fixed charge configuration at t_0 and another fixed configuration at t_1 is a natural motion, if, and only if, the variational indicator [equation (67)] vanishes for arbitrary admissible variations in charge."

Again it is appropriate to recall that an admissible variation in charge δq_1 is one which does not infringe the current continuity constraint (Kirchhoff's Current Law). Similarly, a "natural" motion of the circuit is one for which Kirchhoff's Voltage Law holds.

The complementary form of Lagrange's equations of motion which follow from the complementary form of Hamilton's principle for electrical circuits are

$$\frac{d}{dt}\left(\frac{\partial L^*}{\partial \dot{q}_j}\right) - \frac{\partial L^*}{\partial q_j} + \frac{\partial G}{\partial \dot{q}_j} = V_j, \qquad j = 1, 2, \ldots, g. \tag{68}$$

An example of loop variational analysis of an electrical circuit will serve to demonstrate the salient features of the technique. The electrical circuit shown in Fig. 7.20 has three independent charge constraints, hence the mesh charges (q_1, q_2, q_3) defined as the time integral of the mesh currents form a complete, independent set of generalized charge coordinates. The charge in the third mesh is constrained by a current source $i(t)$ such that

$$q_3(t) = - \int_0^t i(t)dt, \qquad \delta q_3 = 0.$$

The variational coordinates $\delta q_1, \delta q_2$ are therefore a complete independent set. The system co-inductive energy is

$$T^* = \tfrac{1}{2}L_1\dot{q}_2^2 + \tfrac{1}{2}L_2(\dot{q}_2 - \dot{q}_3)^2.$$

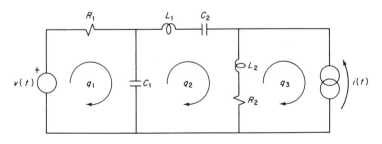

Fig. 7.20.

The system capacitative energy is

$$U = \frac{1}{2C_1}(q_1 - q_2)^2 + \frac{1}{2C_2}q_2^2.$$

The circuit co-Lagrangian is

$$L^* = \frac{1}{2}\left(L_1\dot{q}_2^2 + L_2(\dot{q}_2 - \dot{q}_3)^2 - \frac{1}{C_1}(q_1 - q_2)^2 - \frac{1}{C_2}q_2^2\right).$$

The content of the system is

$$G = \tfrac{1}{2}R_1\dot{q}_1^2 + \tfrac{1}{2}R_2(\dot{q}_2 - \dot{q}_3)^2.$$

Lagrange's equation for the q_1 coordinate is

$$\frac{d}{dt}\left(\frac{\partial L^*}{\partial \dot{q}_1}\right) - \frac{\partial L^*}{\partial q_1} + \frac{G}{\partial \dot{q}_1} = v(t),$$

$$\frac{1}{C_1}(q_1 - q_2) + R_1\dot{q}_1 = v(t). \tag{69}$$

Lagrange's equation for the q_2 coordinate is

$$\frac{d}{dt}\left(\frac{\partial L^*}{\partial \dot{q}_2}\right) - \frac{\partial L^*}{\partial q_2} - \frac{\partial G}{\partial \dot{q}_2} = 0,$$

$$(L_1 + L_2)\ddot{q}_2 - L_2\ddot{q}_3 + \frac{1}{C_1}(q_2 - q_1) + \frac{1}{C_2}q_2 + R_2(\dot{q}_2 - \dot{q}_3) = 0. \tag{70}$$

The q_3 coordinate is constrained by the current source $i(t)$ to be

$$\dot{q}_3 = -i(t). \tag{71}$$

Equations (69), (70) and (71) constitute the equations of motion of the electrical circuit.

7. VARIATIONAL ANALYSIS OF FLUID SYSTEMS

The variational analysis of lumped fluid systems is of limited practical use, since they are rarely sufficiently complex to merit it. A possible exception to this rule is the instance where non-linear constitutive relations occur (such as sealed tank flow stores, and turbulent flow dissipators). An additional possibility is that a fluid sub-system may form part of a multi-media energy handling system which is to be analysed by a variational approach. There are, of course, two complementary variational analysis procedures, one based on loop concepts, the other upon node variables. Both are equally useful, although the latter is intuitively more acceptable since it uses readily identifiable pressure coordinates.

7.1. Nodal variational analysis of fluid systems

The nodal variational analysis of fluid systems is based upon consideration of admissible configurations of *fluid momentum* Γ, which is defined as the time integral of fluid pressure P measured with respect to some pressure datum. That is,

$$\Gamma = \int_0^t P(t)\mathrm{d}t, \qquad \dot{\Gamma} = P.$$

The analysis commences with the definition of a complete, independent set of generalized fluid momentum coordinates $(\Gamma_1, \Gamma_2, \ldots, \Gamma_m)$. If the fluid momentum configuration is holonomically constrained by pressure sources and multi-ports, a set of variational coordinates $(\delta\Gamma_1, \delta\Gamma_2, \ldots, \delta\Gamma_l)$ can be defined which determines the infinitesimal changes in fluid momentum configuration. The nodal variational indicator (equation (25)) can be written in terms of fluid variables as

$$\delta V = \int_{t_0}^{t_1} \left[\delta L - \sum_{j=1}^{l} \left(\frac{\partial J}{\partial \dot{\Gamma}_j} - Q_j \right) \delta\Gamma_j \right] \mathrm{d}t, \tag{72}$$

where the fluid system Lagrangian L is defined by

$$L = U^*(\dot{\Gamma}_1, \dot{\Gamma}_2, \ldots, \dot{\Gamma}_m) - T(\Gamma_1, \Gamma_2, \ldots, \Gamma_m),$$

where $U^* =$ the total co-potential energy of the system fluid flow stores; $T =$ the total kinetic energy of the system fluid inertances; also $J =$ the co-content of the fluid dissipators; $Q_j =$ the generalized fluid flow source associated with the jth fluid momentum coordinate.

Hamilton's principle for a fluid system which is subject to holonomic constraints is:

"An admissible motion of a fluid system between a specified fluid momentum configuration at time t_0 and another specified configuration at time t_1 is a natural motion if, and only if, the variational indicator [equation (72)] vanishes for arbitrary admissible variations in the fluid momentum configuration."

It is appropriate to recall that an admissible variation in fluid momentum configuration is one which does not infringe pressure compatibility constraints. A natural motion is one which at all times maintains the fluid flow continuity constraints in the system.

Hamilton's principle applied to the variational indicator (equation (72)) results in the fluid system obeying the following set of Lagrange's equations of motion:

$$\frac{\mathrm{d}}{\mathrm{d}t}\left(\frac{\partial L}{\partial \dot{\Gamma}_j} \right) - \frac{\partial L}{\partial \Gamma_j} + \frac{\partial J}{\partial \dot{\Gamma}_j} = Q_j, \qquad j = 1, 2, \ldots, l. \tag{73}$$

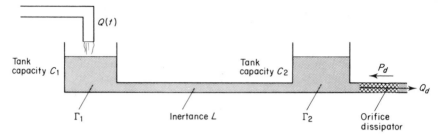

Fig. 7.21.

An example is now given which illustrates the use of nodal variational analysis on a fluid system. Figure 7.21 shows a fluid flow system consisting of two open tanks of capacity C_1, C_2 respectively. The first tank is fed by a flow source $Q(t)$, and linked to the second tank by a long pipe of inertance L. The second tank discharges to atmospheric pressure through an orifice dissipator whose constitutive relation is

$$P_d = \frac{1}{D} Q_d^2.$$

P_d and Q_d are respectively the pressure drop across and the flow rate through the dissipator.

The system has two independent fluid momentum coordinates, and the generalized coordinates (Γ_1, Γ_2) form a suitable complete independent set. In physical terms these momenta are just the time integrals of the pressures at the bases of the tanks. The system co-potential energy is given by

$$U^* = \tfrac{1}{2} C_1 \dot{\Gamma}_1^2 + \tfrac{1}{2} C_2 \dot{\Gamma}_2^2.$$

The system co-kinetic energy is

$$T = \frac{1}{2L} (\Gamma_1 - \Gamma_2)^2.$$

The system has Lagrangian:

$$L = \frac{1}{2} C_1 \dot{\Gamma}_1^2 + \frac{1}{2} C_2 \dot{\Gamma}_2^2 - \frac{1}{2L} (\Gamma_1 - \Gamma_2)^2.$$

The system co-content is

$$J = \int_0^{P_d} Q_d \, dP_d = \tfrac{2}{3} D^{1/2} P_d^{3/2} = \tfrac{2}{3} D^{1/2} (\dot{\Gamma}_2)^{3/2}.$$

Lagrange's equations of motion for the system are

$$\frac{d}{dt}\left(\frac{\partial L}{\partial \dot{\Gamma}_1}\right) - \frac{\partial L}{\partial \Gamma_1} + \frac{\partial J}{\partial \dot{\Gamma}_1} = Q(t),$$

$$C_1\ddot{\Gamma}_1 + \frac{1}{L}\Gamma_1 - \frac{1}{L}\Gamma_2 = Q(t); \tag{74}$$

$$\frac{d}{dt}\left(\frac{\partial L}{\partial \dot{\Gamma}_2}\right) - \frac{\partial L}{\partial \Gamma_2} + \frac{\partial J}{\partial \dot{\Gamma}_2} = 0,$$

$$C_2\ddot{\Gamma}_2 + \frac{1}{L}\Gamma_2 - \frac{1}{L}\Gamma_1 + (D\Gamma_2)^{1/2} = 0. \tag{75}$$

The coupled non-linear second-order differential equations (equations (74, 75)) describe the system motion in terms of the generalized fluid momenta (Γ_1, Γ_2).

7.2. Loop variational analysis of fluid systems

The loop variational analysis of fluid systems is based upon consideration of admissible configurations of *fluid volume V*, which is defined as the time integral of fluid flow rate Q measured at some point in the system. That is,

$$V = \int_0^t Q(t)dt, \qquad \dot{V} = Q.$$

The analysis commences with the definition of a complete, independent set of generalized fluid volume coordinates (V_1, V_2, ..., V_r). If the fluid volume configuration is holonomically constrained by flow sources and multi-ports, a set of variational coordinates (δV_1, δV_2, ..., δV_g) can be defined which determine the infinitesimal changes in fluid volume configuration. The loop variational indicator (equation (36)) can be written in terms of fluid variables as

$$\delta Y = \int_{t_0}^{t_1}\left[\delta L^* - \sum_{j=1}^{g}\left(\frac{\partial G}{\partial \dot{V}_j} - P_j\right)\delta V_j\right]dt, \tag{76}$$

where the fluid system co-Lagrangian is defined by

$$L^* = T^*(\dot{V}_1, \dot{V}_2, ..., \dot{V}_r) - U(V_1, V_2, ..., V_r),$$

where T^* = the total co-kinetic energy of the system fluid inertances; U = the total potential energy of the system fluid flow stores; also G = the content of the fluid dissipators; P_j = the generalized fluid pressure source associated with the jth fluid volume coordinate.

The complementary form of Hamilton's principle for a fluid system which is subject to holonomic constraints is:

"An admissible motion of a fluid system between a specified fluid volume configuration at time t_0 and another specified configuration at time t_1 is a natural motion if, and only if, the variational indicator [equation (76)] vanishes for arbitrary admissible variations in the fluid volume configuration."

In this instance an admissible variation in fluid volume configuration is one which does not infringe flow continuity constraints. A natural motion is one which at all times maintains the fluid pressure compatibility constraints in the system. The complementary form of Hamilton's principle results in the fluid system obeying the following set of Lagrange's equations of motion:

$$\frac{\mathrm{d}}{\mathrm{d}t}\left(\frac{\partial L^*}{\partial \dot{V}_j}\right) - \frac{\partial L^*}{\partial V_j} + \frac{G}{\partial \dot{V}_j} = P_j, \qquad j = 1, 2, \ldots, g. \qquad (77)$$

An example is now given which illustrates the use of loop variational analysis on a fluid system. Figure 7.22 shows a fluid system consisting of a pressure source $P(t)$ pumping fluid through a long pipe of inertance L_1, and into an open reservoir with capacity C. The reservoir C itself discharges through a long pipe (inertance L_2) and finally through an orifice dissipator with constitutive relation:

$$P_d = \frac{1}{D} Q_d^2.$$

The system has two independent fluid volume coordinates, and the generalized coordinates (V_1, V_2) form a suitable complete independent set. In physical terms these volumes are the time integrals of the volumetric flow rates through the inertances. The system co-kinetic energy is given by

$$T^* = \tfrac{1}{2} L_1 \dot{V}_1^2 + \tfrac{1}{2} L_2 \dot{V}_2^2.$$

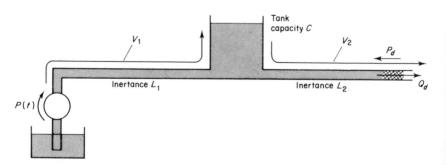

Fig. 7.22.

The system potential energy is given by

$$U = \frac{1}{2C}(V_1 - V_2)^2.$$

The system has co-Lagrangian:

$$L^* = \frac{1}{2}(L_1 \dot{V}_1^2 + L_2 \dot{V}_2^2) - \frac{1}{2C}(V_1 - V_2)^2.$$

The system content is

$$G = \int_0^P P_d dQ_d = Q_d^3/3D = (\dot{V}_2)^3/3D.$$

Lagrange's equations of motion for the system are

$$\frac{d}{dt}\left(\frac{\partial L^*}{\partial \dot{V}_1}\right) - \frac{\partial L^*}{\partial V_1} + \frac{\partial G}{\partial \dot{V}_1} = P(t),$$

$$L_1 \ddot{V}_1 + \frac{1}{C}V_1 - \frac{1}{C}V_2 = P(t); \tag{78}$$

$$\frac{d}{dt}\left(\frac{\partial L^*}{\partial \dot{V}_2}\right) - \frac{\partial L^*}{\partial V_2} - \frac{\partial G}{\partial \dot{V}_2} = 0,$$

$$L_2 \ddot{V}_2 + \frac{1}{C}V_2 - \frac{1}{C}V_1 + \frac{\dot{V}_2^2}{D} = 0. \tag{79}$$

The coupled non-linear second-order differential equations (equations (78, 79)) describe the system motion in terms of the generalized fluid volumes (V_1, V_2). An incidental point to notice is that the systems of Fig. 7.21 and Fig. 7.22 are *complete duals*. As would be anticipated, the application of complementary variational methods leads to equation formulations which are dual (cf. equations (74, 75), and (78, 79)).

8. VARIATIONAL ANALYSIS OF COMPOSITE SYSTEMS

This section is concerned with the variational analysis of systems which are composite in the sense that they consist of several different energy handling sub-systems linked by multi-ports. The variational analysis of mechanical systems involving coupled rotation and translation has already been dealt with; for this reason the current discussion explicitly avoids this aspect of variational analysis, and concentrates upon the general formulation of Lagrange's equations (a) in the presence of power conserving two-ports, and (b) in the presence of two-ports which are intrinsically energy storage devices.

The analysis of composite systems is made by formulating a composite variational indicator which consists of the *sum* of appropriate indicators for the sub-systems. A composite set of variational variables is then defined which consists of the appropriate variational variables for the sub-systems. An admissible variation is one which preserves the appropriate interconnective constraint for the individual sub-systems *and* the "external" constraints imposed by the multi-ports which couple them. Once the composite set of generalized variables is fixed, a composite Lagrangian is formed by taking the sum of the individual sub-system Lagrangians and co-Lagrangians, *plus* any energy stored in the coupling devices. A composite co-content is likewise formed which is the sum of the individual sub-system co-contents and contents. Lagrange's equations of motion are then obtained for all of the composite system's degrees of freedom.

8.1. Variational analysis involving power conserving two-ports

For all practical purposes the only power conserving two-ports which need be considered are the pure transformer and the pure gyrator. These devices neither dissipate nor store energy, their only function is to mutually constrain the configurations of the sub-systems which they couple together. As a consequence, the variational analysis of such composite systems requires careful attention during the selection of generalized coordinates and genera-lized sources. Whether a multi-port constraint manifests itself in the genera-lized coordinates or as an external source depends upon the choice of variational indicator for the sub-systems and the nature of the constraint. In the case of two sub-systems coupled by a pure transformer, if like variational indicators are employed the transformer constrains the generalized coor-dinates; however, if complementary variational indicators are used the transformer constraint appears as a generalized source. In the case of a gyrator coupling two sub-systems, the converse is true. In either instance, the constraint on the system is holonomic since both types of constraint on the generalized coordinates can be put into the form

$$g(q_1, q_2, \ldots, q_m) = 0,$$

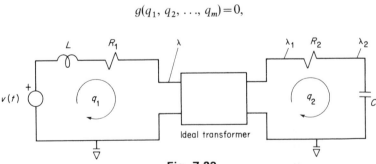

Fig. 7.23.

where $(q_1, q_2, \ldots, q_m)$ are a composite generalized coordinate set. For example, consider the composite electrical system shown in Fig. 7.23, which consists of two sub-systems mutually constrained by an ideal transformer with constitutive relation:

$$\dot{q}_2 = n\dot{q}_1, \qquad \lambda = n\lambda_1. \tag{80}$$

If loop variational analysis is employed in both sub-systems the generalized charge coordinates (q_1, q_2) are constrained by

$$nq_1 - q_2 = \text{constant},$$
$$\delta q_2 = n\delta q_1. \tag{81}$$

Thus the set (δq_1) suffices to define the variational charge configuration completely and independently. If it is assumed that the initial charge state is zero, the constant in equation (81) is zero, and the system capacitative energy is

$$U = \frac{1}{2C} q_2^2 = \frac{n^2}{2C} q_1^2.$$

The system co-inductive energy is

$$T^* = \tfrac{1}{2} L\dot{q}_1^2.$$

The system co-Lagrangian is

$$L^* = \frac{1}{2} L\dot{q}_1^2 - \frac{n^2}{2C} q_1^2.$$

The system content is

$$G = \tfrac{1}{2} R_i \dot{q}_1^2 + \tfrac{1}{2} n^2 R_2 \dot{q}_1^2.$$

Lagrange's equation of motion for the system is

$$L\ddot{q}_1 + \frac{n^2}{C} q_1 + (R_1 + n^2 R_2)\dot{q}_1 = v(t). \tag{82}$$

The alternative manner in which power conserving two-ports influence variational analysis of composite systems is illustrated by considering the circuit of Fig. 7.23 when complementary variational methods are used in the sub-system. If this is the case the composite set of generalized coordinates $(q_1, \lambda_1, \lambda_2)$ define in a complete, independent manner the system configuration. For the first sub-system the co-Lagrangian is

$$L^* = \tfrac{1}{2} L_1 \dot{q}_1^2.$$

For the second sub-system the total inductive energy is zero. The total co-capacitative energy U^* is also the Lagrangian:

$$L = U^* = \tfrac{1}{2} C\dot{\lambda}_2^2.$$

The composite system Lagrangian is therefore

$$\mathscr{L} = L^* + L = \tfrac{1}{2} L\dot{q}_1^2 + \tfrac{1}{2} C\dot{\lambda}_2^2.$$

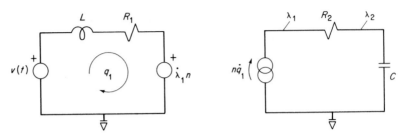

Fig. 7.24.

The content of the first sub-system is

$$G = \tfrac{1}{2} R_1 \dot{q}_1^2.$$

The co-content of the second sub-system is

$$J = \frac{1}{2R_2} (\dot{\lambda}_1 - \dot{\lambda}_2)^2.$$

The composite system co-content is therefore

$$\mathscr{J} = \tfrac{1}{2} R_1 \dot{q}_1^2 + \frac{1}{2R_2} (\dot{\lambda}_1 - \dot{\lambda}_2)^2.$$

Because of the choice of variational methods, the effect of the transformer is to introduce source elements into the sub-systems as indicated in Fig. 7.24. Lagrange's equations of motion are therefore:

$$\frac{\mathrm{d}}{\mathrm{d}t} \left(\frac{\partial \mathscr{L}}{\partial \dot{q}_1} \right) - \frac{\partial \mathscr{L}}{\partial q_1} + \frac{\partial \mathscr{J}}{\partial \dot{q}_1} = v(t) - \dot{\lambda}_1 n,$$

$$L\ddot{q}_1 + R_1 \dot{q}_1 + \dot{\lambda}_1 n = v(t); \tag{83}$$

$$\frac{\mathrm{d}}{\mathrm{d}t} \left(\frac{\partial \mathscr{L}}{\partial \dot{\lambda}_1} \right) - \frac{\partial \mathscr{L}}{\partial \lambda_1} + \frac{\partial \mathscr{J}}{\partial \dot{\lambda}_1} = n\dot{q}_1,$$

$$\frac{1}{R_2} (\dot{\lambda}_1 - \dot{\lambda}_2) = n\dot{q}_1; \tag{84}$$

$$\frac{\mathrm{d}}{\mathrm{d}t} \left(\frac{\partial \mathscr{L}}{\partial \dot{\lambda}_2} \right) - \frac{\partial \mathscr{L}}{\partial \lambda_2} + \frac{\partial \mathscr{J}}{\partial \dot{\lambda}_2} = 0,$$

$$C\ddot{\lambda}_2 + \frac{1}{R_2} (\dot{\lambda}_2 - \dot{\lambda}_1) = 0. \tag{85}$$

Equations (83, 84, 85) describe the composite system motion in terms of the coordinates $(q_1, \lambda_1, \lambda_2)$.

The constraints imposed by a set of transformers or gyrators which couple different sub-systems can always be handled by an extension of the procedure illustrated here.

8.2. Variational analysis involving energy storing two-ports

A number of multi-ports depend upon an intrinsic energy storing property in order to perform the coupling or energy converting task. Specific examples are the moving plate capacitor and solenoid, both of which depend upon the storage of energy in a field. The variational analysis of composite systems involving such devices differs from the previous analysis in that additional energy terms are introduced into the Lagrangian which *implicitly* couple the equations of motion of the sub-systems. In order to illustrate this point an example of a composite electromechanical system is given. However, before this can be done the variational analysis of electromechanical systems must be discussed.

The variational analysis is begun by defining an appropriate mechanical variational indicator and an appropriate electrical variational indicator. A composite set of variational variables is then formed consisting of the mechanical and electrical variational variables. An admissible variation is one which preserves both the appropriate mechanical and the appropriate electrical interconnective constraints. The constitutive relation of the energy storing multi-port which constrains the electrical and mechanical circuits is represented by its energy in the composite Lagrangian.

There are two mechanical and two electrical variational indicators, thus the composite indicator can take four possible forms. For all practical purposes, however, the complementary mechanical variational indicator can be discarded and only the composite forms which examine admissible displacement/charge coordinates or displacement/flux linkage coordinates need be considered. In the former case a composite variational indicator is formed by adding the indicators (equation (55) and equation (67)). This leads to a composite set of Lagrange's equations of the form

$$\frac{\mathrm{d}}{\mathrm{d}t}\left(\frac{\partial \mathscr{L}}{\partial \dot{z}_j}\right) - \frac{\partial \mathscr{L}}{\partial z_j} + \frac{\partial \mathscr{J}}{\partial \dot{z}_j} = F_j, \qquad j = 1, 2, \ldots, l_m,$$

$$\frac{\mathrm{d}}{\mathrm{d}t}\left(\frac{\partial \mathscr{L}}{\partial \dot{q}_j}\right) - \frac{\partial \mathscr{L}}{\partial q_j} + \frac{\partial \mathscr{J}}{\partial \dot{q}_j} = V_j, \qquad j = 1, 2, \ldots, g_e,$$

where the generalized displacement coordinates have been relabelled (z_1, z_2, ..., z_{m_m}) to avoid confusion with the generalized charge coordinates. The composite system Lagrangian $\mathscr{L}$ is given by

$$\mathscr{L} = L_{\mathrm{mech}} + L^*_{\mathrm{elec}},$$

$$\mathscr{L} = U^*_{\mathrm{mech}} + T^*_{\mathrm{elec}} - (T_{\mathrm{mech}} + U_{\mathrm{elec}}).$$

The composite system co-content $\mathscr{J}$ is defined by

$$\mathscr{J} = J_{\text{mech}} + G_{\text{elec}}.$$

The (F_j) and (V_j) are generalized force and voltage sources for the mechanical and electrical circuits respectively. In addition the composite system is holonomically constrained such that the mechanical and electrical parts have respectively l_m and g_e degrees of freedom. Note that the coupling device will have its energy included in the Lagrangian just *once*, either referred to the electrical port or to the mechanical port.

The alternative form of composite variational procedure combines the study of admissible displacement coordinates in the mechanical part with admissible flux linkage configurations in the electrical part. A composite variational indicator is then formed by combining the indicators, equation (55) and equation (62). This leads to a composite set of Lagrange's equations of the form:

$$\frac{d}{dt}\left(\frac{\partial \mathscr{L}}{\partial \dot{z}_j}\right) - \frac{\partial \mathscr{L}}{\partial z_j} + \frac{\partial \mathscr{J}}{\partial \dot{z}_j} = F_j, \qquad j = 1, 2, \ldots, l_m,$$

$$\frac{d}{dt}\left(\frac{\partial \mathscr{L}}{\partial \dot{\lambda}_j}\right) - \frac{\partial \mathscr{L}}{\partial \lambda_j} + \frac{\partial \mathscr{J}}{\partial \dot{\lambda}_j} = I_j, \qquad j = 1, 2, \ldots, l_e.$$

The generalized coordinates of the system are now the generalized displacement coordinates $(z_1, z_2, \ldots, z_{m_m})$ and the generalized flux linkage coordinates $(\lambda_1, \lambda_2, \ldots, \lambda_{m_e})$. The composite system is assumed to be holonomically constrained with l_m degrees of freedom in displacement and l_e degrees of freedom in flux linkages. The composite system Lagrangian in this revised formulation is given by

$$\mathscr{L} = L_{\text{mech}} + L_{\text{elec}},$$

$$\mathscr{L} = U^*_{\text{mech}} + U^*_{\text{elec}} - (T_{\text{mech}} + T_{\text{elec}}).$$

The composite system co-cotent $\mathscr{J}$ is now defined as

$$\mathscr{J} = J_{\text{mech}} + J_{\text{elec}}.$$

The (F_j) and (I_j) are generalized force and current sources for the mechanical and electrical circuits respectively. Note that the coupling device will have its energy included in the Lagrangian just *once* either referred to the electrical port or the mechanical port.

A representative example of the variational analysis of a composite system involving an energy storing two-port is the composite electromechanical system shown in Fig. 7.25. The electrical sub-system contains a voltage source $v(t)$ which passes current $\dot{q}$ through a resistor R and a solenoid of inductance $L(z)$, where z is the position of the solenoid core. The mechanical sub-system is the core of mass m which is constrained to move horizontally and is restrained by a linear spring and dissipator. The system may be analysed by considering

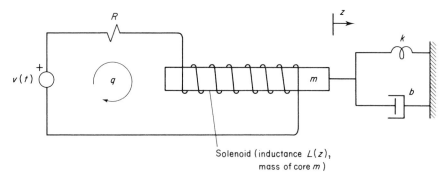

Solenoid (inductance $L(z)$,
mass of core m)

Fig. 7.25.

admissible variations in the generalized coordinates (q, z) as labelled in the diagram. The co-Lagrangian of the electrical sub-system is

$$L^*_{\text{elec}} = \tfrac{1}{2} L(z) \dot{q}^2,$$

which is actually the co-inductive energy of the solenoid. The Lagrangian of the mechanical sub-system is

$$L_{\text{mech}} = \tfrac{1}{2} m \dot{z}^2 - \tfrac{1}{2} k z^2.$$

The composite Lagrangian is

$$\mathscr{L} = \tfrac{1}{2} m \dot{z}^2 + \tfrac{1}{2} L(z) \dot{q}^2 - \tfrac{1}{2} k z^2.$$

The composite co-content of the system is

$$\mathscr{J} = \tfrac{1}{2} R \dot{q}^2 + \tfrac{1}{2} b \dot{z}^2.$$

Lagrange's equations of motion are therefore

$$\left(\frac{\partial \mathscr{L}}{\partial \dot{q}} \right) - \frac{\partial \mathscr{L}}{\partial q} + \frac{\partial \mathscr{J}}{\partial \dot{q}} = v(t),$$

$$L(z) \ddot{q} + R \dot{q} = v(t); \tag{86}$$

$$\frac{\mathrm{d}}{\mathrm{d}t} \left(\frac{\partial \mathscr{L}}{\partial \dot{z}} \right) - \frac{\partial \mathscr{L}}{\partial z} + \frac{\partial \mathscr{J}}{\partial \dot{z}} = 0,$$

$$m \ddot{z} + b \dot{z} + k z - \tfrac{1}{2} (\dot{q})^2 \partial L(z) / \partial z = 0. \tag{87}$$

The non-linear coupled differential equation pair (equations (86, 87)) represent the equations of motion in terms of the charge q and displacement z.

9. NOTES AND REFERENCES

[1] Differential variational indicators such as the virtual work principle are discussed in

Den Hartog, J. P. (1948). "Mechanics". Dover, London.

Somerfield, A. (1964). "Mechanics — Lectures on Theoretical Physics", Vol. 1. (Translated by M. D. Stern). Academic Press, London and New York.

[2] The use of differential indicators in determining the constitutive relations of large multi-port systems is discussed in
Karnopp, D. (1969). "Power conserving transformations". *Journal of the Franklin Institute* **288**, 175–201.

[3] Useful texts on variational methods in system modelling are
Yourgrau, W. and Mandelstam, S. (1968). "Variational principles in dynamics and quantum theory". Pitmans, London.
Crandall, S. H., Karnopp, D. C., Kurtz, E. F. and Pridmore-Brown, D. C. (1968). "Dynamics of mechanical and electromechanical systems". McGraw-Hill, New York.
MacFarlane, A. G. J. (1970). "Dynamical system models". Harrap, London.
The material in this chapter is based upon the second of these books.

[4] The Calculus of Variations is covered in
Forray, M. J. (1968). "Variational calculus in science and engineering". McGraw-Hill, New York.

[5] The use of variational methods as a means of numerically solving modelling equations is discussed in
Biot, M. (1970). "Variational principles in heat transfer". OUP, Oxford.
See also:
Civil Engineering Dept., University of Southampton. (1973). "Variational methods in engineering". Southampton University Press.

[6] An excellent description of classical variational methods (using nodal variational methods) is given in:
Lanczos, C. (1966). "The variational principles of mechanics". University of Toronto Press, Toronto.
See also:
Pars, L. A. (1962). "An introduction to the calculus of variations". Heinemann, London.

10. PROBLEMS

10.1. Solve problems 9.1 and 9.2 of chapter 5 by a variational method. Obtain the set of second-order differential equations which describe the system's behaviour.

10.2. Figure 7.26 shows an automobile suspension test bed in which the suspension units have been idealized and are each represented by a spring in parallel with a damper. The suspension units are loaded by a mass M which simulates the automobile body. If the system is perturbed by the application of a force $F(t)$ applied at the edge A, use a variational method to determine the transfer functions relating the displacements q_1, q_2 and the input force. Assume that (a) the system moves only in the plane of the paper, (b) deflections are small, and the moment of inertia of the load about the centre of gravity is I.

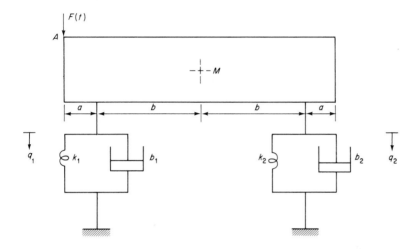

Fig. 7.26.

10.3. Use a variational technique to determine the equations of motion for the system shown in Fig. 7.27. The system is an idealized form of a gantry crane consisting of a trolley of mass m_1, sliding on an elevated track with a load of mass m_2 suspended beneath it by means of a light rigid of length L. The trolley is pulled along the rails by a motor which applies a force $F(t)$ through a flexible cable. The cable can be represented by a single lumped spring, (stiffness k), and the trolley sliding friction is linear with coefficient b. Use generalized coordinates x_1, x_2, θ. Compare your results with Case Study 2.

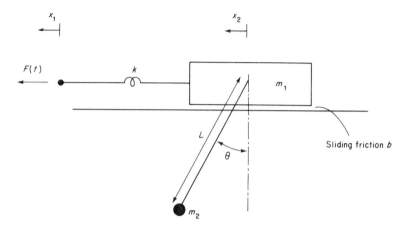

Fig. 7.27.

10.4. Use a variational method involving (a) flux linkage coordinates (b) charge coordinates to determine the differential equations describing the linear electrical system shown in Fig. 7.28.

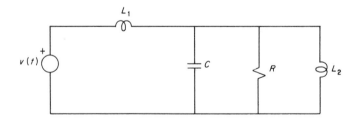

Fig. 7.28.

10.5. Use a variational method to determine the transfer function relating $F_1(t)$ to $x_2(t)$ for the hydro-mechanical system shown in Fig. 7.29. Assume linear components throughout.

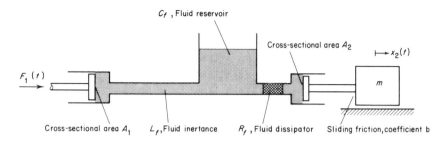

Fig. 7.29.

10.6. An idealized representation of a vibration instrumentation scheme is shown in Fig. 7.30. A mass m is constrained to move horizontally subject to the displacement $x_0(t)$ of a vibrator which is connected to the mass by a linear spring and dissipator. The movements of the mass m are detected by utilizing the mass as one plate of a movable plate capacitor. The capacitor is charged by the ideal constant voltage source v_0, and the resistor R models the input resistance of a signal amplifier. The capacitance C_1 models stray capacitance in the circuit. Assume that the movable plate capacitance is electrically linear and use a Lagrangian approach to determine the equations of motion of the system in terms of the displacements $x_0(t)$, $x(t)$ and the voltage $V(t)$ developed across the input to the signal amplifier.

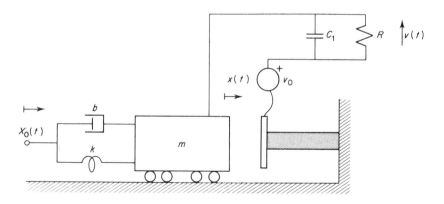

Fig. 7.30.

10.7. Fig. 7.31 shows a disk of mass M and radius r rolling without slip on a cylindrical surface of radius R. Take θ as the generalized coordinate and use a variational method to obtain the equations of motion for the disk under the influence of gravity. Explain by means of a root locus diagram how you would expect the motions of the disk to be influenced by: (i) R small; (ii) R large; (iii) R negative.

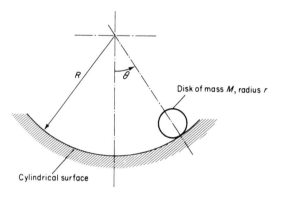

Fig. 7.31.

Assume that the disk moves in the plane of the paper and has moment of inertia $\frac{1}{2}Mr^2$. Compare your results with Case Study 3.

Bond Graph Methods

8

INTRODUCTION

This chapter deals with a graphical approach to system modelling known as bond graph analysis. The essential feature of the bond graph approach is the representation of energetic interactions between systems and system components by a single line or energy bond. In a sense such a convention is just an alternative to the network approach. However, bond graphs have certain advantages over network models, the main one being that a bond graph model is generally more compact and orderly than an equivalent system graph. In particular, bond graph elements exist which allow multiport elements to be modelled explicitly, whereas network models, even of simple two-port elements, are awkward to draw and manipulate.

For example, consider the coupled electric drives considered in Case Study 5 and redrawn in Fig. 8.1. The linear network graph for this system (Fig. 8.1(b)) is ungainly and, as a result, unhelpful in studying the interconnective structure. On the other hand, the bond graph (Fig. 8.1(c)) is a more orderly graphical interpretation of the system, and yet contains all the dynamical and interconnective information required to formulate a mathematical model.

From a practical viewpoint the relatively compact nature of bond graphs commends the technique as the basis for computer-aided modelling. This, coupled with the development of low-cost, high-speed interactive computer systems, distinguishes the bond graph approach as potentially the most useful of the systematic modelling techniques.

1. WORD BOND GRAPHS

The fundamental component of a bond graph is the energy bond used to couple the energy ports of system components, and in order to convey a preliminary feeling for energetic bonding, it is useful to first discuss the word

193

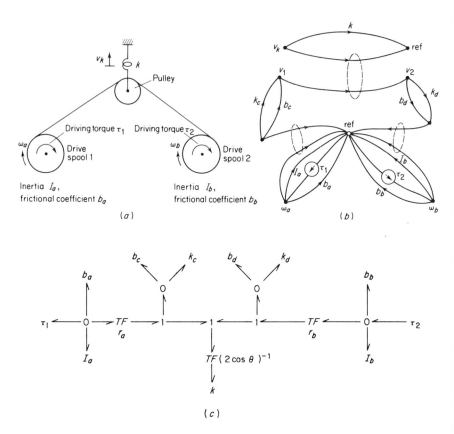

Fig. 8.1. (*a*) Coupled electric drives. (*b*) Network representation of the coupled drives (cf. Case Study 5). (*c*) Bond graph representation of coupled drives.

bond graph of a representative system. Word bond graphs are primarily a heuristic means of exploring the possible energetic interconnections within a system prior to a detailed analysis. For the present they will serve to introduce the basic concepts of system modelling by bond graphical procedures.

Consider the two-stage gas turbine shown in schematic form in Fig. 8.2(*a*). This particular turbine is of the type used for high-power road transport vehicles, and as such differs slightly from conventional turbines. In addition to the normal input, fuel mass flow rate ($\dot{m}_f$), a set of adjustable nozzles are provided in the power turbine. These constitute a second input which can be manipulated to optimize the engine efficiency over the wide operating range required of an automotive engine. The automotive gas turbine therefore consists of a gas generator comprising a compressor, fuel burner and

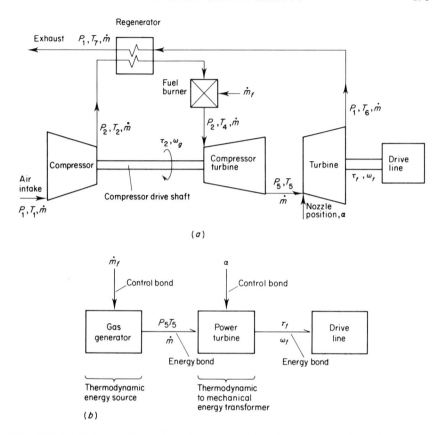

Fig. 8.2. (*a*) Schema of an automotive gas turbine. (*b*) Basic word bond graph of the automotive gas turbine.

compressor turbine, feeding hot gases into the second stage, which is simply the power turbine. In addition, an attempt to withdraw the remaining energy from the exhaust gases is made by passing the exhaust through a regenerator, which in turn pre-heats the gases from the compressor. In bond graph terms the automotive gas turbine can be thought of as a controlled source of thermodynamic energy (the gas generator), coupled to a converter of thermodynamic energy to mechanical energy (the power turbine). Figure 8.2(*b*) is the bond graph of the gas turbine when thought of in these terms. The heavy lines between the system elements are the energy bonds which denote the component coupling with half-arrows which indicate the assumed direction of positive energy flow. The variables written alongside the energy bonds are the quantities required to define the energy being transmitted on that bond. For

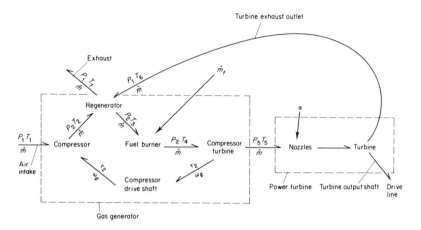

Fig. 8.3. Expanded bond graph of the automotive gas turbine.

the bond which represents the gas stream coupling the thermodynamic energy source and the energy converter the energy variables are the gas pressure p_5, the temperature T_5 and the mass flow rate $\dot{m}$. For the bond connecting the energy converter to the vehicle drive-line, the energy is given by the torque, τ_t and angular velocity ω_t of the power turbine output shaft.

In addition to the energy bonds which connect system elements, control bonds are shown in Fig. 8.2(b). These indicate that the constitutive properties of the system element in question are modulated by the variable indicated on the controlling bond. Hence the output of the energy source is controlled by the fuel mass flow rate $(\dot{m}_f)$ and the energy converter is controlled by the position (α) of the turbine nozzles. Thus control bonds transmit information but no significant amounts of energy.

The word bond graph of Fig. 8.2(b) can be expanded as indicated in Fig. 8.3 to include all the major system components. At this stage the word bond graph is just a formalized version of Fig. 8.2(a). However it is one of the features of the bond graph method that a graph may be readily extended to include more detailed behaviour as required. This point will be taken up again later, for the moment it is sufficient to note that the components indicated in Fig. 8.3 can be modelled as they stand in terms of their gross constitutive properties. Alternatively they may be further decomposed to obtain a more detailed model of the system.

2. BASIC BOND GRAPH COMPONENTS

The word bond graph discussed above referred to highly specialized system components which are particular to turbine systems. In most cases systems are modelled in terms of the basic energy handling components (energy stores, sources and dissipators), suitably interconnected in series and parallel combinations with possibly some transforming or gyrating elements. It is therefore necessary to define initially the bond graph conventions for the basic one-port elements.

2.1. One-port components: energy sources

There are two basic energy storing devices, one for each of the system variable pair required to specify an energy flow. Thus in mechanical systems there are sources of force and velocity. In the same spirit, electrical systems have sources of electrical current and voltage. Fluid systems commonly involve sources of fluid pressure and fluid flow rate. Likewise thermal systems can be thought of as being driven by temperature and heat flow sources, although these two variables do not constitute a true pair of energy variables, because their product is energy not power as with the remaining sets of system variables.

In terms of generalized system variables the basic bond graph sources are the effort source and the flow source, these two components together with their equivalents in various energy domains are given in Fig. 8.4. Notice that the

Effort source		*Flow source*	
$SE \longrightarrow$ e	generalized component	$SF \longrightarrow$ f	
$SE \longrightarrow$ v Voltage source	electrical	$SF \longrightarrow$ i Current source	
$SE \longrightarrow$ P Pressure source	fluid	$SF \longrightarrow$ Q Fluid flow source	
$SE \longrightarrow$ v Velocity source	mechanical translation	$SF \longrightarrow$ F Force source	
$SE \longrightarrow$ ω Angular velocity source	mechanical rotation	$SF \longrightarrow$ τ Torque source	
$SE \longrightarrow$ T Temperature source	thermal	$SF \longrightarrow$ Q Heat flow source	

Fig. 8.4.

half-arrow alluded to previously is included in the source bond to indicate the normal direction of positive energy flow. In this case sources are assumed normally to supply energy and the power arrow is directed away from the components.

2.2. Energy stores

In common with source components there are two basic forms of energy stores. For generalized elements these are the flow store and the effort store. The former device stores energy as the time integral of the flow variable applied to its port, the device effort is then given by the time integral of the flow variable and the material properties of the device.

If the flow accumulation is defined by

$$f_a = \int_0^t f \, dt, \tag{1}$$

in general, the component effort is given by a non-linear function of the accumulation of flow:

$$e = \varphi^{-1}(f_a). \tag{2a}$$

	Dynamic relation	Linear constitutive relation
Generalized component	$f_a = \int f \, dt$	$e = \dfrac{1}{C} f_a$
Electrical component [capacitor, q = charge]	$q = \int i \, dt$	$v = \dfrac{1}{C} q$
Fluid component [fluid reservoir, V = fluid volume]	$V = \int Q \, dt$	$P = \dfrac{1}{C_f} V$
Mechanical component [inertia, p = translational momentum, h = rotational momentum]	$p = \int F \, dt$	$v = \dfrac{1}{m} p$
	$h = \int \tau \, dt$	$\omega = \dfrac{1}{I} h$
Thermal component [thermal capacity, H = total heat]	$H = \int Q \, dt$	$T = \dfrac{1}{C_t} H$

Fig. 8.5. Flow store conventions: symbol $\dfrac{e}{f} C$.

In the linear case, the flow store effort is given by

$$e = C^{-1}f_a. \tag{2b}$$

The bond graph convention for the flow store together with the equivalent components in the various energy domains is shown in Fig. 8.5. In this diagram linear constitutive relations are assumed for simplicity, the convention does not alter for non-linear constitutive relations. Notice that in the case of passive one-ports the power arrow is directed towards the component, indicating that power is normally absorbed by the device.

The complementary storage device is the effort store, this device stores energy as the time integral of the effort variable applied at its port. The corresponding flow is then given by the time integral of the effort variable and the material properties of the device. If the effort accumulated in the component is defined by

$$e_a = \int_0^t e \, dt, \tag{3}$$

in general, the component flow is given by a non-linear function of the accumulation of effort:

$$f = \varphi^{-1}(e_a). \tag{4a}$$

	Dynamic relation	Linear constitutive relation
Generalized component	$e_a = \int e\,dt$	$f = \dfrac{1}{L}e_a$
Electrical component [inductor, λ = flux linkages]	$\lambda = \int v\,dt$	$i = \dfrac{1}{L}\lambda$
Fluid component [fluid inertance, Γ = pressure momentum]	$\Gamma = \int P\,dt$	$Q = \dfrac{1}{L_f}\Gamma$
Mechanical component [compliance, x = translational displacement, θ = rotational displacement]	$x = \int V\,dt$ $\theta = \int \omega\,dt$	$F = kx$ $\tau = k\theta$
Thermal component		no equivalent

Fig. 8.6. Effort store conventions: symbol $\dfrac{e}{f} L$.

	Linear constitutive relation
Generalized component	$e = Rf$
Electrical component [resistor]	$v = Ri$
Fluid component [fluid dissipator]	$P = R_f Q$
Mechanical component [friction]	$F = bV$
	$\tau = b\omega$
Thermal component [Fourier's Law]	$T = RQ$

Fig. 8.7. Dissipator conventions: symbol $\dfrac{e}{f} R$.

In the linear case, the effort store flow is given by

$$f = L^{-1} e_a \qquad (4b)$$

The bond graph convention for the effort store, together with the equivalent components in the various energy domains is given in Fig. 8.6. Again linear constitutive relations are quoted for simplicity.

2.3. Energy dissipators

A single type of energy dissipator is required in order to model the basic phenomena encountered in electrical resistors, mechanical dashpots, and the like. In terms of generalized system elements an energy dissipator is a device whose effort and flow variables are statically constrained by a non-linear function, e.g.

$$e = \varphi(f). \qquad (5)$$

In the linear case this constraint is written as

$$e = Rf. \qquad (6)$$

The bond graph convention for a dissipator, together with the equivalent components in various energy domains are given in Fig. 8.7. Linear constitutive properties are assumed.

3. INTERCONNECTION OF BOND GRAPH COMPONENTS

The main functional difference between bond graphs and networks occurs in the way in which basic components are interconnected. Because bond graphs are port-oriented it is necessary to introduce explicit bond graph components to allow the interconnection of more than two energy ports together. By

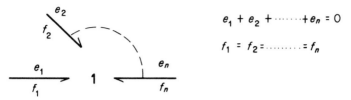

$$e_1 + e_2 + \cdots + e_n = 0$$

$$f_1 = f_2 = \cdots = f_n$$

Fig. 8.8. The effort junction.

contrast, network methods are terminal-oriented and interconnective constraints are implicitly introduced by appropriately joining terminals. It will emerge subsequently that the need for explicit elements to denote component interconnection is an important structural feature of the bond graph, since it allows the interconnective structure of a system to be isolated as a distinct part of the model.

There are two fundamental interconnective constraints which need to be modelled in the bond graph language, these are the generalized compatibility constraint on effort variables, and the generalized continuity constraint on flow variables.

3.1. The generalized compatibility constraint

This constraint is modelled in bond graph terms by an n-port device known as an effort junction. This is a device which is represented symbolically in Fig. 8.8, and has constitutive relation:

$$e_1 + e_2 + e_3 + \ldots + e_n = 0,$$
$$f_1 = f_2 = f_3 = \ldots = f_n, \tag{7}$$

where the signs in the constitutive relation refer specifically to the inward power flow convention used in Fig. 8.8. If any power arrow is reversed the sign of the appropriate effort variable in equation (7) should be reversed.

The effort junction is an abstract representation of the effort compatibility constraint. In physical terms it is a general statement of Kirchhoff's Voltage Law (KVL) for electrical systems, while in mechanical systems it refers to the fact that velocities measured round a closed loop sum to zero. In the same spirit, in fluid and thermal systems it refers to the basic physical law that pressures and temperatures respectively round closed loops balance to zero. In terms of networks, the effort junction is the multi-port which allows components to be connected in series. Some examples of simple systems involving one-ports interconnected by an effort junction are given in Fig. 8.9.

3.2. The generalized continuity constraint

The continuity of flow constraint is modelled in bond graph terms by an n-port

System   Bond graph model

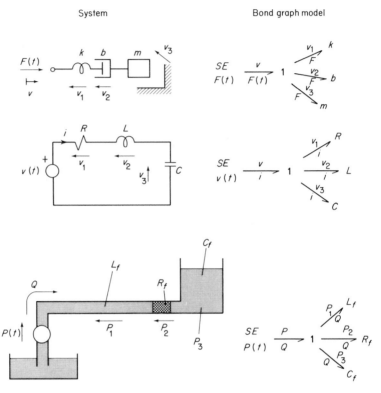

Fig. 8.9. Simple systems employing the effort junction.

device known as a flow junction. This component, which is indicated in symbolic form in Fig. 8.10, as an n-port whose constitutive relation is

$$f_1 + f_2 + f_3 + \ldots + f_n = 0,$$
$$e_1 = e_2 = e_3 = \ldots = e_n,$$ (8)

where the signs in the constitutive relation refer specifically to the inward power flow convention used in Fig. 8.10. If any power arrow is reversed the sign of the appropriate flow variable in equation (8) should be reversed.

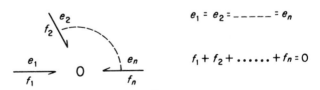

$$e_1 = e_2 = \text{-----} = e_n$$

$$f_1 + f_2 + \ldots\ldots + f_n = 0$$

Fig. 8.10. The flow junction.

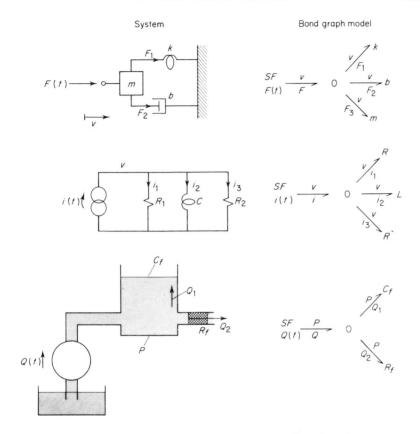

Fig. 8.11. Simple systems employing the flow junction.

It is useful to note that the flow junction is a representation of Kirchoff's Current Law (KCL) for electrical systems. In mechanical systems it corresponds to the force balance, while in fluid and thermal systems it refers to the continuity of material at a junction, and the conservation of thermal energy, respectively. A network interpretation of the flow junction is as a multi-port which allows the parallel connection of components. Examples of simple systems involving one-ports interconnected by a flow junction are given in Fig. 8.11.

3.3. Use of the effort and flow junctions

With the two series and parallel connection multi-ports and the basic one-ports, a wide range of systems can be modelled. However, some care is needed in applying these basic multi-ports, because it is often not immediately obvious

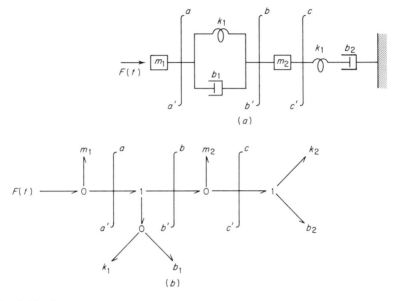

Fig. 8.12. Illustrating the construction of a bond graph for a mechanical system: (a) the system; (b) the bond graph.

how one should use the effort and flow junctions to obtain a valid bond graph model. Probably the simplest approach is to work sequentially through the system, mentally looking for points at which interconnective constraints can be applied, and replacing such points by the appropriate 0 or 1 junction. The most useful guide in this respect is the fact that at an effort junction all components have a common flow, and at a flow junction all components have a common effort. Thus junctions can be associated with the occurrence of the same flow or effort variable on one or more components. The following examples illustrate these points.

Consider the mechanical system shown in Fig. 8.12(a). The force source, the mass m_1 and the link crossing line aa' share the same velocity, they therefore connect to a flow junction. The elements k_1, b_1, are in parallel with each other and are connected via a flow junction. However the pair of variables are effectively in series with the links crossing line aa' and bb' so that the flow junction connecting k_1, b_1, must itself be connected by an effort junction to the main system. The links crossing bb' and cc' share a common velocity with m_2, which is therefore connected to a flow junction with bonds associated with the links crossing bb' and cc'. Finally, the link crossing cc' and components k_2, b_2, share a common force, and so the bond graph is completed with an effort junction joining k_2, b_2 and the bond from the previously constructed part of the graph.

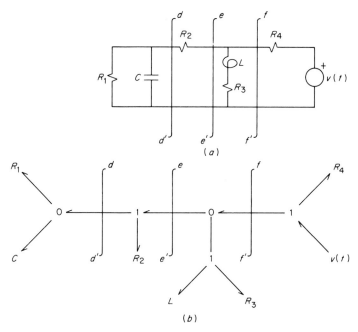

Fig. 8.13. Illustrating the construction of a bond graph for an electrical system: (*a*) the system; (*b*) the bond graph.

A similar example, this time drawn from electrical engineering is shown in Fig. 8.13. In part (*a*) of the diagram a simple circuit is shown divided for convenience by the lines dd', ee', ff'. The components R_1 and C share a common voltage with the wire crossing dd', and they are therefore connected to a flow junction. The component R_2 shares a common current with the wires crossing dd' and ee' and is therefore connected to an effort junction. The components L and R_3 are mutually coupled by an effort junction, but are as a whole in parallel with the wires crossing ee' and ff'. The effort junction joining the two components is therefore bonded by a flow junction into the main graph. The bond graph is completed by noting that the voltage source and resistor are in series with the rest of the graph and can be bonded to it via an effort junction.

4. OTHER USEFUL BOND GRAPH COMPONENTS

4.1. Power conserving two-ports

To model systems where energy transforming phenomena occur, or where different sub-systems (say mechanical and fluid) are coupled, it is necessary to

$$\xrightarrow{\quad \frac{e_1}{f_1} \quad} TF \atop n \xrightarrow{\quad \frac{e_2}{f_2} \quad} \qquad \xrightarrow{\quad \frac{e_1}{f_1} \quad} GY \atop r \xrightarrow{\quad \frac{e_2}{f_2} \quad}$$

(a)   (b)

Fig. 8.14. Bond graph representation of transformers and gyrators: (a) transformer; (b) gyrator.

consider two-port devices. The simplest class of two-port components are the power conserving kind, and within this class the most important devices are the transformer and the gyrator.

In bond graph terms the transformer is represented by the symbol given in Fig. 8.14(a) and has the constitutive relation:

$$e_2 = ne_1, \qquad f_1 = nf_2. \tag{9}$$

By the same token, the gyrator is represented by the symbol given in Fig. 8.14(b) and has the constitutive relation:

$$e_2 = rf_1, \qquad e_1 = rf_2. \tag{10}$$

Physical examples of transformers are the electrical transformer, mechanical gear trains and levers. Gyrators are less frequently encountered within any one energy handling domain, the gyroscope is the only familiar example. However, gyrators and transformers occur with equal frequency when a change in energy handling media is encountered. Which of the two devices occurs depends upon the choice of effort and flow variables in either energy domain. For example, a fluid ram as shown in Fig. 8.15 can be represented as either a transformer or gyrator by a simple switch in the effort and flow

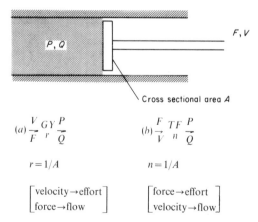

$$(a)\, \frac{V}{F}\, GY \atop r\, \frac{P}{Q} \qquad\qquad (b)\, \frac{F}{V}\, TF \atop n\, \frac{P}{Q}$$

$$r = 1/A \qquad\qquad n = 1/A$$

$$\begin{bmatrix} \text{velocity} \to \text{effort} \\ \text{force} \to \text{flow} \end{bmatrix} \qquad \begin{bmatrix} \text{force} \to \text{effort} \\ \text{velocity} \to \text{flow} \end{bmatrix}$$

Fig. 8.15. Alternative transformer and gyrator representations of a hydraulic piston.

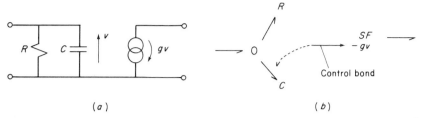

(a)   (b)

Fig. 8.16. (a) Equivalent circuit for common emitter transistor. (b) Bond graph equivalent with controlled source.

variable on one of the ports. According to the convention assumed here the gyrator representation of Fig. 8.15(a) would normally be used, but if force is assumed to be an effort variable and velocity a through variable, the transformer representation of Fig. 8.15(b) is obtained.

4.2. Controlled sources and modulated two-ports

It frequently occurs that the material properties of a component are dependent upon an external input or system variable. The two most commonly occurring cases are the controlled source and the modulated two-port. Controlling the output of a source is the most common manner in which inputs are applied to a system model, although controlled sources also arise frequently in models of active electrical devices. Consider for example the common emitter transistor equivalent circuit given in Fig. 8.16(a). The output current is a direct function of the voltage across capacitor C. The bond graph reflects this by the inclusion of a controlling bond on the current source. As mentioned before the control bond carries no energy, only information.

Modulated two-ports occur frequently in the study of mechanical systems involving coupled translation and rotation. In practice what happens is the transformer coefficient n or gyrator coefficient r is a function of some other system variable. This is indicated on the bond graph by changing the two-port symbols as shown in Fig. 8.17. Examples of modulated transformers and gyrators are given in the case studies of the gantry crane, the ball and beam problem and the automotive engine test rig.

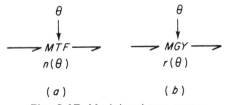

(a)   (b)

Fig. 8.17. Modulated two-ports.

5. DYNAMIC EQUATION FORMULATION

The bond graph can be used to obtain the system dynamical equations in either transfer function or state space form. However, the most natural form in which to frame the equations of motion for bond graph purposes is the state space description. The reason for this lies in the concept of input/output causality which has been developed for the bond graph method. Causality, when added to a bond graph shows up immediately certain degeneracies in the system, and makes the compilation of state equations a fairly straightforward affair.

5.1. Causality

The input/output causality of system components is not usually discussed in explicit terms during equation formulation. It is however rather useful in bond graph modelling since it allows the input/output roles of effort and flow to be added explicitly to the graph. This is done using the causal stroke convention illustrated in Fig. 8.18. In the first part of this diagram the causal stroke indicates that effort is the output of the bond and that flow is the input to the bond. Conversely, Fig. 8.18(b), indicates the convention adopted when flow is the output variable and effort is the input variable. It is important to distinguish between causality and power flow, since they serve completely different purposes. The power flow arrow indicates the *assumed* direction of positive flow on a particular bond, whereas the causal stroke indicates which of the system variables is *assumed* input to a bond. For example, the causal form shown in Fig. 8.19(a) for an effort source indicates that effort is the output variable of the device. The power arrow, on the other hand, indicates that positive power is assumed to flow out of the device. If at some time power flow was into the source this would not affect the causal convention but would show up as a negative product of effort and flow on the source bond.

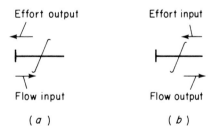

Fig. 8.18. Causal stroke convention.

$$SE \longrightarrow\!\!\mid \qquad SF \mid\!\!\longrightarrow$$

$$(a) \qquad\qquad (b)$$

Fig. 8.19. (*a*) Causal form for effort sources. (*b*) Causal form for flow sources.

5.1.1. Causality for the one-ports

The input/output causality for the energy sources is fixed by definition. Thus, effort sources can only have the "effort output" causality shown in Fig. 8.19(*a*), and flow sources can only have the "flow output" causality shown in Fig. 8.19(*b*).

There is more freedom associated with the causality of energy stores, although there is a "natural" causal form, known as integral causality, which stems from the way in which one intuitively conceives of energy storage. For example, the effort store can be thought of as a device which integrates the input effort to give an effort accumulation. The output flow is then a function of the material properties of the device and the accumulated effort. Figure 8.20

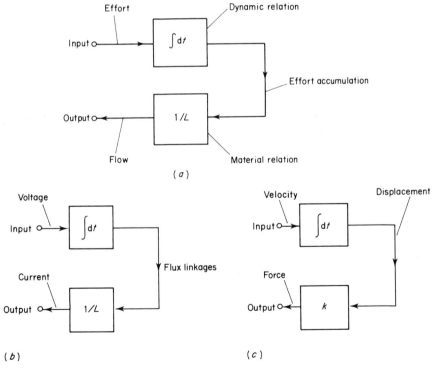

Fig. 8.20. Computing diagrams for integral causal effort stores: (*a*) general effort store; (*b*) electrical inductor; (*c*) mechanical spring.

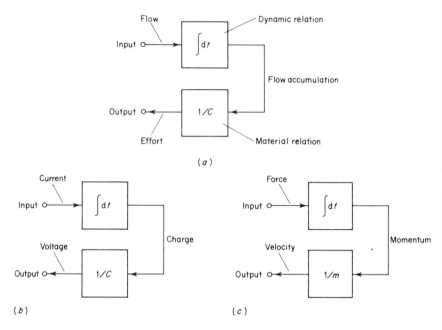

Fig. 8.21. Computing diagrams for integral causal flow stores: (*a*) general flow store; (*b*) electrical capacitor; (*c*) mechanical inertia.

gives a computing diagram of this integral causal form for effort stores, together with corresponding computing diagrams for the electrical and mechanical effort stores (inductor and spring respectively). Note that although linear material properties are assumed throughout, this has no influence on the causal form. The corresponding computing diagram for the integral causal form for flow stores is given in Fig. 8.21. Again, examples drawn from electrical and mechanical systems are included to illustrate the point.

To summarize, the preferred causality for effort stores is "effort input/flow output", as indicated in the bond graph notation of Fig. 8.22(*b*). Likewise the preferred causality for flow stores is "flow input/effort output" as indicated in Fig. 8.22(*a*).

$$\longmapsto C \qquad \longrightarrow\!\!\shortmid L$$

(*a*)   (*b*)

Fig. 8.22. Preferred (integral) casuality for stores: (*a*) flow store; (*b*) effort store.

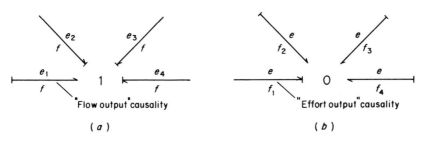

Fig. 8.23. Causal patterns for effort and flow junctions: (a) "flow output" causality; (b) "effort output" causality.

By definition, dissipators have a constitutive relation which statically constrains the effort and flow imposed upon the device. For this reason, there is no preferred causality associated with energy dissipators, and either of the possible causal forms are feasible. Exceptions to this rule are certain non-linear, multi-valued, constitutive relations where only one causal form is physically meaningful. A particular instance is the tunnel diode, this device can be considered as an electrical dissipator, but for certain voltages the diode can have one of three values of current. In this regime it would be incorrect to use voltage as an input variable.

5.1.2. Causality for the effort and flow junctions

Because the interconnective constraints are embodied in explicit bond graph elements, it is necessary to determine the causal possibilities associated with these devices before causality can be assigned to an entire graph. The permitted causal pattern associated with the effort junction maybe determined by noting that all bonds on an effort junction share a common flow. Hence only one bond on an effort junction is permitted to have flow as an output variable, resulting in the causal pattern shown in Fig. 8.23(a). In the same spirit, all bonds on a flow junction share a common effort, consequently only one bond on a flow junction can have effort as an output variable. As a result the causal pattern of Fig. 8.23(b) is the only one possible.

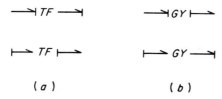

Fig. 8.24. Causal patterns for transformers and gyrators.

5.1.3. Causality for two-ports

The causal patterns which are possible in the transformer and gyrator follow from their definitions. Since a transformer only modifies the ratio by which effort and flow jointly transport energy, then the causality of the output bond is the same as that of the input bond and the causal forms of Fig. 8.24(a) are possible. On the other hand, the gyrator reverses the roles of effort and flow, hence the causality of the output bond on a gyrator is the opposite to that on the input bond and the causal forms of Fig. 8.24(b) are possible.

5.2. Assigning causality to a graph

The causal pattern of an entire graph is obtained by first noting that there is a hierarchy in the causal requirements of the basic one-ports. Firstly, the source elements *must* have certain prescribed causalities. Secondly, the storage elements have a *preferred* causality, and finally the dissipators can have *either* causality. Bearing this natural order in mind, the causality of a graph may be obtained in the following way.

(1)   Assign the required causality to each source component, and follow the causal consequences by assigning whatever causality the sources force upon the remaining system components via the required causality of the system multiports.

(2)   So far as is possible, assign the preferred (integral) causality to the storage components, and follow the causal consequences by assigning whatever causality the stores force upon the remaining unassigned components via the required causality of the system multi-ports.

(3)   If any dissipators remain which have no causal assignments, give them arbitrary causality and thus complete the causality of the graph.

Depending upon the nature of the graph, three things may happen during the assignment of causality. The most straightforward possibility from the point of view of state space equation formulation is that steps (1) and (2) above are sufficient to completely specify the causality of the remaining graph components. Now, causal assignment is the complementary procedure to selecting a normal tree in state space network analysis, and thus the corresponding phenomenon in network methods is that there is only one normal tree which includes all effort sources and flow stores and yet excludes all flow sources and effort stores. The second possibility during causal assignment is that steps (1) and (2) are insufficient to determine the causality of the graph, and some dissipators must be given arbitrary causality in order to complete the causal assignment in the graph. In state space network analysis terms this corresponds to the existence of several normal trees. The remaining causal possibility produces redundancy in the system, this occurs when not all storage devices can be given integral causality, and some are forced by

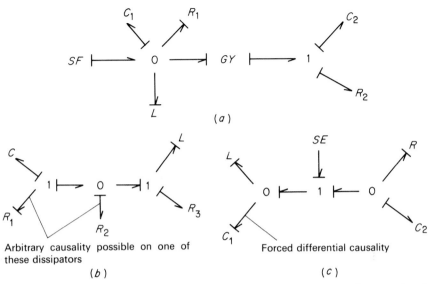

Arbitrary causality possible on one of these dissipators

(b)

Forced differential causality

(c)

Fig. 8.25. (a) Causality completed by sources and stores. (b) Causality completed by arbitrary causal assignment of some dissipators. (c) Differential causality on some stores.

appropriately placed sources and stores to have differential causality. In physical terms this corresponds to the existence in the graph of compatibility constraints involving only flow stores and effort sources and/or continuity constraints involving only effort stores and flow sources. Either of these phenomena imply that there is linear dependence among the stored energy variables and the state dimension is not, as one would normally assume, equal to the number of energy stores in the system. Rather it is given by the number of energy stores with integral causality in the system. Again in network terms, the "system complexity" is the number of stores with integral causality.

At this stage it is probably useful to assign causality to some typical graphs, and thus illustrate the features mentioned above. Consider the graph shown in Fig. 8.25(a). After assigning the required causality to the source and the preferred causality to the storage devices, the causality of the remaining components is completely specified. The graph in Fig. 8.25(b) illustrates the case when the assignment of causality to the stores and sources is not sufficient to fix the causal pattern in the graph. In this instance it is necessary to assign arbitrarily the causality of either R_1 or R_2 to fix the overall graph causal pattern.

The redundancy mentioned above is illustrated in Fig. 8.25(c). In this case the causality of C_1 is forced to be differential. An electrical circuit correspond-

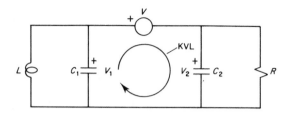

Fig. 8.26. Illustrating the cause of differential causality: electrical circuit for the graph of Fig. 25(c).

ing to this graph is shown in Fig. 8.26. The cause of the problem is then evident, for if Kirchhoff's voltage law (the voltage compatibility constraint) is applied around the loop indicated the following equation results:

$$v + v_2 - v_1 = 0, \tag{11}$$

or

$$v + q_2/C_2 - q_1/C_1 = 0. \tag{12}$$

Thus the system states q_1, q_2 (which in this case are the capacitor charges) are linearly constrained by equation (12).

The complementary source of degeneracy occurs when flow sources and effort stores can be combined in a single continuity constraint, as illustrated (again for an electrical system), in Fig. 8.27. An attempt to assign integral causality on all stores will fail due to the linear constraint on the flux linkages in L_1, L_2, L_3.

5.3. State space equation formulation by pencil and paper

For fairly small bond graphs the state space description can be obtained in a straightforward manner by hand. For larger systems the computing algorithm

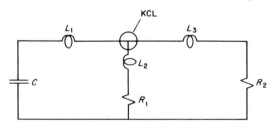

Fig. 8.27. Illustrating the complementary cause of degeneracy using an electrical circuit with KCL involving only inductors.

described later is more appropriate. The normal form for the state space model of a system is

$$\dot{x} = f(x, u), \tag{13a}$$

or in the linear case

$$\dot{x} = Ax + Bu, \tag{13b}$$

where x is a vector of state variables, u is a vector of inputs. In physical terms, the state variables are the effort and flow accumulations in the system stores and the system inputs are the outputs of the system source components. Accordingly, equation (13) can be interpreted for causally assigned bond graphs as saying:

$$\left. \begin{array}{l} \text{inputs to} \\ \text{integrally} \\ \text{causal} \\ \text{stores} \end{array} \right\} = \left\{ \begin{array}{l} \text{outputs of remaining system} \\ \text{components, expressed as a} \\ \text{function of the effort and flow} \\ \text{accumulation and the source variables} \end{array} \right\} \tag{14}$$

The hand algorithm for determining the state space model is just a systematic way of arriving at equation (14). It runs as follows:

(1)   Write the input system variables for the stores as functions of outputs of the junction components to which they are connected.

(2)   Work through the junction structure using the constitutive relations of the effort and flow junctions, transformers and gyrators to arrive at a stage where the *inputs* to the stores are expressed as a function of the outputs of other system one-ports.

(3)   Use the constitutive relations of the system one-ports to re-express the *outputs* of the system one-ports as functions of their *inputs*.

(4)   Work back through the junction structure as in stage (2), until the inputs to the system stores are expressed only in terms of the effort and flow accumulations and source variables in the system.

Notice that at stages (2) and (3) of this algorithm the causal strokes help by indicating which way to go in order to eliminate a redundant variable. Specifically, by tracing a path of like causality through the interconnective structure the analyst is led to the appropriate point.

During these computations, two difficulties may arise, either the system effort and flow accumulations may be statically constrained or the inputs to dissipator components may be mutually constrained. The former phenomenon occurs when differential causality is imposed upon some storage devices. The latter situation arises when the causality of sources and stores is insufficient to completely specify the graph causality. In either case there are algebraic constraints to be solved before the state equations can be obtained.

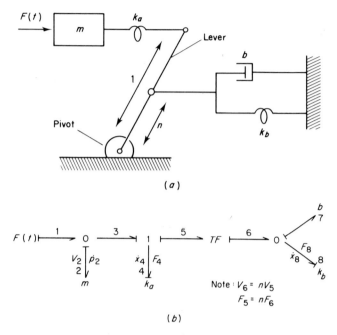

Fig. 8.28. Example 1 of state space equation formulation: (*a*) the system; (*b*) the bond graph.

Example 1

Consider the mechanical system shown in Fig. 8.28(*a*) and whose causally assigned bond graph is given in Fig. 8.28(*b*). The causality of the graph is determined by the source and storage devices, and no store has forced differential causality. The vector of system store inputs is $[\dot{p}_2, \dot{x}_4, \dot{x}_8]$, where the suffixes correspond to the bond numbering used in Fig. 8.28(*b*), and the symbols are defined in Figs. 8.4 to 8.7. Applying step (1) of the hand algorithm gives

$$\dot{p}_2 = F(t) - F_3, \qquad \dot{x}_4 = V_3 - V_5, \qquad \dot{x}_8 = V_7, \tag{15}$$

where forces F and velocities V are numbered according to the bonds where they occur. Working through the junction structure as suggested in step two of the hand algorithm gives

$$\dot{p}_2 = F(t) - F_4, \qquad \dot{x}_4 = -n^{-1}V_7 + V_2, \qquad \dot{x}_8 = V_7. \tag{16}$$

Then, assuming the linear constitutive relations quoted in Figs. 8.4 to 8.7 gives

$$\dot{p}_2 = -k_a x_4 + F(t), \qquad \dot{x}_4 = m^{-1}p_2 - (nb)^{-1}F_7, \qquad \dot{x}_8 = b^{-1}F_7, \tag{17}$$

and, after a final pass through the junction structure to eliminate the force F_7, the state equations are obtained as

$$\begin{bmatrix} \dot{p}_2 \\ \dot{x}_4 \\ \dot{x}_8 \end{bmatrix} = \begin{bmatrix} 0 & -k_a & 0 \\ m^{-1} & -n^{-2}b^{-1}k_a & (nb)^{-1}k_b \\ 0 & (nb)^{-1}k_a & -b^{-1}k_b \end{bmatrix} \begin{bmatrix} p_2 \\ x_4 \\ x_8 \end{bmatrix} + \begin{bmatrix} F(t) \\ 0 \\ 0 \end{bmatrix} \quad (18)$$

All bond graphs are in principle amenable to this algorithm with the proviso that certain algebraic dependences need to be eliminated if differential causality occurs or if some dissipators can be assigned causality in an arbitrary fashion. The following two examples illustrate these cases.

Example 2

An example of a system whose bond graph involves differential causality is given in Fig. 8.29(a), this system is a rudimentary hydraulic drive in which a fluid pump is represented by a pure pressure source and dissipator. The pump drives a piston which in turn is connected to a mechanical load represented by

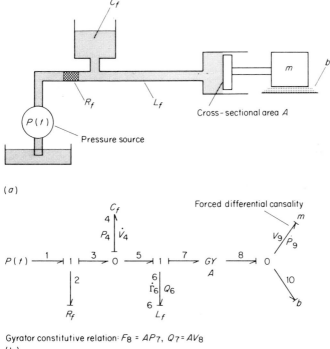

Fig. 8.29. Example 2 of state space equation formulation: (a) the system; (b) the bond graph.

a mass m sliding with viscous friction coefficient b. The fluid line connecting the pump and piston is described by a fluid flow store C_f and a fluid inertance L_f, and the shaft connecting the piston and mass is assumed rigid.

The bond graph of this system is shown in Fig. 8.29(b); notice that on assigning causality either the fluid inertance or the mass must have differential causality. Physically the momentum of the fluid in the connecting line and the momentum of the mass m are statically constrained by the presence of the piston. The vector of integral causal store inputs is $[\dot{V}_4, \dot{\Gamma}_6]$, where the suffixes correspond to the bond numbering used in Fig. 8.29(b). Applying step (1) of the hand algorithm gives

$$\dot{V}_4 = Q_3 - Q_5, \qquad \dot{\Gamma}_6 = P_5 - P_7. \tag{19}$$

Working through the junction structure as suggested in step two of the hand algorithm gives

$$\dot{V}_4 = Q_2 - Q_6, \qquad \dot{\Gamma}_6 = P_4 - \frac{1}{A}(F_9 + F_{10}). \tag{20}$$

But $F_9 = \dot{P}_9$, i.e. the differentiated state of a store. We eliminate this variable by seeking the constraint which links Γ_6 and P_9. From the gyrator constitutive relation

$$Q_6 = V_9 A,$$

or

$$\frac{\Gamma_6}{L_f} = A\left(\frac{P_9}{m}\right), \tag{21}$$

that is

$$P_9 = \frac{m}{A L_f} \Gamma_6.$$

Using this constraint and the constitutive relations of the system elements gives

$$\dot{V}_4 = \frac{P_2}{R_f} - \frac{\Gamma_6}{L_f},$$

$$\dot{\Gamma}_6 = \frac{V_4}{C_f} - \frac{m}{A^2 L_f} \dot{\Gamma}_6 - \frac{b}{A} V_{10}. \tag{22}$$

After rearranging, and a final pass through the junction structure, the state equations are

$$\dot{V}_4 = \frac{-V_4}{C_f R_f} - \frac{\Gamma_6}{L_f} + \frac{P(t)}{R_f},$$

$$\dot{\Gamma}_6 = \left(1 + \frac{m}{A L_f}\right)^{-1} \left(\frac{V_4}{C_f} - \frac{b}{A L_f} \Gamma_6\right). \tag{23}$$

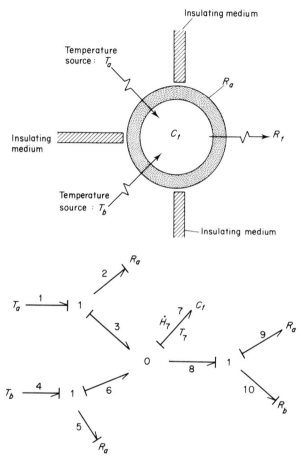

Fig. 8.30. Example 3 of state space equation formulation: (*a*) the system; (*b*) the bond graph.

Example 3

A system in which arbitrary causal assignment can be made to some of the dissipators is the thermal system shown in Fig. 8.30(*a*). This shows, in schematic form, a heat exchanger in which heat from two pure temperature sources $T_a(t)$, $T_b(t)$ is passed to a thermal load (represented by a thermal dissipator R_b) through a medium with thermal capacity C_t. Temperature loss due to conduction through the medium is represented by lumping a thermal dissipator R_a around the periphery of the medium. The bond graph for this device is given in Fig. 8.30(*b*), notice that to complete causal assignment, either of two dissipators must be given an arbitrary causality.

The vector of system store inputs is $\dot{H}_7$ where H_7 is the total heat stored in the medium. Applying step one of the hand algorithm gives

$$\dot{H}_7 = Q_3 + Q_6 - Q_8.$$

Working through the junction structure gives

$$\dot{H}_7 = Q_2 + Q_5 - Q_9.$$

The system store input is now expressed as the outputs of the system one-ports, but bond 9 had the possibility of arbitrary causal assignment, indicating a static constraint among the system variables, specifically

$$Q_9 = Q_{10} = \frac{T_{10}}{R_b} = \frac{T_8 - T_9}{R_b} = \frac{T_8 - Q_9 R_a}{R_b}.$$

Using this constraint and the constitutive properties of the elements gives

$$\dot{H}_7 = \frac{T_2}{R_a} + \frac{T_6}{R_a} - \frac{T_8}{R_a + R_b}.$$

After a final pass through the junction structure, the state equation is

$$\dot{H}_7 = -\left(\frac{2}{R_2} + \frac{1}{R_a + R_b}\right)\frac{H_7}{C_t} + \frac{T_a}{R_a} + \frac{T_b}{R_b}. \tag{24}$$

5.4. Systematic state space equation formulation

A key feature of the bond graph formulation is the way in which it allows systems to be sub-divided into distinct energy handling segments or fields. In particular, any graph may be split up into the following sections:

(i)   a source field, containing all source elements;
(ii) a dissipator field, containing all dissipator elements;

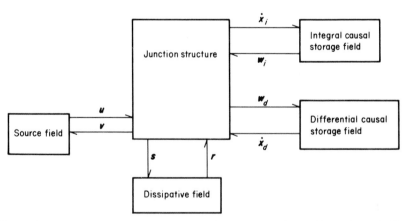

Fig. 8.31. Showing the decomposition of a bond graph into its various fields.

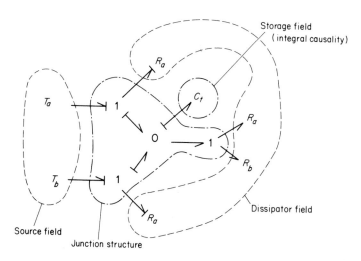

Fig. 8.32. Example of a bond graph decomposition.

(iii)   an integral causal storage field, containing all stores to which it has been possible to assign integral causality;

(vi)   a differential causal storage field, containing all stores to which differential causality has been assigned;

(v)   a junction structure, containing all the effort and flow junctions together with other power conserving multi-ports.

The sub-division of a bond graph in this way is indicated in Fig. 8.31 and can be illustrated by reference to the bond graph of Fig. 8.30. This is redrawn in Fig. 8.32 with the various fields indicated.

In this section the sub-division of bond graphs in this way is used to formulate state space descriptions in a manner suited to computer implementation. To begin with, consider the junction structure and its associated input/output behaviour.

5.4.1. Junction structure

Each multi-port within the junction structure can have its constitutive relation written as a vector–matrix input–output relation. Thus for the jth multi-port:

$$\begin{bmatrix} g_0^j \\ h_0^j \end{bmatrix} = \begin{bmatrix} J_{11}^j & J_{12}^j \\ J_{21}^j & J_{22}^j \end{bmatrix} \begin{bmatrix} g_i^j \\ h_i^j \end{bmatrix} \qquad (25)$$

where g_0^j is a vector of external bond output variables for the jth multi-port; h_0^j is a vector of internal bond output variables for the jth multi-port; g_i^j is a vector of external bond input variables for the jth multi-port; h_i^j is a vector of internal bond input variables for the jth multi-port.

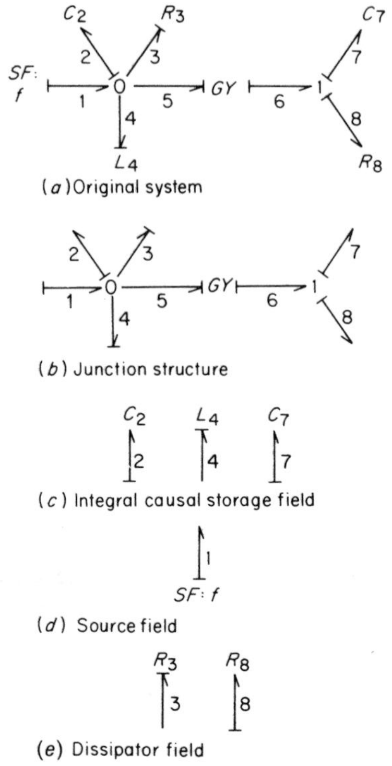

C2
R3
C7
SF:
f
GY
L4
R8
(a) Original system
GY
(b) Junction structure
C2
L4
C7
(c) Integral causal storage field
SF: f
(d) Source field
R3
R8
(e) Dissipator field

Fig. 8.33.

In this context the term internal bond means a bond which is linked to another multi-port within the junction structure. An external bond is one which is linked to one of the external device fields. In addition, the role of input or output is determined by the causality assignment. For example, the flow junction in Fig. 8.33(*b*) has the constitutive relation:

$$\begin{bmatrix} e_1 \\ f_2 \\ e_3 \\ e_4 \\ e_5 \end{bmatrix} = \begin{bmatrix} 0 & 1 & 0 & 0 & 0 \\ 1 & 0 & -1 & -1 & -1 \\ 0 & 1 & 0 & 0 & 0 \\ 0 & 1 & 0 & 0 & 0 \\ 0 & 1 & 0 & 0 & 0 \end{bmatrix} \begin{bmatrix} f_1 \\ e_2 \\ f_3 \\ f_4 \\ f_5 \end{bmatrix}. \tag{26a}$$

The gyrator has constitutive relation:

$$\begin{bmatrix} f_5 \\ f_6 \end{bmatrix} = \begin{bmatrix} 0 & 1/r \\ 1/r & 0 \end{bmatrix} \begin{bmatrix} e_5 \\ e_6 \end{bmatrix}. \tag{26b}$$

The effort junction has constitutive relation:

$$\begin{bmatrix} f_7 \\ f_8 \\ e_6 \end{bmatrix} = \begin{bmatrix} 0 & 0 & 1 \\ 0 & 0 & 1 \\ -1 & -1 & 0 \end{bmatrix} \begin{bmatrix} e_7 \\ e_8 \\ f_6 \end{bmatrix} \tag{26c}$$

The vector–matrix entries in equations set (26) can be identified with the corresponding entries in equation (25).

The constitutive relations for the individual multi-ports can be combined to yield the equivalent relation for the junction structure itself. Thus:

$$\begin{bmatrix} g_o \\ h_o \end{bmatrix} = \begin{bmatrix} J_{11} & J_{12} \\ J_{21} & J_{22} \end{bmatrix} \begin{bmatrix} g_i \\ h_i \end{bmatrix} \tag{27}$$

where g_o = a vector of external bond output variables for the junction structure; h_o = a vector of internal bond output variables for the junction structure; g_i = a vector of external bond input variables for the junction structure; h_i = a vector of internal bond input variables for the junction structure.

However, h_i must be a reordered form of h_o since they both relate to internal junction structure bonds. It follows that by reordering h_o the vector h_i can be obtained and hence eliminated. Let P be a permutation matrix which reorders the elements of h_o to obtain h_i

$$h_i = Ph_o \tag{28}$$

The internal bond input and output vectors are now eliminated using equations (28) and (27) to obtain the junction structure constitutive relation in input–output form:

$$g_o = [J_{11} - J_{12}P(J_{22}P - I)^{-1}J_{21}]g_i. \tag{29}$$

As an example consider the junction structure shown in Fig. 8.33(b). The constitutive relations are combined into an overall junction structure description (cf. equation (27)) thus:

$$\begin{bmatrix} e_1 \\ f_2 \\ e_3 \\ e_4 \\ f_7 \\ f_8 \\ e_5 \\ f_5 \\ f_6 \\ e_6 \end{bmatrix} = \begin{bmatrix} 0 & 1 & 0 & 0 & 0 & 0 & 0 & 0 & 0 & 0 \\ 1 & 0 & -1 & -1 & 0 & 0 & -1 & 0 & 0 & 0 \\ 0 & 1 & 0 & 0 & 0 & 0 & 0 & 0 & 0 & 0 \\ 0 & 1 & 0 & 0 & 0 & 0 & 0 & 0 & 0 & 0 \\ 0 & 0 & 0 & 0 & 0 & 0 & 0 & 0 & 0 & 1 \\ 0 & 0 & 0 & 0 & 0 & 0 & 0 & 0 & 0 & 1 \\ 0 & 1 & 0 & 0 & 0 & 0 & 0 & 0 & 0 & 0 \\ 0 & 0 & 0 & 0 & 0 & 0 & 0 & 0 & 1/r & 0 \\ 0 & 0 & 0 & 0 & 0 & 0 & 0 & 1/r & 0 & 0 \\ 0 & 0 & 0 & 0 & -1 & -1 & 0 & 0 & 0 & 0 \end{bmatrix} \cdot \begin{bmatrix} f_1 \\ e_2 \\ f_3 \\ f_4 \\ e_7 \\ e_8 \\ f_5 \\ e_5 \\ e_6 \\ f_6 \end{bmatrix} \tag{30}$$

The column vector corresponding to h_i can be reordered to correspond with h_o using

$$P = \begin{bmatrix} 0 & 1 & 0 & 0 \\ 1 & 0 & 0 & 0 \\ 0 & 0 & 0 & 1 \\ 0 & 0 & 1 & 0 \end{bmatrix}, \tag{31}$$

leading to the junction structure equations (cf. equation (29)):

$$\begin{bmatrix} e_1 \\ f_2 \\ e_3 \\ e_4 \\ f_7 \\ f_8 \end{bmatrix} = \begin{bmatrix} 0 & 1 & 0 & 0 & 0 & 0 \\ 1 & 0 & -1 & -1 & -1/r & -1/r \\ 0 & 1 & 0 & 0 & 0 & 0 \\ 0 & 1 & 0 & 0 & 0 & 0 \\ 0 & 1/r & 0 & 0 & 0 & 0 \\ 0 & 1/r & 0 & 0 & 0 & 0 \end{bmatrix} \begin{bmatrix} f_1 \\ e_2 \\ f_3 \\ f_4 \\ e_7 \\ e_8 \end{bmatrix}. \tag{32}$$

The junction structure equations can, alternatively, be obtained by direct manipulation of the junction structure variables.

5.4.2. The component fields

Consider the component fields and how they couple to the junction structure. From Fig. 8.31:

For the source field:

u = the vector of source field output variables;
v = the vector of source field input variables.

For the integral causal storage field:

$\dot{x}_i$ = the vector of integral causal storage field input variables;
w_i = the vector of integral causal storage field output variables.

The vector of state variables x_i for the system is related to the co-state vector w_i by the constitutive relation:

$$w_i = Z_i x_i. \tag{33}$$

For the differential causal storage field:

w_d = the vector of differential causal storage field input variables;
$\dot{x}_d$ = the vector of differential causal storage field output variables.

The vector of dependent state variables x_d for the system is related to the co-state vector w_d by the vector–matrix constitutive relation:

$$x_d = Y_d w_d. \tag{34}$$

For the dissipator field:

r = the vector of dissipator field output variables;
s = the vector of dissipator field input variables.

The vector–matrix constitutive relation for the dissipator field is:

$$r = Ds \tag{35}$$

By way of illustration, for the system shown in Fig. 8.33 the integral storage field is defined by

$$\begin{bmatrix} e_2 \\ f_4 \\ e_7 \end{bmatrix} = \begin{bmatrix} 1/C_2 & 0 & 0 \\ 0 & L_4 & 0 \\ 0 & 0 & 1/C_7 \end{bmatrix} \begin{bmatrix} q_2 \\ p_4 \\ q_7 \end{bmatrix}, \tag{36}$$

where as before

$$q = \int f(t)\, dt \quad \text{and} \quad p = \int e(t)\, dt.$$

The dissipator field is defined by

$$\begin{bmatrix} f_3 \\ e_8 \end{bmatrix} = \begin{bmatrix} 1/R_3 & 0 \\ 0 & R_8 \end{bmatrix} \begin{bmatrix} e_3 \\ f_8 \end{bmatrix}. \tag{37}$$

The differential storage field is empty.

5.4.3. Systems with integral causality

In the absence of the differential storage field the junction structure input and output vectors can be rearranged in the form:

$$g_o = \begin{bmatrix} \dot{x}_i \\ v \\ s \end{bmatrix} \quad \text{and} \quad g_i = \begin{bmatrix} w_i \\ u \\ r \end{bmatrix}. \tag{38}$$

The junction structure constitutive matrix can be split into block entries which correspond to this form:

$$\begin{bmatrix} \dot{x}_i \\ v \\ s \end{bmatrix} = \begin{bmatrix} J_{xw} & J_{xu} & J_{xr} \\ J_{vw} & J_{vu} & J_{vr} \\ J_{sw} & J_{su} & J_{sr} \end{bmatrix} \begin{bmatrix} w_i \\ u \\ r \end{bmatrix}. \tag{39}$$

Deleting the second block row gives

$$\begin{bmatrix} \dot{x}_i \\ s \end{bmatrix} = \begin{bmatrix} J_{xw} & J_{xu} & J_{xr} \\ J_{sw} & J_{su} & J_{sr} \end{bmatrix} \begin{bmatrix} w_i \\ u \\ r \end{bmatrix}. \tag{40}$$

Substitution for the store and dissipator constitutive relations from equations (33) and (35) gives

$$\begin{bmatrix} \dot{x}_i \\ s \end{bmatrix} = \begin{bmatrix} J_{xw} Z_i & J_{xu} & J_{xr} D \\ J_{sw} Z_i & J_{su} & J_{sr} D \end{bmatrix} \begin{bmatrix} \dot{x}_i \\ u \\ s \end{bmatrix}. \tag{41}$$

Eliminating the vector s from equations (41) gives the state equations as required:

$$\dot{x} = A\dot{x}_i + Bu. \tag{42}$$

where

$$A = [J_{xw}Z_i + J_{xr}D(I - J_{sr}D)^{-1}J_{sw}Z_i], \tag{43}$$

$$B = [J_{xu} + J_{xr}D(I - J_{sr}D)^{-1}J_{su}]. \tag{43}$$

Applying this procedure to the junction structure and device field constitutive relations (specified by equations (32), (36) and (37)), for the system in Fig. 8.33 yields

$$
\begin{bmatrix} \dot{q}_2 \\ \dot{p}_4 \\ \dot{q}_7 \end{bmatrix} =
\begin{bmatrix} -\dfrac{1}{C_2}\left(\dfrac{1}{R_3} - \dfrac{R_8}{r}\right) & -L_4 & -\dfrac{1}{rC_7} \\ 1/C_2 & 0 & 0 \\ 1/rC_2 & 0 & 0 \end{bmatrix}
\begin{bmatrix} q_2 \\ p_4 \\ q_7 \end{bmatrix} +
\begin{bmatrix} f \\ 0 \\ 0 \end{bmatrix} \tag{44}
$$

5.4.4. Systems with differential causality

For systems with differential causality on some of the stores the procedure for equation formulation is more involved. The junction structure input and output vectors are rearranged in the form:

$$
g_0 = \begin{bmatrix} \dot{x}_i \\ w_d \\ v \\ s \end{bmatrix} \quad \text{and} \quad g_i = \begin{bmatrix} w_i \\ \dot{x}_d \\ u \\ r \end{bmatrix} \tag{45}
$$

The junction structure constitutive matrix can be split into block entries which correspond to this form and the block row corresponding to v deleted:

$$
\begin{bmatrix} \dot{x}_i \\ w_d \\ s_d \end{bmatrix} =
\begin{bmatrix} J_{xw} & J_{xd} & J_{xu} & J_{xr} \\ J_{dw} & 0 & J_{du} & 0 \\ J_{sw} & J_{sd} & J_{su} & J_{sr} \end{bmatrix}
\begin{bmatrix} w_i \\ \dot{x}_d \\ u \\ r \end{bmatrix} \tag{46}
$$

The zero entries in the second block row of equation (46) occur because by definition the dependent state variables are functions only of the integrally causal states and the system inputs.

The constitutive relations are then used to eliminate w_i, $\dot{x}_d$ and r on the right-hand side of equation (46):

$$
\begin{bmatrix} \dot{x}_i \\ w_d \\ s_d \end{bmatrix} =
\begin{bmatrix} J_{xw}Z_i & J_{xd}Y_d & J_{xu} & J_{xr}D \\ J_{dw}Z_i & 0 & J_{du} & 0 \\ J_{sw}Z_i & J_{sd}Y_d & J_{su} & J_{sr}D \end{bmatrix}
\begin{bmatrix} \dot{x}_i \\ \dot{w}_d \\ u \\ s \end{bmatrix} \tag{47}
$$

Differentiation of the second block row gives

$$\dot{w}_d = J_{dw}Z_i\dot{x}_i + J_{du}\dot{u}. \tag{48}$$

The equation set (47) can now be rearranged such that $\dot{x}_i$ and $\dot{x}_d$ occur on the left-hand side.

$$
\begin{bmatrix} I & -J_{xd}Y_d \\ -J_{dw}Z_i & I \\ 0 & -J_{sd}Y_d \end{bmatrix}
\begin{bmatrix} \dot{x}_i \\ \dot{w}_d \end{bmatrix} =
\begin{bmatrix} J_{xw}Z_i & J_{xu} & 0 \\ 0 & 0 & J_{du} \\ J_{sw}Z_i & J_{su} & 0 \end{bmatrix}
\begin{bmatrix} J_{xr}D \\ 0 \\ J_{sr}D-I \end{bmatrix}
\begin{bmatrix} x_i \\ u \\ \dot{u} \\ s \end{bmatrix}. \tag{49}
$$

Eliminating s from the right-hand side

$$
\begin{bmatrix} I & K_{xd} \\ -J_dZ_i & I \end{bmatrix}
\begin{bmatrix} \dot{x}_i \\ \dot{w}_d \end{bmatrix} =
\begin{bmatrix} K_{xw} & K_{xu} & 0 \\ 0 & 0 & J_{du} \end{bmatrix}
\begin{bmatrix} x_i \\ u_i \\ \dot{u}_i \end{bmatrix} \tag{50}
$$

where

$$K_{xd} = -J_{xd}Y_d + J_{xr}D(J_{sr}D-I)^{-1}J_{sd}Y_d,$$

$$K_{xw} = J_{xw}Z_i - J_{xr}D(J_{sr}D-I)^{-1}J_{sw}Z_i,$$

$$K_{xu} = J_{xu} - J_{xr}D(J_{sr}D-I)^{-1}J_{su}.$$

Finally, the vector $\dot{w}_d$ is eliminated from the left-hand side to produce the system state space equations:

$$\dot{x} = Ax + Bu + E\dot{u},$$

where

$$A = (I + K_{xd}J_{dw}Z_i)^{-1}K_{xw},$$

$$B = (I + K_{xd}J_{dw}Z_i)^{-1}K_{xu},$$

$$E = (I + K_{xd}J_{dw}Z_i)^{-1}K_{xd}J_{du}.$$

6. TRANSFER FUNCTIONS FROM BOND GRAPHS

Transfer function models can be obtained from a bond graph in a number of ways. The most direct method for small graphs is to replace the dynamic relations for the stores by their Laplace transform equivalents and eliminate variables until the required transfer function is obtained. By the same token the loop and node techniques of network analysis can be adapted by identifying meshes with effort junctions and nodes with flow junctions. However, these methods have the difficulty that certain multi-ports cannot be easily accommodated. The method given here is based upon the junction structure approach used in the previous section to develop state equations and avoids some of these difficulties.

For bond graphs with no causal conflicts, write the differentially causal junction structure constitutive relation (cf. section 5.4.3.) as

$$\begin{bmatrix} w_i \\ v \\ s \end{bmatrix} = \begin{bmatrix} K_{wx} & K_{wu} & K_{wr} \\ K_{vx} & K_{vu} & K_{vr} \\ K_{sx} & K_{su} & K_{sr} \end{bmatrix} \begin{bmatrix} \dot{x}_i \\ u \\ r \end{bmatrix} \tag{52}$$

eliminate the unwanted components of vector v and assemble the output variables into a vector y to give

$$\begin{bmatrix} v \\ w_i \\ s \end{bmatrix} = \begin{bmatrix} K_{yx} & K_{yu} & K_{yr} \\ K_{wx} & K_{wu} & K_{wr} \\ K_{sx} & K_{su} & K_{sr} \end{bmatrix} \begin{bmatrix} \dot{x}_i \\ u \\ r \end{bmatrix} \tag{53}$$

The storage field constitutive relation is

$$x_i = Z_i^{-1} w_i = Y_i w_i, \tag{54}$$

Differentiating and taking Laplace transforms with zero initial conditions we obtain

$$\dot{x}_i = Y_i S w_i, \tag{55}$$

where S is the diagonal matrix with the Laplace operator in each diagonal entry.

Eliminate $\dot{x}$ and r from equation (53):

$$\begin{bmatrix} y \\ w \\ s \end{bmatrix} = \begin{bmatrix} K_{yx}Y_iS & K_{yu} & K_{yr}D \\ K_{wx}Y_iS & K_{wu} & K_{wr}D \\ K_{sx}Y_iS & K_{su} & K_{sr}D \end{bmatrix} \begin{bmatrix} w \\ u \\ s \end{bmatrix}. \tag{56}$$

Eliminate the vector s and take the vector w to the left-hand side:

$$\begin{bmatrix} I & -MS \\ 0 & I-NS \end{bmatrix} \begin{bmatrix} y \\ w \end{bmatrix} = \begin{bmatrix} P \\ Q \end{bmatrix} u. \tag{57}$$

where

$$M = (K_{yx} - K_{yr}D(K_{sr}D - I)^{-1}K_{sx})Y_i,$$

$$N = (K_{wx} - K_{wr}D(K_{sr}D - I)^{-1}K_{sx})Y_i,$$

$$P = K_{yu} - K_{yr}D(K_{sr}D - I)^{-1}K_{su},$$

$$Q = K_{wu} - K_{wr}D(K_{sr}D - I)^{-1}K_{su}.$$

Eliminate the vector w to obtain

$$y = F(s)u, \tag{58}$$

which is the required transfer function relation in which the matrix transfer function $F(s)$ is given by

$$F(s) = P + MS(I - NS)^{-1}Q. \tag{59}$$

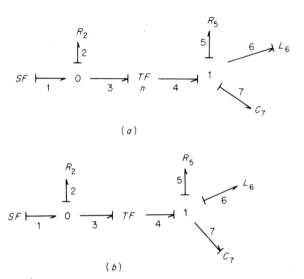

Fig. 8.34. (a) Graph with integral causality. (b) Graph with differential causality.

Note that the procedures followed here relate to the mixed transform method of transfer function formulation from a network with the additional feature that a reduced set of outputs is obtained directly. An example will serve to illustrate the method.

Consider the bond graph shown in Fig. 8.34. For the graph with differential causality the junction structure constitutive relation is (cf. equation (52))

$$
\begin{bmatrix} f_6 \\ e_7 \\ e_1 \\ f_2 \\ f_5 \end{bmatrix} = \begin{bmatrix} 0 & 1 & 0 & 0 & 0 \\ -1 & 0 & 0 & n & -1 \\ 0 & 0 & 0 & 1 & 0 \\ 0 & -n & 1 & 0 & 0 \\ 0 & 1 & 0 & 0 & 0 \end{bmatrix} \begin{bmatrix} e_6 \\ f_7 \\ f_1 \\ e_2 \\ e_5 \end{bmatrix} . \quad (60)
$$

Selecting the output vector $y' = [e_2, e_5]$ and eliminating $v = e_1$ from the equations gives (cf. equation (53))

$$
\begin{bmatrix} e_2 \\ e_5 \\ f_6 \\ e_7 \\ f_2 \\ f_5 \end{bmatrix} = \begin{bmatrix} 0 & 0 & 0 & 1 & 0 \\ 0 & 0 & 0 & 0 & 1 \\ 0 & 1 & 0 & 0 & 0 \\ -1 & 0 & 0 & n & -1 \\ 0 & -n & 1 & 0 & 0 \\ 0 & 1 & 0 & 0 & 0 \end{bmatrix} \begin{bmatrix} e_6 \\ f_7 \\ f_1 \\ e_2 \\ e_5 \end{bmatrix} . \quad (61)
$$

The constitutive equation for the storage field is, in transform form (cf. equation (55))

$$\begin{bmatrix} e_6 \\ f_7 \end{bmatrix} = \begin{bmatrix} sL_6 & 0 \\ 0 & sC_7 \end{bmatrix} \begin{bmatrix} f_6 \\ e_7 \end{bmatrix}. \tag{62}$$

The constitutive equation for the dissipator field is

$$\begin{bmatrix} e_2 \\ e_5 \end{bmatrix} = \begin{bmatrix} R_2 & 0 \\ 0 & R_5 \end{bmatrix} \begin{bmatrix} f_2 \\ f_5 \end{bmatrix}. \tag{63}$$

Eliminating $\dot{x}$ and $\dot{r}$ from equation (61) gives (cf. equation (56))

$$\begin{bmatrix} e_2 \\ e_5 \\ f_6 \\ e_7 \\ f_2 \\ f_5 \end{bmatrix} = \begin{bmatrix} 0 & 0 & 0 & R_2 & 0 \\ 0 & 0 & 0 & 0 & R_5 \\ 0 & sC_7 & 0 & 0 & 0 \\ -sL_6 & 0 & 0 & nR_2 & -R_5 \\ 0 & -snC_7 & 1 & 0 & 0 \\ 0 & sC_7 & 0 & 0 & 0 \end{bmatrix} \begin{bmatrix} f_6 \\ e_7 \\ f_1 \\ f_2 \\ f_5 \end{bmatrix} \tag{64}$$

Eliminating the vector s and w gives

$$\begin{bmatrix} (1+sn^2R_2C_7+s^2C_7L_6) & -snR_2C_7 \\ -snR_5C_7 & (1+sR_5C_7+s^2C_7L_6) \end{bmatrix} \begin{bmatrix} e_2 \\ e_5 \end{bmatrix}$$
$$= \begin{bmatrix} (1+s^2C_7L_6)R_1 \\ 0 \end{bmatrix} f_1, \tag{65}$$

which, on inverting the left-hand side matrix, gives the required result.

7. RELATIONSHIPS WITH NETWORK METHODS

Bond graph techniques are strongly related to the linear graphs used in network analysis of systems, and while the two types of graph are pictorially rather different, there exist systematic techniques for converting one graph to another. Only the conversion from linear graph to bond graph is discussed here, although the converse procedure is straightforward.

7.1. Conversion from linear graphs to bond graphs

There are two ways of converting a linear graph to a bond graph. One procedure uses loop concepts, while the other depends upon nodal ideas. Each procedure produces apparently different but actually equivalent bond graphs.

7.1.1. Nodal conversion

Consider a line segment (A, B) representing a two-terminal element connected between graph nodes A and B. The element can then be thought of as being in

Fig. 8.35. A linear graph line segment and its nodal bond graph equivalent.

series with two bonds, one of which is connected to node A and the other to node B, (see Fig. 8.35). If all line segments in a linear graph are replaced in this manner, and all the graph nodes are replaced by flow junctions, then an equivalent bond graph is obtained. Figure 8.36 illustrates an example of this procedure for a simple bond graph. Notice that the complete bond graph of Fig. 8.36(b) is a good deal less compact than would be expected. This is because

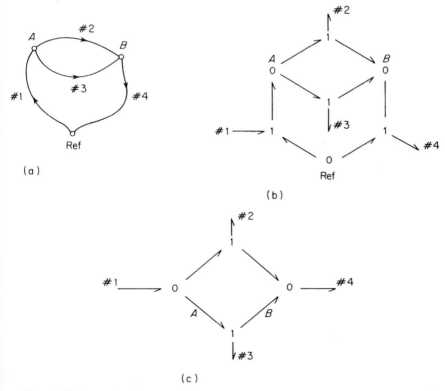

Fig. 8.36. Example of nodal conversion of a linear graph: (a) linear graph; (b) complete bond graph; (c) reduced bond graph.

$$A \quad e \left(\begin{array}{c} f \quad B \end{array} \right. \qquad \rightarrow \qquad \begin{array}{c} A \\ 1 \xrightarrow{\ f_a\ } 0 \xrightarrow{\ f_b\ } 1 \end{array} \quad \begin{array}{c} B \\ \end{array} \qquad f = f_a - f_b$$

Fig. 8.37. A linear graph line segment and its loop bond graph equivalent.

there is redundancy in bond graphs produced in this way. Specifically, it is not normal to include a reference flow junction explicitly on a graph. Usually such a common point is assumed to exist, and all appropriate effort variables are implicitly measured with respect to it. Thus, the reference flow junction can be removed, and a reduced bond graph obtained, as shown in Fig. 8.36(c).

This procedure may be summarized as follows:

(a) Replace each line segment by two bonds, one incident on each of the appropriate nodes. The free ends of the bonds are made incident to a three-port effort junction which has the element represented by the line segment attached to its remaining free port.

(b) Replace each node by a flow junction with as many ports as there are incident line segments.

(c) Reduce the resultant bond graph by deleting the reference flow junction.

7.1.2. Loop conversion

Consider a line segment representing a two-terminal element which is common to two loops A and B in a linear graph. The element can then be

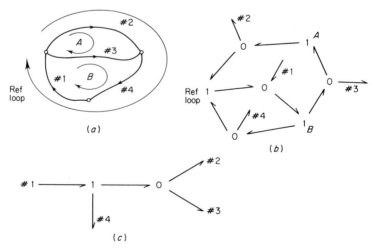

Fig. 8.38. Example of loop conversion of a linear graph: (*a*) linear graph; (*b*) complete bond graph; (*c*) reduced bond graph.

visualized as being connected in parallel with two bonds, one of which is incident on loop A and the other on loop B, (see Fig. 8.37). If this procedure is repeated for every element in a linear graph, and the system loops are replaced by effort junctions then a loop bond graph is obtained. Note that in this case the external loop which defines the exterior of a planar linear graph serves the role of "reference loop". In an analogous manner to that adopted for nodal bond graphs, the loop bond graph can be reduced by removing the reference effort junction associated with the external linear graph loop as indicated in the example in Fig. 8.38. The particular line graph used in this example is the same as that used to illustrate the nodal conversion rule. Note that although the two bond graphs are dissimilar they are in fact equivalent, as expected.

7.2. Dual bond graphs

Dual physical systems are systems in which the role of effort and flow are interchanged. Two systems are structural duals if just the equations of interconnection are exchanged, and thus two bond graphs are duals if their junction structures are the same except that flow junctions are replaced by effort junctions and vice versa. Two systems are complete duals if, in addition to structural duality, the graph storage, source and dissipator fields are the same except that effort stores are replaced by flow stores, effort sources are replaced by flow sources and so on.

It is interesting to note that while dual bond graphs of non-planar linear graphs do not exist, the bond graph of a non-planar linear graph will be usually planar, so there is no indication that such a bond graph does not have a proper dual. Nevertheless, an attempt to construct a dual will meet with failure, due to short circuits introduced by interchanging the effort and flow junctions.

8. NOTES AND REFERENCES

[1] The bond graph technique was invented by H. M. Paynter, see:
Paynter, H. M. (1961). "Analysis and design of engineering systems" MIT Press, Cambridge, Mass.

[2] The technique has been developed as a computer-aided modelling tool by Karnopp and Rosenberg, see:
Karnopp, D. and Rosenberg, R. (1971). "Systems Dynamics — A unified approach". Wiley, New York.

[3] See also the special issue on bond graphs of:
"Transactions ASME Journal of Dynamic Systems" (September, 1972).

In general bond graph articles appear in the above transactions or The Journal of the Franklin Institute.

[4]   The systematic methods of equation formulation given here are based upon:
   Rosenberg, R. C. (1971). "State space formulation for bond graph models of multi-port systems". *Trans. ASME Journal of Dynamic Systems Measurement and Control.* **93**, 1.

   White, B. R. (1974). Ph.D. Thesis, University of Manchester.

[5]   The notion of redundancy and system complexity is discussed in:
   Balanian, B. and Bickhart, J. (1970). "Electrical network theory". Wiley, New York.

[6]   The bond graph model of an automotive gas turbine is taken from:
   Wellstead, P. E. and Nuske, D. J. (1976). "Identification of an automotive gas turbine". *International Journal of Control* **24**, 3.

9. PROBLEMS

9.1.   Draw bond graphs for the systems discussed in Problems 9.1, 9.2, 9.5 of chapter 5. Hence obtain state space descriptions in terms of the natural state variables.

9.2.   Draw bond graphs for the systems discussed in Problems 9.4 and 9.5 of chapter 6. Hence obtain state space descriptions in terms of the natural state variables.

9.3.   Draw bond graphs for the systems discussed in Problems 10.2 and 10.4 of chapter 7. Hence obtain state space descriptions in terms of the natural state variables.

9.4.   Figure 8.39 shows a simple fluid system consisting of a fluid reservoir with capacity C_f, a fluid transmission line with inertance L_f, and a load which can be represented by a linear fluid dissipator with coefficient $R_{f\,1}$. The system is supplied by a fluid pump which is actuated by a reciprocating piston with cross-sectional area A. The piston is driven alternately in directions X and Y by a force $F(t)$.

When the piston moves in direction Y fluid is drawn from a tank into the pump cylinder via valve 2 and valve 1 remains closed. When the piston moved in direction X, valve 2 closes and fluid from the pump cylinder passes through valve 1. Assume that the valves are identical and have the constitutive relation shown.

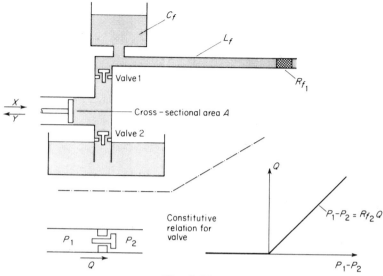

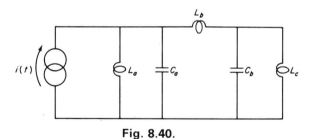

Fig. 8.39.

Write state space equations which describe the behaviour of the system and pump for the following cases:

(i) The piston moving in direction x.

(ii) The piston moving in direction y.

Sketch an analogous electrical system and comment on its possible uses.

9.5. Obtain a state space model for the electrical system shown in Fig. 8.40. Note any significant properties of the system and draw an analogous hydraulic system.

Fig. 8.40.

Part 3: Case Studies

In this part the ideas and techniques of parts 1 and 2 are applied to the mathematical modelling of a representative set of engineering systems.

Case Study 1

The Paper Machine Flow or Head-box

INTRODUCTION

The essential feature of the Fourdrinier paper making process consists of the continuous delivery of a dilute fibrous solution (paper stock) onto a moving wire mesh. After draining most of the water through the wire, drying and pressing, a continuous sheet of paper is obtained. In order to obtain paper of a good consistent quality, the paper stock must be delivered to the wire in a consistent uniform flow; this is done by forcing the stock through a long narrow slit. The requirement for uniform flow can now be interpreted as good control over the stock pressure (or head) at the slit. The classical approach to this problem is to hold a reservoir of stock and control the pressure by regulating the stock input flow-rate (e.g. a straightforward first-order hydraulic system). For moderate wire speeds this control scheme gives satisfactory performance. However, modern paper machines involve high wire speeds, and hence require large stock reservoirs to obtain the required stock pressures. In addition to being physically large such reservoirs have unsatisfactory dynamic response.

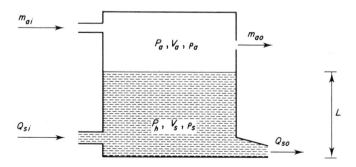

Fig. CS.1. Schema of a paper machine head-box.

An alternative scheme is to maintain a modest stock reservoir and augment the stock pressure by pressurizing a sealed air pad above the stock. This basically is the modern head-box illustrated in Fig. CS.1. The system is multivariable with two inputs (air flow and stock flow) and two outputs (stock pressure and stock level). Dynamically, the system consists of two first-order systems which interact via the transforming action of the pneumatic–fluid interface.

1. DIRECT DERIVATION OF THE DYNAMIC EQUATION

1.1. Definition of relevant variables

With reference to Fig. CS.1, the variables of interest are

System inputs: air mass flow rate m_{ai}
stock volumetric flow rate Q_{si}

System outputs: stock level L
stock head $H = L + (P_a - P_{atm})/g\rho_s$

with the additional variables

P_a = absolute pressure in air pad; C_a = coefficient of discharge (air bleed);
P_{atm} = atmospheric pressure; C_s = coefficient of discharge (stock slit);
ρ_s = mass density of stock; A_a = cross-sectional area of air bleed;
Q_{so} = output stock flow rate; A_s = cross-sectional area of stock slit;
V_a = air pad volume; M_a = mass of air in air pad;
T = absolute temperature; V_s = volume of stock in the box;
R = gas constant; A cross-sectional area of the box.

1.2. Mass balance on the air pad

The basic mass flow balance on the air mass above the stock is

$$\dot{M}_a = m_{ai} - m_{ao}. \tag{1}$$

Assuming that the volumetric variations of the air are isothermal, the air pad flow store has material relation:

$$M_a = (V_a/RT)P_a. \tag{2}$$

Similarly, the material relation for the air bleed dissipator is

$$m_{ac} = C_a A_a [(2(P_a - P_{atm})P_a)/(RT)]^{1/2}. \tag{3}$$

Substituting these material relations into the mass balance and recalling that V_a is a variable yields the air pad differential equation:

$$[(V_a\dot{P}_a + P_a\dot{V}_a)/RT] + C_a A_a [2(P_a - P_{atm})P_a]/RT]^{1/2} = m_{ai}. \tag{4}$$

1.3. Flow balance on the stock reservoir

The basic flow balance on the stock reservoir is

$$\dot{V}_s = Q_{si} - Q_{so}. \tag{5}$$

Using the material relationship for the slit dissipator:

$$Q_{so} = C_s A_s (2Hg)^{1/2} \tag{6}$$

The stock flow balance differential equation can be written

$$A\dot{L} = Q_{si} - C_s A_s (2Hg)^{1/2} \tag{7}$$

1.4. The linear transfer function model

Equations (4) and (7) together define the fundamental dynamic character of the system. It remains now to linearize the equations and obtain a transfer function model which has inputs m_{ai}, Q_{si} and outputs L and H. By considering small variations (H, L, m_{ai}, Q_{si}) about the steady-state values of air pressure $\tilde{P}_a$, air volume $\tilde{V}_a$ and stock head $\tilde{H}$ the following linearized transform equations are obtained:

$$\begin{bmatrix} H(s) \\ L(s) \end{bmatrix} = \Delta^{-1} \begin{bmatrix} k_4 s & (k_1 + k_2)s + k_3 \\ -k_5 & k_1 s + k_3 \end{bmatrix} \begin{bmatrix} m_{ai}(s) \\ Q_{si}(s) \end{bmatrix}, \tag{8}$$

where

$$\Delta = \det \begin{bmatrix} (k_1 s + k_3) & -[(k_1 + k_2)s + k_3] \\ k_5 & k_4 s \end{bmatrix},$$

$$k_1 = \tilde{V}_a g \rho_s (RT)^{-1}, \qquad k_2 = \tilde{P}_a A (RT)^{-1},$$

$$k_3 = g\rho_s C_a A_a (2\tilde{P}_a - P_{atm})[2RT\tilde{P}_a(\tilde{P}_a - P_{atm})]^{-1/2},$$

$$k_4 = A, \qquad k_5 = C_s A_s g(2\tilde{H}g)^{-1/2}.$$

2. A BOND GRAPH MODEL

The head-box provides a simple but interesting example of coupled pneumatic and fluid systems involving energy transformation at the air–stock interface. The bond graph modelling can therefore be logically divided into two stages: modelling of the pneumatic circuit and modelling of the fluid circuit. The two circuits are subsequently linked by a unity modulus transformer representing the air–stock interface.

2.1 The pneumatic circuit

A convenient energy pair for pneumatic systems are mass flow rate and pressure; however, this causes difficulties when coupling to fluid systems, hence it will prove convenient to model the pneumatic system in terms of

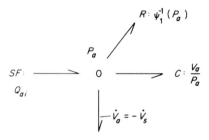

Fig. CS.2. Sub-bond graph of the head-box pneumatic circuit.

volumetric flow rate and pressure. Such a procedure is quite legitimate provided it is adjusted for in the equation formulation stage. Rewriting equation (4) with air density divided out:

$$Q_{ai} = \dot{V}_a + \left(\frac{V_a}{P_a}\right)\dot{P}_a + \psi_1^{-1}(P_a), \tag{9}$$

where $\psi_1^{-1}(P_a)$ is the non-linear dissipator coefficient associated with the air bleed hole. Equation (9) gives rise to the bond graph sub-graph shown in Fig. CS.2.

2.2. The fluid circuit

The fluid circuit is modelled in a similar way. Rewriting equation (7) in terms of the total head pressure P_h and the stock pressure P_s (i.e. that part of P_h due to the stock alone) yields

$$Q_{si} = \left(\frac{A}{\rho_s g}\right)\dot{P}_s + \psi_2^{-1}(P_h), \tag{10}$$

where $P_s = P_h - P_a$ and $\psi_2^{-1}(P_h)$ is the non-linear dissipator coefficient

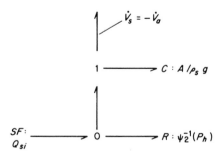

Fig. CS.3. Sub-bond graph of the head-box fluid circuit.

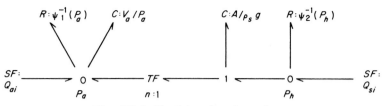

Fig. CS.4. Head-box bond graph.

associated with the stock slit. Noting that the stock flow store has material relation given by

$$P_s = \frac{\rho_s g}{A} V_s, \qquad (11)$$

then the fluid system has the sub-graph given by Fig. CS.3. The overall bond graph, obtained by inserting a unity modulus transformer, is shown in Fig. CS.4.

2.3. The state space equations

Figure CS.5 shows the head-box bond graph with causality added. The linearized constitutive relations can be obtained from physical reasoning and have the general form:

$$P_2 = V_2/C_2, \qquad P_6 = V_6/C_6,$$
$$P_3 = Q_3 R_3, \qquad P_8 = Q_8 R_8,$$

where the numerical suffixes refer to the bond numbering of Fig. CS.5.

By using V_2 and V_6 as the system states, the following state-space equation set is readily found:

$$\begin{bmatrix} \dot{V}_2 \\ \dot{V}_6 \end{bmatrix} = \begin{bmatrix} -(C_2 R_3)^{-1} - (C_2 R_8)^{-1} & -(C_6 R_8)^{-1} \\ -(C_2 R_8)^{-1} & -(C_6 R_8)^{-1} \end{bmatrix} \begin{bmatrix} V_2 \\ V_6 \end{bmatrix} + \begin{bmatrix} 1 & 1 \\ 0 & 1 \end{bmatrix} \begin{bmatrix} Q_{ai} \\ Q_{si} \end{bmatrix} (12)$$

Also the system outputs, head pressure (P_8) and the intrinsic stock pressure (P_6) are given by

$$\begin{bmatrix} P_8 \\ P_6 \end{bmatrix} = \begin{bmatrix} C_2^{-1} & C_6^{-1} \\ 0 & C_6^{-1} \end{bmatrix} \begin{bmatrix} V_2 \\ V_6 \end{bmatrix}. \qquad (13)$$

Fig. CS.5. Head-box bond graph linearized and with causality added.

2.4. The transfer function matrix

Equations (12) and (13) may be substituted into the equation

$$y(s)/u(s) = \boldsymbol{C}(\boldsymbol{I}s - \boldsymbol{A})^{-1} \boldsymbol{B}$$

where $(\boldsymbol{A}, \boldsymbol{B}, \boldsymbol{C})$ is the matrix triple which defines the state-space form. This leads to the following transfer function matrix:

$$\begin{bmatrix} P_8 \\ P_6 \end{bmatrix} = \Delta^{-1} \begin{bmatrix} sC_6 & R_3^{-1} + s(C_2 + C_6) \\ -R_8^{-1} & R_3^{-1} + sC_2 \end{bmatrix} \begin{bmatrix} Q_{ai} \\ Q_{si} \end{bmatrix}, \tag{14}$$

where

$$\Delta = s^2 C_6^2 + (R_8^{-1} + sC_6)[R_3^{-1} + s(C_2 + C_6)].$$

Compare equation (14) with the transfer function matrix found by direct means (equation (8)). Note that the apparent anomaly $k_4 \neq k_2$ is removed if Q_{ai} is expressed as a mass flow rate of air since actually coefficients k_4, k_2 are related by

$$k_2 = \rho_a k_4.$$

3. NOTES AND REFERENCES

[1]   In the nomenclature of control engineering the flow-box is a multivariable control system with two outputs and two inputs. For a controller design exercise applied to this plant see:

Rosenbrock, H. H. (1974). "Computer aided control system design". Academic Press, London and New York.

Astrom, K. J. (1972). "Lecture notes on paper machine control". Division of automatic control, Lund Institute of Technology, Lund, Sweden.

[2]   The paper machine head-box is a fairly straightforward process system. It is however related to more complex coupled pneumatic/hydraulic systems. For example the drum type boiler is a head-box system but with boiling fluid replacing the paper stock and water vapour instead of air.

For a good introduction to this form of system see the theme problem used in the early chapters of:

Franks, R. (1972). "Modelling and simulation in chemical engineering". Wiley, New York.

4. PROBLEMS

4.1.   Draw an electrical analogue circuit of the flow-box system. How would you construct a mechanical analogue (hint: use levers as ideal 1:1 transformers)?

4.2. If the fluid input to the flow-box were not paper-stock, but two immiscible liquids, how would one model the system in terms of the two fluids and the pneumatic sub-system?

4.3. A variation on the head-box shown in Fig. CS.1 is to replace the air bleed by a slit which is gradually obscured as the stock-level rises until an equilibrium is achieved. Use the normal laws for flow through an orifice to model this situation.

Case Study 2

An Overhead Gantry Crane

INTRODUCTION

The unloading of bulk materials from ships is usually performed using an overhead crane. Typically, the crane consists (Fig. CS.6) of a rope-operated grab which is suspended from a movable trolley. The trolley is arranged to traverse a gantry between the ship and unloading point. With reference to the figure, the cycle of operation is (a) position the trolley over the ship hold, (b) lower and load grab, (c) lift grab and traverse the trolley to the quayside hopper, (d) lower grab and discharge the load. The grab is then lifted, the trolley is returned to the ship and the cycle is repeated.

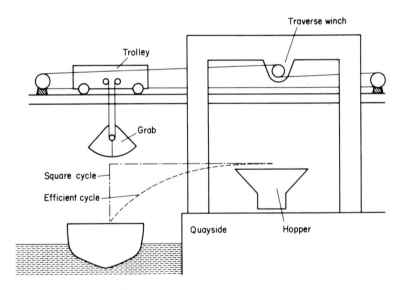

Fig. CS.6. Schema of the gantry crane.

246

The modelling of gantry crane dynamics is a useful exercise because of the need for a dynamical model on which to test automatic control strategies. Automation of the crane work cycle is aimed at reducing cargo handling times at docks and container transfer depots. Specifically, the grab can be moved in a cautious fashion using the square cycle (shown in Fig. CS.6) or using the more efficient cycle. Basically the mathematical model is required in order to calculate and compare the trajectories of these cycles.

The crane cycle is an interesting exercise for us because it is ideally suited to Langrangian methods, and in what follows the variational model will be derived along with a direct application of the laws of motion.

1. DIRECT DERIVATION OF THE MODEL

With reference to Fig. CS.7(a), assume that the crane cable does not flex or stretch during the control cycle. It can then be assumed to be a rigid rod whose length l is controlled by a motor, possibly mounted on the crane trolley, which applies a tension $F_2(t)$ to the cable. If the cable which moves the crane trolley along applies a force $F_1(t)$ then the free body diagram shown in Fig. CS.7(b) can be drawn. Neglecting friction the following force balance is computed by resolving forces in the x_1 direction:

$$M\ddot{x}_1 = F_1(t) + F_2(t)\sin\theta. \tag{1}$$

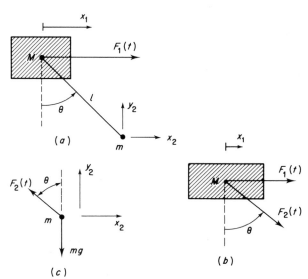

Fig. CS.7. (a) Schema of the gantry crane trolley and load. (b) Free body diagram for the trolley. (c) Free body diagram for the load.

Similarly, the free body diagram for the load m can be drawn (Fig. CS.7(c)), and the following two force balances written:

$$m\ddot{x}_2 = -F_2(t)\sin\theta,$$
$$m\ddot{y}_2 = F_2(t)\cos\theta - mg. \tag{2}$$

Also, by inspection the following geometric relations can be written:

$$x_2 = x_1 + l\sin\theta,$$
$$y_2 = -l\cos\theta. \tag{3}$$

We further have the constitutive relations for the masses:

$$p_{x_1} = M\dot{x}_1, \qquad p_{x_2} = m\dot{x}_2, \qquad p_{y_2} = m\dot{y}_2 \tag{4}$$

where p_{x_1} = the momentum of M in direction $x_1 : p_{x_2}$ = the momentum of m in direction $x_2 : p_{y_2}$ = the momentum of m in direction y_2.

The dynamical equations can now be written in state space form by combining equations (1), (2) and (4). Using the system momenta as the states the basic set of state equations are

$$\dot{p}_{x_1} = F_1(t) + F_2(t)\sin\theta,$$
$$\dot{p}_{x_2} = -F_2(t)\sin\theta,$$
$$\dot{p}_{y_2} = F_2(t)\cos\theta - mg. \tag{5}$$

If the basic system outputs are taken as the velocities $\dot{x}_1, \dot{x}_2, \dot{y}_2$, these are given in terms of the system states via the constitutive relations as

$$\dot{x}_1 = M^{-1}p_{x_1}, \qquad \dot{x}_2 = m^{-1}p_{x_2}, \qquad \dot{y}_2 = m^{-1}p_{y_2}. \tag{6}$$

In order to solve the basic state equation set the velocities $\dot{\theta}, \dot{l}$ are required. These are obtained by differentiating the geometric constraint equations to obtain the following kinetic transformation:

$$\dot{\theta} = l^{-1}[(\dot{x}_2 - \dot{x}_1)\cos\theta + \dot{y}_2\sin\theta],$$
$$\dot{l} = (\dot{x}_2 - \dot{x}_1)\sin\theta - \dot{y}_2\cos\theta. \tag{7}$$

Then substituting in terms of the system states (using equation (6)) the following supplementary state equations are obtained

$$\dot{\theta} = l^{-1}\left[\left(\frac{p_{x_2}}{m} - \frac{p_{x_1}}{M}\right)\cos\theta + \left(\frac{p_{y_2}}{m}\right)\sin\theta\right],$$
$$\dot{l} = \left(\frac{p_{x_2}}{m} - \frac{p_{x_1}}{M}\right)\sin\theta - \left(\frac{p_{x_2}}{m}\right)\cos\theta. \tag{8}$$

Equations (5) and (8) are a full state space description of the gantry crane with inputs $F_1(t)$ and $F_2(t)$. The basic system outputs are the velocity set $\{\dot{x}_1, \dot{x}_2, \dot{y}_2\}$ with $\dot{\theta}$ and $\dot{l}$ defined via the transformation of equation (7). If displacement outputs are required, equations (6) can be used to augment the state equations (5) and (8). The displacements x_1, x_2, y_2 then join θ and l as system states.

2. LAGRANGIAN MODEL

As previously, consider the case depicted in Fig. CS.7(a) in which the system moves without friction and the tension in the load cable $F_2(t)$ and trolley cable $F_1(t)$ are the system inputs. From a variational point of view the fact that the tension $F_2(t)$ is externally constrained simplifies the modelling if the normal "nodal" variational solution is applied. To be specific, there are no external geometric constraints between M and m. The mutual coupling is specified by the external $F_2(t)$ and its angle of application plus some dynamical coupling which is difficult to write down explicitly, but will automatically appear in the Lagrangian solution.

The equations of motion can therefore be obtained by applying Lagrange's equations to the composite system comprising the sub-system s_1 consisting of the trolley (Fig. CS8(a)) and the sub-system s_2 consisting of the mass m in the following manner (cf. the composite Lagrangian models of Ch. 7).

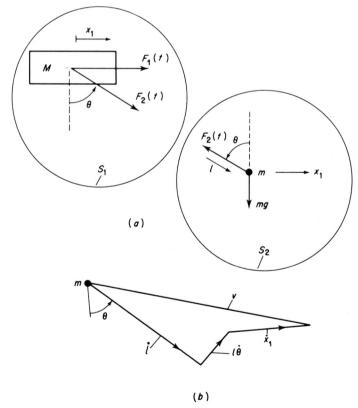

(a)

(b)

Fig. CS.8. (a) Defining the subsystems. (b) Defining kinetic relations for mass m.

Form the sub-Lagrangian L_{s_1} using x_1 as the generalized coordinate:

$$L_{s_1} = \tfrac{1}{2}M(\dot{x}_1)^2. \tag{9}$$

Next consider the mass m as shown in Fig. CS.8(b). The position of m is fixed by the coordinates x_1, l, θ. Therefore, (x_1, l, θ) are a complete independent set of generalized coordinates. However, the variation of x_1 is externally constrained by the sub-system s_1. Therefore, a complete independent set of variational co-ordinates for s_2 is $(\delta l, \delta \theta)$.

The sub-Lagrangian for s_2 is

$$L_{s_2} = \tfrac{1}{2}mv^2, \tag{10}$$

where v is the velocity of the mass m, which is expressed in the terms of the generalized coordinates (see Fig. CS.8(b)) as

$$v^2 = (\dot{l} + \dot{x}_1 \sin \theta)^2 + (\dot{\theta}l + \dot{x}_1 \cos \theta)^2. \tag{11}$$

Now form the composite Lagrangian as

$$L = L_{s_1} + L_{s_2} = \tfrac{1}{2}M(\dot{x}_1)^2 + \tfrac{1}{2}mv^2. \tag{12}$$

For sub-system s_1 (the mass M) the Lagrange equation is

$$\frac{\mathrm{d}}{\mathrm{d}t}\left(\frac{\partial L}{\partial \dot{x}_1}\right) - \frac{\partial L}{\partial x_1} = F_1(t),$$

$$(m+M)\ddot{x}_1 + m\frac{\mathrm{d}}{\mathrm{d}t}[l(\sin \theta + \theta \cos \theta)] = F_1(t), \tag{13}$$

where $F_2(t)$, the cable tension, is considered 'internal" to s_1.

For sub-system s_2 (the mass m) Lagrange's equations are

$$\frac{\mathrm{d}}{\mathrm{d}t}\left(\frac{\partial L}{\partial \dot{l}}\right) - \frac{\partial L}{\partial l} = mg \cos \theta - F_2(t), \tag{14a}$$

$$m[\ddot{l} + \ddot{x}_1 \sin \theta - l(\dot{\theta})^2] = mg \cos \theta - F_2(t); \tag{14b}$$

$$\frac{\mathrm{d}}{\mathrm{d}t}\left(\frac{\partial L}{\partial \dot{\theta}}\right) - \frac{\partial L}{\partial \theta} = -mgl \sin \theta, \tag{15a}$$

$$\ddot{\theta}l + \ddot{x}_1 \cos \theta + 2\dot{\theta}\dot{l} = -g \sin \theta; \tag{15b}$$

where the terms on the right-hand side of equations (14a) and (15a) are respectively external torque in the direction l and the generalized external torque in the direction θ.

Equations (13), (14b) and (15b) are the equations of motion of the gantry crane operated under forced control of trolley position and cable length. Notice that equation (15b) is, as anticipated, a generalized description of a simple pendulum in which the pivot is moving and the length varying.

3. NOTES AND REFERENCES

[1] The modelling and control of gantry cranes has been considered by many authors. Some references are:

Alsop, C. F., Forster, G. A. and Holmes, F. R. (1965). "Ore unloader automation — a feasibility study", pp. 295–305. Proc. IFAC Tokyo Symposium.

Meyer, S. and Zimmermann, W. (1972). "Automatic compensation of load swinging of grab drives". *Siemens Review* **XXXIX**(1), 37–39.

Oyler, J. F. and Withrow, M. F. (1974). "Automated control for ship unloaders" *Trans. ASME, Journal of Engineering for Industry* (August)) pp. 778–784.

[2] A reference which includes an optimal control study of overhead cranes in container handling is:

Martensson, K. (1972). "New approaches to the numerical solution of optimal control problems". Report 7206 Division of Automatic Control, Lund Institute of Technology, Lund, Sweden.

4. PROBLEMS

4.1. Use the kinetic transformation which relates $(\dot{x}_1, \dot{x}_2, \dot{y}_2)$ and $(\dot{\theta}, l)$ to establish the junction structure, and hence show that Fig. CS.9 is a bond graph of the gantry crane. Derive state space equations from the bond graph and compare with the direct solution.

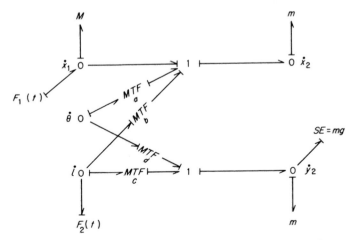

Fig. CS.9. Gantry crane bond graph, where the modulated transformers have coefficients a, b, c, d, given by: $a = l\cos\theta$, $b = \sin\theta$, $c = -\cos\theta$, $d = l\sin\theta$.

4.2. Use a variational approach to determine the equations of motion for the gantry crane when the load cable length is constant. Use the variational solution for variable length to check your results (e.g. put $\dot{l}=l=0$ and eliminate $F_2(t)$).

4.3. Derive a mathematical model of the jib crane shown in Fig. CS.10. Assume that the jib trolley is at a fixed radius R from the centre of rotation of the jib upright and that the jib is rotating under the action of a torque $T(t)$. Check your result by verifying that the equation of motion of the load corresponds to a spherical pendulum with variable length and rotating pivot. Neglect friction, and flexing or stretching of the load cable.

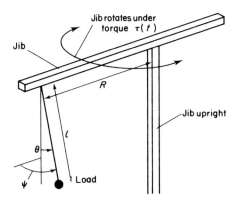

Fig. CS.10. Schema of jib crane.

Case Study 3

The Ball and Beam Problem

INTRODUCTION

A simple mechanical system which is used to demonstrate a fairly difficult control problem is the ball and beam device shown in Fig. CS.11. It consists of a rigid beam which is free to rotate in the plane of the paper around a centre pivot, with a solid ball rolling along a groove in the top of the beam. The control problem is to position the ball at a desired point on the beam using a torque or force applied to the beam as a control input. The nature of this task may be appreciated by thinking of the ball as a mass sliding on a frictionless plane AB, inclined at an angle α, as shown in Fig. CS.12. Resolving the forces parallel to the plane:

$$mg \sin \alpha = m\ddot{x}. \tag{1}$$

Then for small inclinations the relationship between ball position and the angle of the slope is

$$\alpha = g^{-1}\ddot{x}. \tag{2}$$

Thus the position of the ball x cannot be controlled directly, but only through its acceleration $\ddot{x}$. The presence of the two integrators, plus the dynamical properties of the beam results in a difficult, open loop unstable control problem.

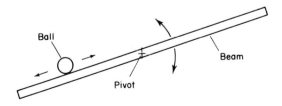

Fig. CS.11. Schema of the ball and beam system.

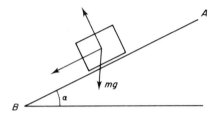

Fig. CS.12. Simplified model.

1. MATHEMATICAL MODEL

The physical details of the ball and beam may vary considerably, the specific arrangement studied here is illustrated in Fig. CS.13. It consists of a straight rigid beam, free to rotate about its centre. The beam angle q_2 is controlled by a force $F(t)$ applied a distance l from the pivot. A linear spring k and dissipator b which are associated with the actuator used to apply the force are also shown.

Applying variational methods, and assuming that the ball is a point mass, the coordinate pair (q_1, q_2) form a complete independent set. Moreover, since neither the ball position nor the beam angle are geometrically constrained the pair $(\delta q_1, \delta q_2)$ are a complete independent set of variational coordinates.

The kinetic co-energy of the system U^*, is associated with the ball mass m and the beam inertia I:

$$U^* = \tfrac{1}{2}mv^2 + \tfrac{1}{2}I\dot{q}_1^2, \tag{3}$$

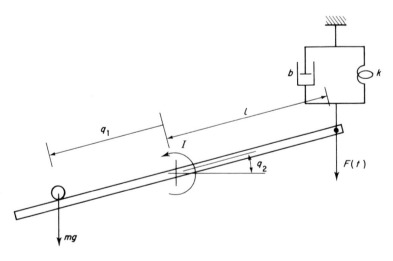

Fig. CS.13. The ball and beam system in a form suitable for modelling.

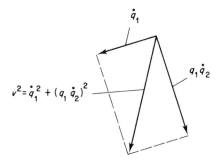

Fig. CS.14. Velocity diagram for the ball and beam.

where the velocity of the ball is obtained from the geometry of Fig. CS.14,

$$v^2 = \dot{q}_1^2 + (q_1 \dot{q}_2)^2. \tag{4}$$

The potential energy of the system is associated with the spring energy, which for small angular deflections is given by

$$T = \tfrac{1}{2} k (l q_2)^2. \tag{5}$$

The system Lagrangian is therefore

$$L = U^* - T$$
$$= \tfrac{1}{2} m v^2 + \tfrac{1}{2} I \dot{q}_1^2 - \tfrac{1}{2} k (l q_2)^2, \tag{6}$$

and the system co-content J is, again for small angular deflections,

$$J = \tfrac{1}{2} b (l \dot{q}_2)^2. \tag{7}$$

Lagrange's equations of motion are thus

$$\frac{\mathrm{d}}{\mathrm{d}t}\left(\frac{\partial L}{\partial \dot{q}_1}\right) - \frac{\partial L}{\partial q_1} + \frac{\partial J}{\partial \dot{q}_1} = F_1(t), \tag{8}$$

$$\frac{\mathrm{d}}{\mathrm{d}t}\left(\frac{\partial L}{\partial \dot{q}_2}\right) - \frac{\partial L}{\partial q_2} + \frac{\partial J}{\partial \dot{q}_2} = \tau_2(t). \tag{9}$$

The generalized force $F_1(t)$ associated with the q_1 coordinate is the component of the gravitational force mg resolved in the q_1 direction:

$$F_1(t) = mg \sin q_2. \tag{10}$$

The generalized torque $\tau(t)$ associated with the q_2 coordinate is made up of two components one due to the input force and another opposing part due to the gravitational force on the ball

$$\tau_2(t) = \cos q_2 (mg q_1 - F(t) l). \tag{11}$$

Substituting into equation (8) gives the equation of motion of the q_1 coordinate:

$$\ddot{q}_1 + q_1 (\dot{q}_2)^2 = g \sin q_2. \tag{12}$$

Similarly, equation (9) leads to the equation of motion of the q_2 coordinate:

$$\frac{d}{dt}(\dot{q}_2(mq_1^2 + I)) + bl^2\dot{q}_2 + kl^2q_2 = \cos q_2(mgq_1 - lF(t)),$$

$$\ddot{q}_2(I + mq_1^2) + \dot{q}_2(bl^2 + 2mq_1) + q_2(kl^2) = \cos q_2(mgq_1 - lF(t)). \tag{13}$$

The equations of motion in this form are a non-linear coupled description of the system. Considerable simplification is possible if the angle q_2 is considered to be small and the mass of the ball is small. Using these approximations, and supposing that $(\dot{q}_2)^2$ is negligible the following linearized equation set is obtained

$$\ddot{q}_1 = gq_2, \qquad \ddot{q}_2I + \dot{q}_2bl^2 + q_2kl^2 = -lF(t). \tag{14}$$

2. BOND GRAPH MODEL

The ball and beam has a bond graph which can be obtained in a straightforward manner using the modulated transformer convention. Specifically, in the chapter on special multi-ports, a crank mechanism was shown to be a transformer whose coefficient is modulated by the cosine of the crank angle. This fact can be used to obtain a bond graph model, by observing that the beam acts as a crank with two input ports. The first is associated with the applied force, and the second with the position of the ball.

The crank input associated with the ball position is complicated by the variable crank radius z which is related to the ball Cartesian coordinates by (see Fig. CS.15(a)):

$$x = z \cos \alpha, \qquad y = z \sin \alpha. \tag{15}$$

By differentiation the kinetic constraints are obtained:

$$\dot{x} = \dot{z} \cos \alpha - \dot{\alpha}z \sin \alpha,$$
$$\dot{y} = \dot{z} \sin \alpha + \dot{\alpha}z \cos \alpha,$$

or

$$\dot{x} = n_1\dot{z} + n_2\dot{\alpha},$$
$$\dot{y} = n_3\dot{z} + n_4\dot{\alpha}, \tag{16}$$

where

$$n_1 = \cos \alpha, \qquad n_2 = -z \sin \alpha,$$
$$n_3 = \sin \alpha, \qquad n_4 = z \cos \alpha, \tag{17}$$

Similarly the velocity on the force input side is constrained by

$$\dot{w} = n_5\dot{\alpha}, \qquad \text{where} \quad n_5 = -l \cos \alpha. \tag{18}$$

The kinetic constraints embodied in equations (16) and (18) are used in Fig. CS.15(b) to construct the junction structure for the ball and beam. The system elements can then be simply attached to the appropriate velocity nodes (0 junctions) as indicated in Fig. CS.16. An attempt to add integral causality to

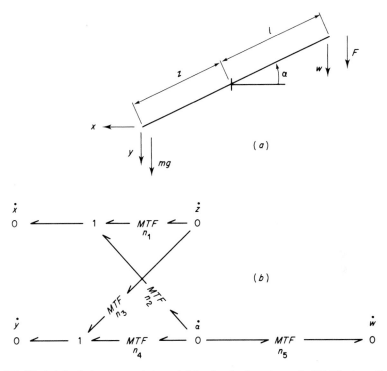

Fig. CS.15. (*a*) Defining geometric variables for the bond graph. (*b*) The junction structure.

the graph fails, with differential causality being inflicted upon one of the inertial energy stores. In Fig. CS.16 it is the mass attached to the $\dot{y}$ velocity node which is constrained, indicating that the momenta in the Cartesian coordinates are linearly constrained by the moment in the angular coordinate. Indeed, from the junction structure, or by direct reasoning, the velocities are constrained by

$$z\dot{\alpha} = \dot{y}\cos\alpha - \dot{x}\sin\alpha, \tag{19}$$

which in turn constrains the momenta p_α, p_x, p_y via the constitutive relations

$$p_\alpha = I\dot{\alpha}, \qquad p_x = m\dot{x}, \qquad p_y = m\dot{y}. \tag{20}$$

The equations of motion for the system can now be obtained. If the set of system states is defined as

p_x = momentum of m in the x direction,
p_y = momentum of m in the y direction,
p_α = angular momentum of the beam,
w = displacement of the spring,

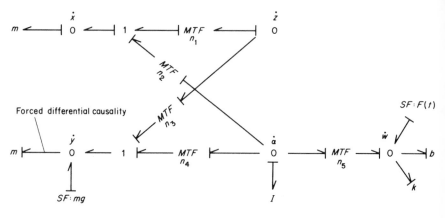

Fig. CS.16. The complete ball and beam bond graph.

only two of the momenta are independent, the third is given by equations (19) and (20).

From the graph two equations connecting the rate of change of momenta can be found. These are

$$\dot{p}_\alpha = n_5[F(t) - kw + n_5(b/I)p_\alpha] - \dot{p}_x[(n_2 n_3 + n_1 n_4)/n_3] \qquad (21a)$$

and

$$\dot{p}_x = n_1^{-1} n_3(\dot{p}_y - mg). \qquad (21b)$$

A further constraint on $\dot{p}_\alpha, \dot{p}_x, \dot{p}_y$ may be found by differentiating equation (19), this allows state equations of the required form to be written for p_α, and p_x. The remaining state equation then follows from the graph as

$$\dot{w} = n_5(p_\alpha/I) = -l \cos \alpha(p_\alpha/I). \qquad (22)$$

3. NOTES AND REFERENCES

[1]   The modelling and control of ball and beam systems is now a fairly standard university laboratory exercise. See for example:

Wellstead, P. E., Crimes, V., Fletcher, P. R., Moody, R. and Robins, A. J. (1977). "The ball and beam control experiment". *International Journal of Electrical Engineering Education.*

[2]   A class of related problems are associated with the balancing of inverted pendulums and multiple inverted pendulums. These amount to open loop unstable systems like the ball and beam. However, unlike the beam problem they do have practical significance since they relate to (among other things) the

dynamics of robot and prosthetic limbs. See for example:
Hemani, H., Welmar, F. C. and Koozekanani, S. H. (1972). "Some aspects of the inverted pendulum problem for modelling of locomotion systems". Joint Automatic Control Conference (J.A.C.C.)

4. PROBLEMS

4.1. Extend the variational solution to the ball and beam problem by modelling the ball more correctly as a sphere of radius r rolling without slip. Show that the only effect is to alter the effective mass of the ball.

4.2. Suppose the force $F(t)$ in Fig. CS.13 is applied via a moving coil actuator by modulating the voltage $v_s(t)$. Extend the variational and bond graph solutions to include the dynamics of the electrical drive circuit.

4.3. A variant of the ball and beam problem involves the use of a curved beam. Derive the equations of motion for a ball rolling on a curved beam. Linearize the equations and show that the pole pair associated with the ball either:

becomes a pair of conjugate imaginary poles for a concave beam; or
becomes a pair of real poles (one in the left half plane and one in the right half plane) for a convex beam.
(Hint: plot a root locus of the ball transfer function with the radius of curvature as parameter.)

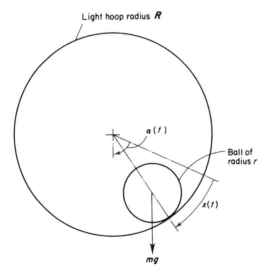

Fig. CS.17.

4.4. A further interesting variant arises if one takes the two ends of the concave beam and joins them together to form a hoop. One can now consider the problem of rotating the hoop so as to position the ball at a specific point on the hoop circumference. Use a variational approach to develop the equations of motion for the ball and hoop shown in Fig. CS.17. Assume that the angular position $\alpha(t)$ of the hoop is the system input and the peripheral position of the ball $x(t)$ is the system output. Linearize and show that the system transfer function is

$$\frac{x(s)}{\alpha(s)} = \frac{(\mathbf{R}s^2 + g)\mathbf{R}}{(\frac{7}{5}\mathbf{R}s^2 + g)} .$$

What is the physical significance of the zero of transmission at $\pm j[g/\mathbf{R}]$?

4.5. Verify the ball and hoop system model using a bond graph approach.

Case Study 4

An Automotive Engine Test Bed

INTRODUCTION

The characteristics of automotive engines are usually measured using a stationary test bed in which the engine is attached to an energy dissipator which may be varied in a way which simulates actual load demands. Figure CS.18 depicts such a test bed. It consists of an automotive internal combustion engine which is connected via a transmission shaft to an eddy current dynamometer. The power output of the engine is controlled by the angle $\theta(t)$ of the throttle control, and the power absorption of the dynamometer is determined by the current $i_f(t)$ which passes through its field windings. Thus, by varying the dynamometer field current the torque/angular velocity characteristics of the engine at various throttle settings can be obtained under controlled conditions.

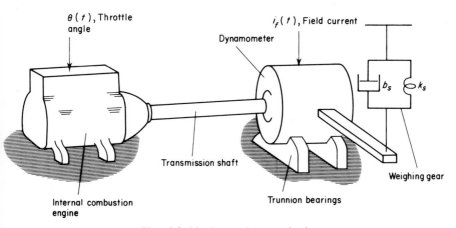

Fig. CS.18. An engine test bed.

261

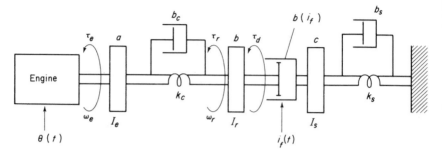

Fig. CS.19. Schema of an engine test bed.

1. THE SYSTEM MODEL

If the engine test data is to be collected accurately and efficiently it is essential that the dynamic behaviour of the overall system be known. Specifically, the mathematical relationships between the system inputs $\theta(t)$, $i_f(t)$ and the system outputs, dynamometer rotor torque $\tau_r(t)$ and rotor speed $\omega_r(t)$ are required. This can be straightforwardly done by constructing a mathematical model of the system based upon any valid technique. Before this is done, however, the literal illustration of the test rig in Fig. CS.18 must be put into a schematic form which depicts its dynamic structure. Figure CS.19 provides such a representation, the engine itself is considered as a non-linear angular velocity source (ω_e) modulated by the throttle setting $\theta(t)$. The engine output torque τ_e is thus given by a constitutive relation of the form:

$$\tau_e = \varphi_e(\omega_e, \theta(t)) \tag{1}$$

A typical engine constitutive relation is shown in Fig. CS.20. Notice that the energy dissipators associated with the engine are incorporated in the constitutive relation, while the energy storage mechanisms are not (this is a consequence of the constitutive relation being measured under steady-state conditions). The preponderant energy storage mechanism in an engine is

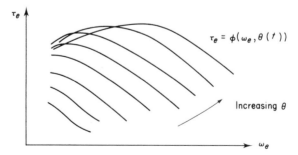

Fig. CS.20. Engine constitutive relation.

associated with the inertia I_e of the rotating parts; this element can be lumped at the output of the engine shaft. The torque transmission shaft is essentially a rotational spring with stiffness k_c; however, in the study upon which this discussion is based the transmission shaft was found to absorb energy; this effect can be modelled by a dissipator b_c in parallel with the shaft. The mass of the transmission shaft can be lumped with the mass of the dynamometer rotor to form an effective inertia I_r at the dynamometer end of the shaft.

The representation of the dynamometer as a modulated dissipator requires some explanation. Basically, an eddy current dynamometer consists of a toothed rotor which is free to rotate in a magnetic field developed by the current $i_f(t)$ passing through the stator windings. In addition, the stator is set in trunnion bearings which allow it to rotate about its principal axis (see Fig. CS.18). Weighing gear, consisting of a spring k_s and dissipator b_s, is attached to the stator in order to restrain its motion and measure the torque developed. The basic dissipator model of a dynamometer can be justified by applying the fundamental laws of electromagnetic energy conversion. From the Lorentz Force Law the torque developed in the rotor τ_r can be approximated by

$$\tau_r = k_1 i_r B, \tag{2}$$

where i_r is the mean eddy current circulating in the rotor; B is the mean flux density of the stator field; and k_1 is a constant of proportionality.

Now the eddy currents flow because of the voltage induced in the rotor v_r by the relative movement of the stator field and the rotor. It is a consequence of Faraday's Law of induction that the following approximation may be said to hold:

$$v_r \simeq k_2 \omega B, \tag{3}$$

where $\omega = (\omega_r - \omega_s)$ is the relative velocity between rotor and stator, and k_2 is a suitable constant of proportionality. The mean voltage developed in the rotor

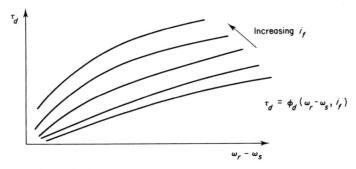

Fig. CS.21. Dynamometer constitutive relation.

is related to the mean rotor current by the effective resistance R_r of the mean path followed by the eddy currents

$$v_r = R_r i_r \qquad (4)$$

These expressions can be combined to yield the approximate constitutive relation for the dynamometer:

$$\tau_r = \frac{k_1 k_2 B^2}{R_r}(\omega_r - \omega_s). \qquad (5)$$

The stator field density B is a function of the field current $i_f(t)$, the constitutive relation can therefore be rewritten as that of a linear modulated dissipator:

$$\tau_r = b(i_f)(\omega_r - \omega_s). \qquad (6)$$

In practice the constitutive relation of an eddy current dynamometer is nonlinear in nature; Fig. CS.21 shows the constitutive relation of a typical dynamometer.

2. A NETWORK MODEL

For the purpose of comparison with the bond graph approach, the system is first studied by network methods. In the network approach the constitutive relations of the engine and dynamometer can be linearized about a specific operating point. Consider first the engine operating at the point A on a straight line L, which is equivalent to a linear modulated source $\tau_m(\theta(t))$ and a linear dissipator b_m connected in parallel, as indicated in Fig. CS.22. Using similar reasoning, the dynamometer can be linearized about an operating point B and represented by a modulated torque source $\tau_l(i_f)$ and a dissipator b_l as depicted in Fig. CS.23.

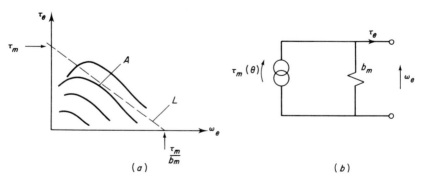

(a) (b)

Fig. CS.22. Linearized engine model.

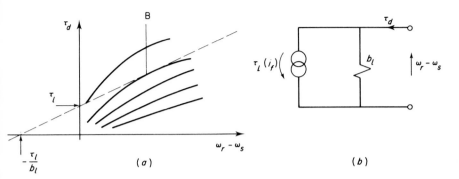

Fig. CS.23. Linearized dynamometer model.

With these approximations in mind the system graph can be drawn directly, as shown in Fig. CS.24. By nodal analysis, the transform equations for the system are

$$
\begin{bmatrix}
(b_c+b_m)+k_cs^{-1}+sI_e & -b_c-k_cs^{-1} & 0 \\
-b_c-k_cs^{-1} & (b_l+b_c)+k_cs^{-1}+sI_r & -b_l \\
0 & -b_l & (b_l+b_s)+k_ss^{-1}+sI_s
\end{bmatrix}
\begin{bmatrix}
\omega_e(s) \\
\omega_r(s) \\
\omega_s(s)
\end{bmatrix}
=
\begin{bmatrix}
\tau_m(s) \\
-\tau_l(s) \\
\tau_l(s)
\end{bmatrix}
\quad (7)
$$

In certain applications the dynamometer stator is clamped. This simplifies the model and leads to the network model shown in Fig. CS.25.

3. A BOND GRAPH MODEL

A word bond graph of the test rig is shown in Fig. CS.26; this illustrates the system structure in bond graph form, and defines the key energy variables. If

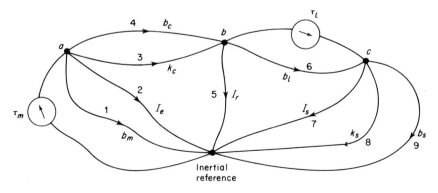

Fig. CS.24. Full system graph.

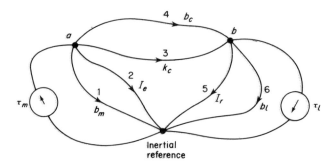

Fig. CS.25. System graph with clamped stator.

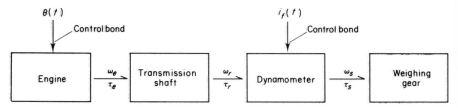

Fig. CS.26. Word bond graph of engine test bed.

the customary assignment of effort → velocity and flow → torque is made, then the bond graph shown in Fig. CS.27 may be drawn. Notice that both the modulated one-ports are drawn as modulated dissipators, with power flow arrows in the normal direction of positive power flow. If the dynamometer stator is clamped, and the modulated one-ports are linearized in the fashion of Fig. CS.22 and CS.23, the reduced bond graph of Fig. CS.28 is obtained.

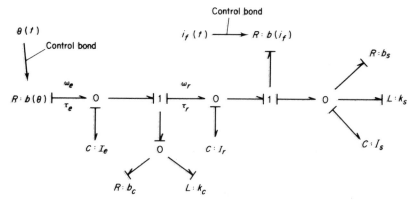

Fig. CS.27. Engine test bed bond graph.

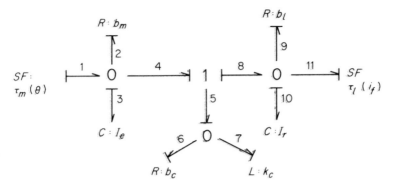

Fig. CS.28. Linearized bond graph with stator clamped.

The internal description of the system behaviour can be deduced directly from Fig. CS.28. Specifically, if the natural state variables are employed, the state space description is

$$
\begin{bmatrix} \dot{h}_r \\ \dot{h}_e \\ \dot{\theta}_c \end{bmatrix} = \begin{bmatrix} -(b_c+b_l)I_r^{-1} & b_c I_e^{-1} & k_c \\ b_c I_r^{-1} & -(b_m+b_c)I_e^{-1} & -k_c \\ -I_r^{-1} & I_e^{-1} & 0 \end{bmatrix} \begin{bmatrix} h_r \\ h_e \\ \theta_c \end{bmatrix} + \begin{bmatrix} 0 & -1 \\ 1 & 0 \\ 0 & 0 \end{bmatrix} \begin{bmatrix} \tau_m(\theta) \\ \tau_l(i_f) \end{bmatrix} \qquad (10)
$$

where h_r = angular momentum of the dynamometer rotor; h_e = angular momentum of the engine; θ_c = angular deflection of the transmission shaft.

4. EXTENSIONS TO THE MODEL

In practice the actual dynamic behaviour of a test rig may be significantly different from that predicted by equations (9) and (10). In particular, a significant time delay occurs between the throttle deflection and the engine response; this is due to the finite time required for the fuel/air vapour to travel from the carburettor to the ignition chamber. This presents no great modelling problem since an appropriate time delay may be readily incorporated into the transfer function or state space model.

A second, more serious, discrepancy is associated with the dynamometer model in which the field current $i_f(t)$ is assumed to modulate directly the dissipator coefficient. Actually the constitutive relation (equation (5)) indicates that it is the dynamometer flux which directly modulates the power absorption. The field current controls the flux through the dynamometer magnetic circuit, thus a complete model of the system must include the dynamic properties of the magnetic circuit.

A rudimentary model can be set up in the following way. The coupling between the electric field circuit and the magnetic field circuit is via a two-port energy coupler. For a field circuit with N effective turns, the flux linkage λ is related to the total flux φ by

$$\lambda = N\varphi. \tag{11}$$

Thus the voltage developed across the field windings v_f is, by Faraday's law,

$$v_f = N\dot{\varphi} \tag{12}$$

The magnetic effort variable which sets up the flux is the magnetomotive force (mmf) M, which is related to the field current i_f by

$$M = Ni_f \tag{13}$$

Equations (12) and (13) are the constitutive relations of a pure gyrator, with gyrational coefficient N (the effective number of field turns). The magnetic effort variable is M, the magnetomotive force and the magnetic flow variable is $\dot{\varphi}$, the rate of change of the total field winding flux.

The behaviour of the magnetic circuit can now be modelled explicitly and related to the remains of the system via the gyrational relationship of equations (12) and (13).

5. NOTES AND REFERENCES

[1] The material for this case study was taken from:
Monk, J. and Comfort, J. (1970). "Mathematical model of an internal combustion engine and dynamometer test rig". *Journal of the Institute of Measurement and Control* **3**, 6.

[2] An additional useful reference is:
Green, A. G. and Lucas, G. G. (1969). "The testing of internal combustion engines". Edinburgh University Press, London.

6. PROBLEMS

6.1. The engine test bed modelled here has a passive load and thus cannot simulate all engine driving conditions. To this end replace the dynamometer with an electric motor/generator set and remodel the system.

6.2. The engine is modelled here as a torque source. Develop a more detailed model which takes into account the reciprocating action of the pistons and the impulsive nature of torque generation. (Hint: use a bond graph method with modulated dissipators for torque injection.)

6.3. Develop an extended form of the engine test bed model which includes the magnetic circuit of the dynamometer as suggested in section 4.

Case Study 5

Coupled Electric Drives

INTRODUCTION

The winding of magnetic tape, wire, textile yarn, paper and plastic strip from one spool to another is often achieved using a pair of electric drives which are coupled by the belt of material being wound (Fig. CS.29). Usually it is necessary to regulate the speed of winding and the tension in the material belt. To this end a spring mounted pulley can be incorporated such that the spring deflection indicates the tension, while the pulley speed is related to the belt speed between the two drives. Physically, the positioning of the pulley might correspond (for example) to that of the read/write heads on a magnetic tape drive.

1. DIRECT DERIVATION OF THE MODEL

Assume that the two drive spools are driven by current-controlled electric motors. For all practical purposes this means that the spools can be assumed to be controlled by ideal torque sources τ_1 and τ_2. The system can thus be

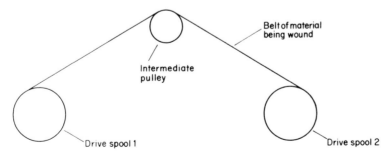

Fig. CS.29. A typical coupled drive system.

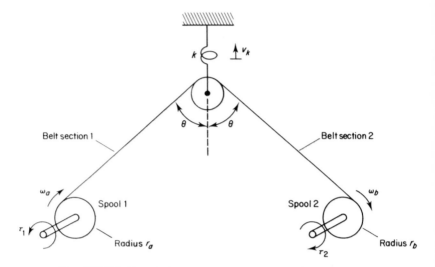

Fig. CS.30. Coupled drives in a form suitable for modelling.

represented (Fig. CS.30) for modelling purposes by a spool 1 of radius r_a coupled to a spool 2 of radius r_b. The belt of material is then wound from spool 1 to spool 2 by torque τ_2, with a reverse tensioning torque τ_1 applied to drive spool 1. The inter-spool pulley is assumed to be light and frictionless, and the spring is assumed to be linear with stiffness k. Moreover, one can assume that the spools 1 and 2 have moments of inertia I_a and I_b respectively and rotational coefficients of friction b_a and b_b respectively. The modelling of the belt sections between the spools and the pulley is in general rather difficult, but generally such components can be represented by a parallel combination of spring and dissipator (cf. modelling the transmission shaft in the automotive test-bed study) as indicated in Fig. CS.31(d).

The modelling now proceeds by considering spools, belt sections and pulley as separate sub-systems. Consider spool 1 as shown in Fig. CS.31(a):

Torque balance: $\qquad F_3 r_a = \tau_1 + b_a \omega_a + \tau_a$ $\qquad$ (1)

Velocity balance: $\qquad v_3 = \omega_a r_a$ $\qquad$ (2)

where

$$h_a = I_a \omega_a \quad \text{and} \quad \tau_a = \dot{h}_a. \qquad (3)$$

In the same spirit, spool 2 (Fig. CS.31(b)) obeys:

Torque balance: $\qquad F_4 r_b = \tau_2 - b_b \omega_b - \tau_b$ $\qquad$ (4)

Velocity balance: $\qquad v_4 = \omega_b r_b$ $\qquad$ (5)

where

$$h_b = I_b \omega_b \quad \text{and} \quad \tau_b = \dot{h}_b. \qquad (6)$$

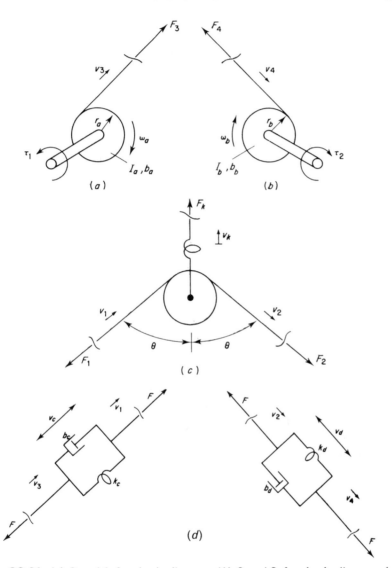

Fig. CS.31. (*a*) Spool 1, free body diagram. (*b*) Spool 2, free body diagram. (*c*) Tensioning pulley, free body diagram. (*d*) Belt sections.

The pulley sub-system is shown in Fig. CS.31(*c*), where since the pulley is massless and without friction $F_1 = F_2 = F$. Then noting that the pulley is a power conserving two-port, one part of the constitutive relation is obtained by resolving forces vertically:

$$F_k = 2 \cos \theta F. \tag{7}$$

The remaining part of the constitutive relation follows from the power conserving constraint:

$$v_k = (2 \cos \theta)^{-1}(v_1 - v_2). \tag{8}$$

The belt sections (Fig. CS.31(d)) obey the force balances:

For belt section 1: $\qquad F = b_c v_c + k_c x_c$ $\qquad\qquad$ (9)

For belt section 2: $\qquad F = b_d v_d + k_d x_d$

where

$$v_c = v_1 - v_3; \qquad v_c = \dot{x}_c \quad \text{and} \quad v_d = v_4 - v_2; \qquad v_s = \dot{x}_d. \tag{10}$$

The state equations for the system follow from equations (1)–(10), by first identifying a suitable set of state variables. In this case the stored energy variables form a suitable set:

h_a = angular momentum of spool 1,

h_b = angular momentum of spool 2,

x_c = extension of belt section 1,

x_d = extension of belt section 2,

x_k = extension of tension-measuring spring.

By combining the system equations and eliminating redundant variables the following equation set is found:

$$\dot{h}_a = \frac{-b_a h_a}{I_a} + \frac{k r_a}{2 \cos \theta} x_k - \tau_1,$$

$$\dot{h}_b = \frac{-b_b h_b}{I_b} - \frac{k r_b}{2 \cos \theta} x_k + \tau_2,$$

$$\dot{x}_c = \frac{-k_c x_a}{b_c} + \frac{k x_k}{2 b_c \cos \theta}, \tag{11}$$

$$\dot{x}_d = \frac{-k_d x_d}{b_d} + \frac{k x_k}{2 b_d \cos \theta},$$

$$\dot{x}_k = \left[\frac{r_a h_a}{I_a} - \frac{r_b h_b}{I_b} - \frac{k_c x_c}{b_c} - \frac{k_d x_d}{b_d} + \left(\frac{1}{b_c} + \frac{1}{b_d} \right) \frac{k x_k}{2 \cos \theta} \right] \frac{1}{2 \cos \theta}$$

2. OTHER MODELLING METHODS

The coupled electrical drives can be modelled by any of the three systematic approaches. This aspect of the problem is left as an exercise for the reader, except insomuch that we wish to compare simplicity of the bond graph of the

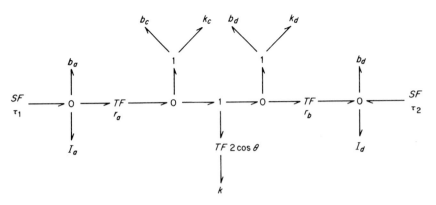

Fig. CS.32. Bond graph for coupled drives.

system (Fig. CS.32) with the system graph given in the first paragraphs of the bond graph chapter.

3. PROBLEMS

3.1. A control problem associated with the coupled electrical drives could be formulated thus:

Use the input variables $\tau_1(t)$ and $\tau_2(t)$ to independently regulate the output variables pulley speed $\omega(t)$ and belt tension (as measured by the spring deflection $x_k(t)$). Obtain a transfer function matrix which relates the inputs to outputs in a form which permits multivariable controller design.

3.2. Show that Fig. CS.32 is a valid bond graph of the coupled drive system. Hence verify the state space model derived previously and the transfer function matrix obtained in the previous problem.

3.3. When used in a textile application, yarn is spooled from drive 1 to drive 2 at a controlled tension and speed. However, the situation is often complicated by heating and twisting action on the yarn between drive 1 and the pulley. How could one extend the model to include these actions?

3.4. Use a variational method to determine the equations of motion of the coupled drive system.

3.5. What happens to the model when the frictional coefficients b_c, b_d become negligible? Examine this phenomenon through the bond graph of Fig. CS.32, and interpret it physically.

Subject Index